MW01485326

Author: One Exam Prep (1-877-804-3959)
www.1examprep.com

ABOUT 1 EXAM PREP

1 EXAM PREP TAKES PRIDE IN BEING THE MOST EFFECTIVE AND EFFICIENT EXAM PREPARATION SCHOOL IN THE INDUSTRY.

All of our Classes and Exam Prep Material is available 24 Hours a Day online when you purchase a online course at www.1examprep.com or call 1-877-804-3959 Access the information whenever and as often as you need.

No Classrooms
No Time Schedules
No Pressure

We provide the TOOLS for YOU to be SUCCESSFUL on YOUR schedule, not ours!
ALL of the Information you need is available at ONE LOW PRICE!

We provide you with exactly what you need to be successful. We are up to date with ALL of our Textbooks. No Bait and switch. No hidden upsells. We invite you to compare......

WE HAVE THE LOWEST TEXT BOOK PRICES IN THE INDUSTRY!!!!!

1 Exam Prep takes pride in our students and in their success. We want you to pass your exam the first time, every time in the most cost efficient way. We offer the most comprehensive, easy to follow, easy to use exam preparation techniques in the industry. We offer both State and County Licensing Exam Prep Courses throughout the United States. We have helped thousands of students successfully pass State and County Licensing Exams and we are seriously committed in helping you!

ALL OF OUR COURSES INCLUDE OUR PROVEN 4 POINT LEARNING SYSTEM UNRIVALED IN THE INDUSTRY YOU WILL RECEIVE:

TABBING AND HIGHLIGHTING INSTRUCTIONS

The most comprehensive, up to date Tabbing and Highlighting instructions found anywhere in the industry. Our experienced instructors will provide you with more tabs, more highlights than any other exam prep school in the country. We know the material cover to cover. We show you what you need to know and where you will find it, when the pressure is on and the clock is moving.

TEST TAKING TECHNIQUES

Learn the strategy on how to be the most efficient and effective on exam day. Learn how to manage the exam, the questions and the clock and make it work to your advantage

PRACTICE QUESTIONS AND ANSWERS

We provide our students with 1000's of Questions and Answers to help you prepare for your exam. We are continually updating and adding relevant questions with answers to prepare for the current exams. Our years of experience and thorough knowledge of the subject matter and testing formats allow us to provide you with the skills needed to address each and every question on the exam.

TEXTBOOK OVERVIEW

You will receive a high level summary on each textbook you receive and is required for your exam. The summary will outline the topics covered in the textbook, where these topics can be located in the textbook and the types of questions most likely to be answered in each textbook. You will also learn which parts of the textbook and which questions are aimed at a particular trade(s). Being thorough, efficient and confident is a huge advantage on exam day. Our Textbook Overview will help you manage your time and efficiency when the pressure is on and you need to stay focused.

TABLE OF CONTENTS

Below is the testing company information you will need concerning your exam.

PSI has examination centers in many other regions across the United States. You may take the written examination at any of these locations by filling out, and faxing the Special Arrangement Form found by using the below link.

For all Virginia specific information please visit - PSI Exam License Page

> Select Your State - Virginia
> Select VA Contractors
> Select Your License Classification

Scope of Work: Home Improvement Contracting (Abbr: HIC) means that service which provides for repairs or improvements to dwellings and townhouses as defined in the USBC or structures annexed to those dwellings or townhouses as defined in the USBC. The RBC classification also provides for this function. The HIC specialty does not provide for electrical, plumbing, HVAC, or gas fitting functions. It does not include new construction functions beyond the existing building structure other than decks, patios, driveways and utility out buildings that do not require a permit per the USBC.

Examination Outline

Open Book

# of Questions 50
Minimum Passing Score 70% 35 correct
Time Allowed 120 Minutes

CONTENT OUTLINE
Subject Area # of Items
Concrete 4
Masonry 4
Painting and Wall Covering 4
Drywall 4
Rough Carpentry and Framing 5
Siding 5
Finish Carpentry 5
Roofing 5
Insulation 5
Safety 5
Windows and Doors 4

Approved References

Painting and Decorating Craftsman's Manual and Textbook, 8th edition
Code of Federal Regulations – Title 29, Part 1926 (OSHA), 2010
Virginia Uniform Statewide Building Code, 2012
International Residential Code, 2012,
Carpentry and Building Construction, 2010 or 2016
The Contractor's Guide to Quality Concrete Construction, 2005, 3rd Edition
Modern Masonry - Brick, Block, Stone, Clois E. Kicklighter, 8th Edition,
Standard Practice for Installation of Rigid Poly Vinyl Chloride (PVC) Siding and Soffit - ASTM D 4756 - 06
Insulation Handbook, 2000
Gypsum Construction Handbook, 2014 Edition
Finish Carpenter's Manual, 1993
ANSI A117.1 - 2017 Accessible and Usable Buildings

Test Taking 101

Read each question carefully and read all the answers before you make a selection. Once you choose the answer to a question, look it up in the reference books. This is especially important even if you believe you know the answer without looking it up. Examination questions are validated by state codes and reference books, not merely according to standard practice. By answering a question solely by experience, you could unknowingly give an incorrect answer. Although experience is helpful, it is still to your benefit to look up each answer.

Sample
Question: The
sky is _____ .

Blue

Green

Red Orange

If the reference book says that the sky is green, guess what the correct answer to the question the sky is green. If you mark blue, you are wrong for not following the directions of finding the correct answer in the book.

This is not a test of what you know, this is a text of problem-solving techniques. The State or County has research that has proven that all good business owners

MUST have problem-solving skills. If they do not possess these skills, they have 4 times more of a chance of going out of business.

<u>For best performance, go through the examination several times.</u>

<u>On the first pass,</u> answer all the easy questions and write what book(s) (and chapter) you

think the answer will be in.

<u>On the second pass,</u> take one book at a time and go from the front to the back of each book, by chapter, and answer the questions in the most efficient manner.

On each successive pass of the test, you will find the harder questions:

DO NOT SPEND 5 MINUTES ON A QUESTION UNTIL THE END OF THE TEST.

ALL MATH QUESTIONS ARE ATTEMPTED LAST.

DO NOT LEAVE ANY ANSWERS UNANSWERED. TAKE OU BEST GUESS, YOU WILL HAVE A 25% CHANCE OF GUESSING CORRECTLY. Many of my students have passed the test on this method only.

    4. Relax, take a 30 second- or 1-minute break every 30-45 mins.

You do not have to answer any of the very hard questions to pass the test. Learn to identify them early in the process, skip them and take 25% at the end.

Most people think that they have 2 minutes and 24 seconds per question (120 mins / 50 questions) . Where if you do not attempt the very hard questions, you will have 3 mins and 10 seconds per question (120 minutes / questions).

Cross out the question on your test after you have found the correct answer.

This will ensure that you do not waste any time rereading a question that you have already answered, thus wasting your most valuable asset..... TIME!

Important Tip: If you are taking a paper and pencil exam, place a small check mark on the answer sheet next to any question you are going to skip.

This will do two things for you:

1.Reserve the answer line of the questions you are skipping

Instantly tell you which questions you need to look at again

Only one answer is right. If two answers mean the same thing, then they are both wrong. - Use scratch paper for math computations and work neatly. Place the number of the question next to the computation, and draw a line to separate it from the rest of your work. That way, if you decide to go back and check your answers, you can easily find your math for a question.

Do not use your scratch paper as an answer sheet. Some candidates number down the side of the scratch paper, record their answers there and then transcribe them onto the answer sheet later. This practice is time-consuming and increases the risk of error. Even worse, some candidates do not remember to transcribe their answers and turn in blank answer sheets!

Remember: only the answer sheet will be scored.

o Your final score will be determined from the answers you record on the answer sheet. Allow time to record an answer for each question, but **DO NOT** mark more than one answer per question. After the time is called, no further marking of the answer sheet will be allowed. If you are unsure of an answer, it may be better to guess, since you will **NOT** receive credit for any question left blank. Select the closest or best answer for each question.

If you want to change an answer, make sure before you do so that you have clearly made an error and have seen the mistake. Then, erase carefully and completely.

When you have finished the examination, take a close look at your answer sheet. Check each line to make sure there is only one answer marked for each question and that you have completely erased any changes, check marks, or stray lines. Candidates taking computer-based tests may scroll back through the test to review and change answers if necessary.

After you finish the examination, raise your hand and wait for the examiner to check your papers for completeness before leaving your seat. You may then leave the room.

Filling Out Your Answer Sheet

For Paper and Pencil testing, you will be given a scan-able answer sheet and will be asked to bubble in your answers to each question. You may also be asked to bubble in some additional information such as your name, social security number, and the test number that is printed on your test booklet. You may be asked to sign a statement that you will comply with the test administration rules, procedures, and guidelines and that you will not divulge the test questions.

For computer-based testing, you will be using a keyboard and/or a mouse to enter your response to each question. You will be given time and a tutorial to familiarize yourself with using the keyboard or mouse to select your answers. If you complete your test and have time remaining, you will be able to review any or all questions and change your responses. You may also be asked to indicate agreement with a statement that you will comply with the test administration rules, procedures, and guidelines and that you will not divulge the test questions. (LOL)

STRATEGIES FOR TAKING A STATE OR COUNTY EXAM

The amount of time spent studying is not the only factor in being prepared. It is also very important to study efficiently. If you want to retain what you are studying, you must set up a system. You are better off if you study for one hour in a quiet, private and relaxed atmosphere than if you study for 15 minutes at a time, 6 or 8 times a day. So, start your exam preparation by setting up a schedule and picking an appropriate area.

<u>Rules to help you study more effectively</u>

Make sure that you know the meaning of words that are unfamiliar to you. Keep a list of the unknown words, look up their definitions and then keep going back to review the list.

Always try to follow your study schedule and plan.

Practice the rules for answering multiple choice questions while you are doing practice questions.

Find your weakest areas and then concentrate your study in those areas.

Write down problem questions and go back over them later. Bring them to the class and ask the instructor to review questions.

Be sure to tab the books and become familiar with the tabs, indexes, and table of contents so you can find things quickly.

Time yourself, so you know how long you are spending on each question.

The Test Day

Remind yourself how well you will do on the exam.

Get a good night's rest. Get up early and remind yourself how well you will do on the exam. Eat a good breakfast. Remind yourself how well you will do on the exam.

Be sure to wear comfortable clothes. Wear or bring a sweater that you can add or remove depending on the room temperature. Remind yourself how well you will do on the exam.

Get to the exam site early. If you have to rush to find the site or get to the room, you may not do as well on the exam. Remind yourself how well you will do on the exam.

Don't get nervous or excited. Remember, if all else fails, there is always another day.

General rules to answer multiple choice questions

Read the directions carefully and be sure that you understand them.

Look over the answer sheet and be sure you understand how to mark your answers.

Be carefully when transferring answers from the test to the answer sheet. Be sure to:

Mark answer completely,

Only mark one answer per question,

Make no extra marks on the answer sheet,

If you make an error, erase,

Be sure to mark the answer in the correct spot on the answer sheet. Repeat the answer to yourself as you transfer it to the answer sheet. And then check it again on the test sheet, repeating it.

Read the question carefully and be sure you understand what it is asking. Cross out any extraneous information. Read the question again.

Read all the answers before you make a choice. Quite often a "possible" answer is listed before the correct answer. **Don't be caught by this trap.**

Eliminate all choices that are wrong choices. After you read all the answers then cross out the wrong answers and chose from the remaining.

Never pick an answer because of a pattern to the answers on previous questions. There is no pattern. Just pick the answer you feel is correct.

Be aware of key words that may help select an answer. Absolute words, such as: always, never, only, all or none. These words usually indicate an incorrect answer. Limiting words such as: some, many, most, sometimes, usually, normally, occasionally, will often indicate the correct answer.

Skip over a question that gives you trouble or is taking too long to solve. Mark it in the question book so you can find it later. Continue through the exam and come back to the question after you are completed. Be sure to save five minutes at the end of the test period, so that if there are any unanswered questions, you can at least guess at the answer.

10.Never leave a question unanswered. There is no penalty for a wrong answer.

Watch for negative question, such as, "Which of the following would make the statement false?"

12. How to make an educated guess. If there are four choices, you have a 25% chance to pick the correct answer. But you may be able to improve those odds.

Eliminate the incorrect answers.

Look for answers with absolute or limiting words.

Look for answers with obviously the wrong sign (+ or -).

Look for two answers with the same meaning, they are probably both wrong.

Look for two answers with the opposite meaning, one of them may be correct. If all else fails and you must guess, always guess the same choice.

13. Be careful changing answers. Remember that your first guess is normally the best. If you have time at the end of the exam you should go back through the test. But, only change answers if you are sure that your first choice is incorrect, *i.e.* you find a calculation error.

GOOD LUCK. Remember to keep reminding yourself that you will do fine and pass the exam!

If you have no confidence in yourself, you are twice defeated in the race of life. With confidence you have won before you've

started-----MARCUS GARVEY

There are 24 hours in a day. If 8 of them are spent sleeping, that gives you 16 hours to get some efficient and productive study done, right? It seems simple enough. There are plenty of hours in a day, so why is it so hard to use this time effectively, especially around exam time? We've found that managing their time effectively is one of the things
that students struggle the most with around exam time. However, time management
is also one of the things that schools never teach – how frustrating?!

In the weeks leading up to study leave, every teacher you have for every class you go to seems to pile on the work: Mrs. Gibb from English class tells you that you have to prepare 3 practice essays for both your visual and written texts, your Geography teacher Miss Wood expects you to do every past exam paper for the last three years before the exam, Mr. West your Math teacher says that you have to finish all of the questions in that darned AME textbook if you want to do well on the exam.

But they expect you to do all of this without giving you any time management tips. Mrs. Gibb, Miss Wood and Mr. West all fail to tell you how it's humanly possible to complete all this work without collapsing when you walk into the exam hall.
That's where we come in!

Read on for the time management tips that your teachers never gave you!

1. Focus on what you must study – not what you don't.
It seems obvious, but think of all the times you've sat down to study, and you've ended up
spending 2 hours studying the concepts you already know like the back of your hand.

It's easier to study the subjects you like. Studying the concepts that you're already confident in is a lot less challenging than studying the concepts that you find the most difficult, as your brain will have to work less to learn this information. Studying what you already know is a bad time management strategy because you'll leave all the important stuff to the last minute meaning you won't have the time to cover these concepts in depth.

The trouble with this tip is that it's often hard to decipher what you know and what you don't.

To figure out what you concept you already know, and what concepts you still need to learn, complete a subject audit. A subject audit involves breaking down a subject into several points or sections and then analyzing how well you know each of these points. You should spend most of your time studying those concepts that you have rated the most difficult. Find our study audit outline form here.

The key for effective time management is to review the easier material, but allow enough time to cover the harder concepts in depth so you're not left to study all of the most difficult concepts the night before the exam.

2. Work in sprints.

You may think that to have good time management skills you have to spend all of your time studying. However, this is a misconception that many students hold.

Think of studying for exams like training for a marathon.

On your first day of training, you wouldn't go out and run 42kms. You would burn-out quickly due to a lack of prior training, and you would probably be put off running for a long time. This would not be a good way to manage your time. The better route to success would be to slowly work up to running the 42kms by running a bit further every day.

This simple idea of training in short bursts has been proven effective in all areas of human performance. You don't have to be a marathon runner to use this strategy!

When studying, you should start out small by studying in short, focused 'sprints' followed by brief
breaks. Start by studying in 15- minute bursts followed by one 10-minute break. Over time, slowly increase the length of time you're studying (and breaking) for.

This strategy is effective because studying for short bursts promotes more intense focus and will give your brain the time to process and consolidate information as opposed to studying for long periods of time which is not effective and may increase your chances of burnout.

Don't think of effective time management as studying for three hours straight with no breaks, think of effective time management as using your time wisely and in ways that will best promote retention of information.

Follow these steps to practice effective time management and become an expert studier (or marathon runner!) in no time:

Set a timer for 15 minutes.

Put in some solid study until the timer goes off, making sure you're spending every minute working with no distractions.

Have a ten-minute break to check your phone, walk around, stretch, get outside etc.

Rinse and repeat.

Increase the amount of time you're studying for as you begin to feel more comfortable studying for extended lengths of time.

Make a study system.

I'm sure you've been lectured by every teacher you've ever had to "make a study plan!!!" Study plans are effective for your time management, however they're sometimes hard to stick to.

Here at Study Time, we find that the 'study system' is an effective strategy for really getting to the root of what you're studying. A study

system is easier to stick to, and therefore fosters better time management
skills, because it breaks tasks down into small chunks.

A study system is basically a simple list of steps that you can make to outline the steps you're going to take when you study. The list should start simple (4-5 things), but over time it should become more complex as you add steps to it.

Just like a workout plan at the gym or for sport, it will give you a clear direction of what action to take, making study much more efficient.

Over time, you can experiment with new study methods, and add them in to optimize the system.

Below is an example study formula that you could use when studying:

Download the "Achievement Standard" from the NCEA website

Turn this into a checklist for what you already know and what you need to know

Break the checklist into main themes using a mind map For each theme, make a summary sheet

After that, break down the key points of each summary and put these onto flash cards Read through your notes and ensure you understand them, and then hit the flash cards

Test yourself on all of them first, then make two piles, one that's wrong and one that's right. Then redo the wrong pile again

Get someone else to test you

Practice exam papers – test yourself using exam papers from the past 2-3 years and time yourself

Work through the answers

Write a sheet of all tips/tricks i.e. things you got wrong in the

practice exam papers Redo exam paper and make model

answers

Adjust flashcards if necessary i.e. make new ones based on

the exam papers Re-test all your flashcards

Creating a study system will keep you on track and it will allow you to effectively plan out your time while studying.

4. Practice distributed learning.
Imagine your Math teacher gave you seven equations to do for homework. How would you answer these questions? Would you do one question per day for seven days, or would you do all seven questions in one day?

You may think that it would be a better time management strategy to do all seven questions at once and get them over and done with. However, this is an ineffective way to manage your time.

The brain works better when it has time to process information. Neuroscience has shown that your brain needs time to consolidate information that has been newly learned, in order to form strong links between neurons and thus strong memories.

If the learning is done in one big chunk, you'll just forget it after three days. However,

if you review it a day after, then you'll retain it for seven days.

When making a study schedule, you should space out when you study for each subject. For example, don't spend one day studying
English, then the next day studying Math, then the next day studying Biology.

Instead, you should alternate studying for these subjects throughout the day. Do one hour of Math, then one hour of English study, then one hour of Biology, and so on.

This is a much better way to manage your time, because the more often you review a concept, the more solidified it will be in your mind. This is because there will be more time to consolidate this into your memory. Also, taking breaks between reviewing certain concepts will give your brain time to process the information.

Try it out!

1 Exam Prep Tabs

Painting and Decorating Craftsman's Manual, 8th Ed.

These 1 Exam Prep Tabs are based on the *Painting and Decorating Craftsman's Manual, 8th Edition*.

Each 1 Exam Prep Tabs sheet has five rows of tabs. Start with the first tab at the first row at the top of the page; proceed down that row placing the tabs at the locations listed below. Place each tab in your book setting it down one notch until you get to the bottom of a page. Then start back at the top again.

1 Exam Prep Tab	**Page #**
Table of Contents	iii
Solvents	10
Pigments	13
Resins	15
Additives	17
Primers	33
Shellacs & Lacquers	36
Elastomeric Coatings	41
Floor Coatings	43
Caulks	51
Efflorescence	59
Surface Preparation	65
Concrete & Masonry Surfaces	81
Hand Tools	85
Mixing	115
Brushing	119
Rolling	121
Spraying Defects	127
Wood Finishes & Types	131
Finishes	133
Types of Brushes	149
Types of Rollers	153
Spray Equipment	155
Ladders	165
Scaffolds	173
Safety	191

Recommended Highlights

	Page #	Description
Chapter 2		
	10	Solvents: Water, Hydrocarbon, (Aliphatic and Aromatic), Turpentines, etc.
	13	Pigments: Color, Hiding, Extender, Barrier, Inhibitive, Sacrificial.
	15	Resins: Natural (Copal), Lac, Rosin). Synthetic (alkyds, Epoxies, Phenolics, Silicones, Vinyls, Acrylics, Polyurethanes, Etc.)
	16	Additives: Driers, Antiskinning Agents, Fungicides, Emulsion, Etc.
	33	Primers: Wood, Concrete, Plaster, Drywall, Steel, Galvanized
	36	Sealers: Shellacs or Varnish for Knots.
	37	Shells, Lacquers, Varnish

1 Exam Prep
Carpentry and Building Construction Manual, 2016 Ed.
Tabs and Highlights

These 1 Exam Prep Tabs are based on the *Carpentry and Building Construction Book, 2016 Edition.*

Each 1 Exam Prep Tabs sheet has five rows of tabs. Start with the first tab at the first row at the top of the page; proceed down that row placing the tabs at the locations listed below. Place each tab in your book setting it down one notch until you get to the bottom of a page. Then start back at the top again.

1 Exam Prep Tab	Pg.#
Table of Contents	v
Bldg. Codes & Planning	33
Plans & Drawings	49
Calculating Board Feet	63
Bar Chart	70
Critical Path	73
Hand Tools	109
Concrete	219
Placing Concrete	223
Site Layout	237
Establishing Lines & Grades	243
Concrete Foundation Walls	265
Laying Block Foundation Walls	279
Concrete Flatwork	295
Estimating Concrete	303
Wood as a Bldg. Material	319
Engineered Lumber	353
Framing Systems	371
Floor Joists Spans	383

*** *This concludes the tabs. Please proceed with the highlights on the following page.* ***

Pg. #	Highlight
35	**Permits and Inspections**
47	**Different Symbols** Highlight: Brick, Concrete Block, Cinder Block and Face Grain Wood.
49	The views of a building include general drawings and detail drawings … They provide information about how parts fit together.
50	**Plan Views:** A site plan, or plot plan, shows the building with lot boundaries … The basic elements of a site plan, are drawn from notes and sketches based upon a survey.
50-51	A foundation plan is a top view of the footings and foundation walls. …This plan is used by foundation contractors.
55	**Detail Drawings:** When precise information is need about a small or complex portion of the building, a detail drawing is made. Details are drawn at larger scales than plan views, such as …. or ¼" = 1'0".
56	**Renderings:** A rendering is sometimes called a presentation drawing. It is more like a picture of the structure. **Schedules:** A schedule is a list or chart. (See example on page 57).
63	**Calculating Board Feet:** A board foot is a unit of measure that represents a piece of lumber … and the thickness of 1" nominal size. Table 2-3: Rules for Estimating Board Feet To determine the number of board feet in one or more pieces of lumber, use the following formula: (equation).
70	**Bar Charts:** A bar chart is an easy way to keep track of a project. It shows how long each tasks will take and when each task will start and end.
72	**Critical Path Method Diagrams:** The Critical Path Method (CPM) of scheduling shows the relationship among tasks as well as how long they take.
109-111	Highlight the following: - Try Square - Combination Square - Sliding T-bevel - Framing Square - Triangular Framing Square - Carpenter's Level - Torpedo Level

Pg. #	Highlight
218	**Understanding Concrete:** Concrete is a hard, strong building material that is made by mixing cement … water in proper proportions.
	Hydration is a chemical reaction that occurs when water combines with cement.
219	Table 8-1: Basic Types of Portland Cement
221	**Admixtures**
222	**Super-Plasticizing Admixtures**. These can make concrete flow very easily, or they can significantly increase its strength.
223	**Mixing**
225	Table 8-3: Mix Proportions for Sand of Various Moisture Content
226	**Slump Testing**: A slump test is a test to measure the consistency of concrete.
227	In a slump test, concrete straight from the mixer is placed into a small sheet metal cone of specific dimensions.
	A measurement is then taken of how much the unsupported mass of concrete slumps, or loses its conical shape.
229	**Reinforcing Bar:** Rebar is most often used in footings and walls, while welded-wire fabric is used mostly in slabs.
	Rebar comes in 20' lengths … A rebar shear is sometimes called a rebar cutter.
237	**Types of Instruments:** Highlights the following: - Builder's Level - Automatic Level - Laser Level
238	**Transits:** A transit can measure horizontal angles and vertical angles as well. It can also be used to determine if a post or wall is plumb.
	A transit is classified by the smallest increment that can be read on its vernier scale … are in minutes or seconds.
239	**Locating a Benchmark:** To layout a building using a transit or a level … called the benchmark.
240-241	**Laying Out a Simple Rectangle:** Layout a simple rectangle parallel to the existing line as follows: Steps 1-6
243	**Grade:** The grade refers to the level of the ground where it will meet the foundation of the completed building.

<u>Pg. #</u>	<u>Highlight</u>

244   **Setting Up Batter Boards:** Steps 1-6.

244-245   **Batter Boards:** A batter board is a board fastened horizontally to stakes … corners of the building will be located.

246   **Measuring Difference in Elevation:** The process of determining differences in elevation between points that are remote from each other is called differential leveling.

249   Table 9-1: Converting Inches to Decimal Fractions of a Foot

257   **Footing Forms**

258   A common type of wall footing form … these boards are sometimes called haunch boards.

Spreaders, or form brackets, are the boards that hold apart the sides of the forms. Lumber formwork is often assembled with duplex head nails to make disassembly easy later on.

259   **Estimating the Job**

260   The vertical step should be poured at the same time as the rest of the footing. … This is the height of a block with a standard 3/8" mortar joint.

A run is a horizontal section between two vertical sections.

The vertical step should be at least 6" thick and be the same width as the rest of the footing.

262   **Footing Drains:** If water builds up on one side of a foundation … This is called hydrostatic pressure.

Footing drains, sometimes called foundation drains or perimeter drains, relieve pressure by allowing water to drain away.

263   The piping can also drain into subsurface drain fields if permitted by code.

The pipes should be placed with the holes facing down … After the pipes are in place, the drainage area should be covered with filter fabric also called (geotextile or landscaping fabric).

264   **Wall Form Details:** Wall forms may be made from wood or metal, depending on how durable they must be … Although any exterior-grade plywood can be used, special form-grade plywood is available."

Form-grade plywood made by member mills of APA … is referred to as plyform.

265   Medium-density overlay (MDO) has a smooth surface and can be reused many times.

High-density overlay (HDO) offers the smoothest finish and can be reused the most.

Mill-oiled plywood … This coating prevents the forms from sticking to the concrete.

Pg. #	Highlight

Forms built on site may be taken apart after the concrete hardens … It is generally more cost effective and efficient to use reusable forms.

268 **Sill-Plate Anchors**

269 A sill sealer is often placed under the sill plate on poured walls … during placement.

Foundation Wall Details

275 **Strengthening Walls:** Adding pilasters to the wall is another way to strengthen it … bottom of the beam or girder they support.

277 **Protecting Block Walls:** Care must be taken to keep blocks dry on the job. They should be stored on planks or other supports, so the edges do not touch the ground … Concrete block must not get wet just before or during installation.

278-279 **Mortar Mixtures**

The following types of mortar are the most common:
- Type N Mortar
- Type M Mortar
- Type S Mortar
- Type O Mortar

279 Table 10-4: Proportions of Mortar Ingredients by Volume

Mixing and Placing Mortar: Mortar stiffened by hydration should be thrown away. It is not easy to tell whether evaporation or hydration is the cause.

Building the Corners: The corners of the wall are built first, usually four or five courses high.

281 A story pole, or course pole, is a board with markings 8" apart. It can be used to gauge the top of the masonry for each course.

285 Table: Estimating Table for Masonry Blocks

287 **Lintels and Bond Beams:** Where openings occur in the foundation, a lintel must be installed over the opening to provide support for the masonry above it. A lintel … One leg of the L fits under the masonry to support it over the opening.

Another type of lintel is made of … It is placed over an opening just as a wood header would be placed.

A third way to create a lintel is to use lintel blocks … The open portions of the blocks are then filled with concrete and reinforced with rebar.

Pg. #	Highlight
	A bond beam is a course of reinforced concrete or reinforced lintel block. It is sometimes called a collar beam.
294	Concrete flatwork consist of flat, horizontal areas of concrete that are usually 5" or less in thickness.
303	Table 11-1: Estimating Materials for Concrete Slab
304	**Screeding:** The first step in finishing any flatwork is screeding … Screeding may also be done with mechanical equipment.
305	**Bullfloating:** Bullfloating makes the concrete surface more even with no high or low spots.
	Bullfloating is done shortly after screeding, while the concrete is still wet enough … there must be no visible water on the concrete.
	Edging and Jointing: "When sheen has left the surface and the concrete has started to stiffen, other finishing operations can be done … The edger is run back and forth, covering coarse aggregate particles.
306	**Troweling:** For a dense, smooth finish, floating is followed by troweling with a steel trowel … Troweling cannot be started until the concrete has hardened enough to prevent fine material and water from working to the surface.
320	**Hardwoods and Softwoods**
	Table 12-1: Principal Commercial Softwoods
324	**Hardwood Grades:** Hardwood are available in three common grades, first and seconds, (FAS), select, and No. 1 common.
	Figure: A Grade Stamp. Know each mark A-E.
352-353	**Engineered Lumber Basics:** Engineered lumber is not suitable for all purposes. It should not be used where it will permanently be exposed to the weather.
382	Table 14-2: Floor Joist Spans
403	Table 15-2: Floor Joist Spans for Common Lumber Species
	Termite Shields (Highlight box in top right corner).
410	**Bridging:** Cross bridging (also called diagonal bridging) is more common because it is very effective and requires less material. Precut 1x3 or 2x2 lumber is sometimes used for cross bridging with nailing flanges may also be used.
421	**Installing Subflooring:** The layer of material directly over the floor joists is called floor sheathing. It forms what is called the subfloor.

Pg. #	Highlight

Pg. #	Highlight

The total rise is the vertical distance from the top of the top plate to the upper end of the measuring line. The unit rise is the number of inches that a roof rises for every 12" of run.

Slope refers to a ratio of rise to run.

474   **Laying Out Common Rafters**

475   The theoretical length of a common rafter is the shortest distance between the outer edge of the plate (A) … rafter meets the ridge line (B).

It may be calculated the following ways: (4 bullets)

481   **Laying Out a Bird's Mouth:** A bird's mouth is a notch made in a rafter with an overhang so that the rafter will fit against the plate … The level cut, which bears on top of the plate, is called the seat cut.

492   **Parts of a Rood Truss**

496   **Bracing Trusses**

505   **Hip Rafter Layout**

550   **Chimney Saddles:** A chimney saddle, or cricket, diverts water around a chimney and prevents ice from building up on the roof behind it.

556-557   **Building a Box Cornice:** Steps 1-9. Highlight the following:
Step 3: Lookouts are generally made from 2 x 4 lumber.
Nail through the back of the ledger into the end of each lookout with two 16d coated nails.
Step 4: Snap a chalk line along the length of the building on the sheathing.
Step 7: The groove should be located about 3/8" up from the bottom edge of the fascia board.
Step 9: Nail the soffit to each lookout and to the ledger strip with 4d galvanized nails about 6" apart.

562-563   **Spans:** The stamp consists of a pair of numbers separated by a slash mark, such as 32/16 or 12/0…Note that greater spans are generally allowed for roof sheathing than for floor sheathing."

577   **Types of Windows**

596   **Types of Doors**

601   **Direction of Swing**

602   Figure: Door Hand. Two Methods. Two ways to determine the swing direction of a door.

605   **Garage Doors:** Mounting clearance required above the top of sectional overhead doors is usually about 12". However, low headroom brackets are available when such clearance is not possible. Overhead doors are usually installed by the door supplier.

Pg. #	Highlight
608	**Preparing the Door:** When hung properly, the door should fit with an opening clearance of 1/16" at the sides and top … If it has a threshold, the bottom clearance should be 1/8" above the threshold."
	Bevel the lock edge so that the inside edge will clear the jamb. This angle is about 3 degrees.
615	**Interior Doors:** Most interior passage doors are 1-3/8" thick. Standard interior door height is 6'-8'. Common minimum widths for single doors are: -Bedrooms and other habitable rooms: 2'-6" -Bathrooms: 2'- 4" -Small closets and linen closets: 2'
617	**Pocket Doors:** A pocket door slides into an opening or pocket inside a wall.
	Standard widths are 2'-0", 2'-4", 2'-6", 2'-8", and 3'-0". Any style of door with a thickness of 1-3/8" can be installed in the pocket to match the other doors in the home.
618	**Installing Interior Doors**
618-619	**Installing the Door Frame:** Plumb the assembled frame in the rough opening using pairs of shingle shims placed between the side jambs and the studs.
619	**Hanging an Interior Door:** "Interior doors are often hung with two 3-1/2" by 3-1/2" loose-pin butt hinges. However, three hinges will strengthen the door and help to prevent it from warping."
620	**Door Stops and Trim:** After the door is in place, permanently nail the stops with 1-1/2" finish nails. Nail the stop on the lock side first, setting it tightly against the door face while the door is latched. Space the nails 16" apart in pairs … Allow a 1/32" clearance from the door face to prevent scraping as the door is opened.
626	**Roofing Terms and Concepts:** One square of roofing is the amount of roofing required to cover 100 sq. ft. of roof surface.
	The amount of weather protection provided by the overlapping of shingles is called coverage.
629	**Roll Roofing**
632	**Underlayment:** Underlayment is a layer of weather-resistant material that is applied to the roof sheathing before the final roofing material is installed.
	Roof underlayment generally has four purposes: (4 bullets).
633	Eaves protection should extend from the end of the eaves to a point at least 22" inside the exterior wall line of the house.
	Flashing: Flashing is a thin metal sheet or strip used to protect a building from water seepage.

| Pg. # | Highlight |

Flashing must be installed so that it sheds water. Metal used for flashing must be corrosion resistant. Galvanized steel (at least 26 gauge), 0.019" thick aluminum, 16 oz. copper, or lead-coated copper can be used.

634   **Drip Edges:** Drip edges are designed and installed to protect edges of the roof.

636   **Installing Underlayment:** Make sure to create a top lap of at least 2" at all horizontal joints and a 4" side lap at all end joints. Lap the underlayment over all hips and ridges for 6" on each side.

637   **Laying Shingles**

638   Two methods for alignment are:
-Method 1: Breaking the joints on halves
-Method 2: Breaking the joints on thirds

Nailing: Nails should be made of hot-dipped galvanized steel, aluminum, or stainless steel … Shanks should be 10-to 12-gauge wire.

In areas where high, local codes may require six nails per shingle …To provide extra resistance to uplift in high wind areas, use six nails for each strip.

642   Table 22-1: Determining Roof Area from a Plan

652   **Installation:** To ensure the correct slope, measure the distance in feet from one end of the fascia to the other. Round up to the nearest whole foot. Multiply this number by 1/16".

658   **Types of Wood Siding**

660   **Flashing:** Metal flashing is used to seal the joints where the siding meets a horizontal surface … Flashing should extend well under the siding and sufficiently over ends of a well-sloped drip cap to prevent water from seeping in.

661   **Protecting the Sheathing:** Sheathing should be covered by a barrier or building paper or housewrap … Every type of siding should be installed over building paper or housewrap.

690   **Brick Basics**

694   **Types of Mortar**
- Type M
- Type S
- Type N
- Type O

697   Figure: Brick Veneer at The Foundation

698   **Flashing and Drainage:** A weep hole is a hole that provides drainage near the bottoms of the walls. Weep holes are often formed … every 18" to 24" along the wall.

Pg. #	Highlight
	Wall Ties: The veneer wall must be tied to the frame of the house with corrosion-resistant fasteners, called wall ties, secured with galvanized nails.
702	**Estimating Brick:** A Rough estimate of bricks needed may be made based on a wall's square footage. Approximately seven standard bricks are needed for every square foot of veneer wall … After calculating the square footage of walls, minus any openings, multiply this figure by 7 to get the number of bricks required.
703	Table 24-2: Modular Brick and Mortar Required for Single-Wythe Walls in Running Bond
706	**Fireplace Construction**
	Hearth: The hearth is the floor of the firebox, plus the fireproof area in front of the fireplace. The hearth has two parts … it is built of or lined with firebrick. It should be at last 4" thick.
711	**Chimney Construction Details**
711-712	**Flue Liners:** A flue liner is a fire-clay or stainless-steel pipe assembled from individual sections that sit within the chimney brick work. This creates a fire hazard.
714	Chimney Saddle: A saddle (sometimes called a chimney cricket) actually diverts water round the chimney. Building code requires … and does not intersect the ridge.
724	**Parts of a Stairway**
726	A stringer is a long piece of 2 X lumber that supports the stairs.
	Balusters are slender vertical members that support the handrail.
	Handrails and Balusters
728	Gooseneck – The curved piece between the main handrail and a newel post.
729	Newel – A newel is a post that supports the handrail at the top and bottom.
	A landing newel, also called a starting newel, is located at the bottom of a stair.
	An angle newel supports the handrail at the landings, particularly where the stair changes direction.
	Stairway Planning
730	Radiating treads called winders can be used instead of a platform when a stairway must change direction.
734	**Calculating Total Run:** The total run is a measurement equal to the unit run times the number of treads in the stairway.

Pg. #	Highlight
	Calculating Unit Rise and Unit Run: (Steps 1-5)
759	**Door Casing**
	Installation: Casings are nailed to the door jamb and to the framing around it, allowing about a 3/16" reveal on the face of the jamb. A reveal is a small offset between a piece of trim and the surface it is applied to.
760	**Window Casing and Shutters:** The stool is a horizontal member that laps the window sill and extends beyond the casing. An apron serves as a finish member below the stool.
	The Window Stool: The window stool is normally the first piece of window trim to be installed. It is notched so that it fits between the jambs and butts against the lower sash.
761	The upper drawing shows the stool in place. The lower drawing shows it laid out and cut, ready for installation.
780-781	**Planning for Cabinets**
783	**Kitchen Cabinet Dimensions:** Wall cabinets are usually 12" deep and are often located beneath a soffit.
	A soffit is an area around the perimeter of the room that is lower than the rest of the ceiling.
894	**Insulation Basics:** R-value is a measure of a material's ability to resist eat transmission.
	Table 31-1: Thermal Properties of various Building Material per Inch of Thickness
900	**Controlling Moisture:** The process by which a vapor turns into a liquid is called condensation.
	Vapor Retarders: A vapor retarder is a material that reduces the rate at which water vapor can move through a material.
901	**Attic Ventilation**
	Reducing Temperatures
902	Where a sloped ceiling is insulated, there should be a free opening of at least 1-1/2" between the sheathing and the insulation to encourage are movement.
906	**Job Safety: Handling Fiberglass**
923	**Installing Drywall**
924	Table 32-1: Nailing Structural Support for Drywall
938	**Installing a Suspended Ceiling** (Steps 1-7).

1 Exam Prep

The Contractors Guide to Quality Concrete Construction, 3rd Edition
Tabs and Highlights

These 1 Exam Prep Tabs are based on The Contractor's Guide to Quality Concrete Construction, 3rd Edition.

Each 1 Exam Prep Tabs sheet has five rows of tabs. Start with the first tab at the first row at the top of the page; proceed down that row placing the tabs at the locations listed below. Place each tab in your book setting it down one notch until you get to the bottom of a page. Then start back at the top again.

Special Note to our Students: If you are a 1 Exam Prep student, here is how to really get the most from these Tabs. Follow the above instructions, but before placing the tab, find the tab's topic in the outline of your appropriate module. Now locate and highlight several items listed in the outline just before the topic, and just after. See how the topic fits in the outline and how it relates as a concept to the broader concept spelled out in the outline. If you take a few minutes to do this, when you take the test key words in the test questions will remind you of where the information is in the manual!

1 Exam Prep Tab	Page	Subjects Covered/Highlight
Table of Contents	7	
Organizing for Quality	9	CHAPTER 1
The Concrete Mix	13	CHAPTER 2
	13	**Slump:** The slump test is used to measure the consistency of the concrete…..Variations in slump are caused by changes in water content, air content, admixtures, aggregate proportions and gradation, delivery time, and temperature…
	13	**Figure 2.2 -** Measuring the slump of fresh concrete. The cone is filled with concrete in three layers of equal volume. Each layer is rodded 25 times with a steel tamping rod.
	14-15	**Compressive Strength Test:** The compressive strength of concrete is measured by testing concrete cylinders (usually 6 in. in diameter and 12 in. high) in the laboratory… Cylinders are tested for two purposes: for acceptance testing and to estimate the strength of the concrete at any given time.
	15	**Figure 2.5** - Cylinders must be kept at a controlled temperature while stored on the jobsite….
	17	**Basic Types of Portland Cement:** - Type I: Is a general-purpose cement, that is used in the vast majority of concrete - Type II: Is generally used where reduced heat of hydration is needed or where moderate sulfate resistance is desired - Type III: Is a high-early-strength cement - Type IV: Is a low-heat-of-hydration cement, limited in use to massive structures such as dams - Type V: Is a sulfate-resistant cement, limited to use where high sulfate soils, solutions, or groundwater are found.

1 Exam Prep Tab	Page	Subjects Covered/Highlight
	17	**Fly Ash:** Fly ash is a byproduct of coal-burning power plants and is classified as a pozzolan.....Fly ash usually reduces the air content in air-entrained concrete, so a larger amount of air-entraining agent is needed to maintain the required amount of air
	20	**Admixtures:** Admixtures, when properly used, can increase early strength, increase ultimate strength, accelerate or retard setting time, increase workability, improve uniformity, reduce permeability, and improve durability.....They are dispensed into the batch in measured amount in a liquid form
	20	**Water reducers:** Water-reducing admixtures enhance the workability of the concrete, making it possible to reduce the water by 5 percent or more.
	20	**High-Range Water Reducers:** Commonly known as super plasticizers, high-range water reducers may reduce the amount of water in the mix by over 30 percent....
	20	**Retarders:** A retarder is usually used in hot weather to extend setting time, allowing more time for placement and finishing, and often causing a reduction in early strength...
	20	**Accelerators:** An accelerator is used to shorten setting time or to produce high early strengths.....
	21	**Water-Reducing Retarders:** Retardation and water reduction are often combined in the same admixture
	21	**Water-Reducing Accelerators:** Acceleration and water reduction are often combined in the same admixture
	21	**Air-Entraining Agents:** In addition to being essential for durability when concrete is exposed to freezing and thawing and the application of deicing salts, strained air benefits concrete in other ways.
	22	**Table 2.2** – Relationship between Water-Cement Ratio and Compressive Strength
	22	**Table 2.3** – Maximum Permissible Water – Cement Ratios for Concrete in Severe Exposures
Concrete Specifications	27	CHAPTER 3
	30	**Delivery Time for Ready-Mixed Concrete:** Unless special conditions are involved, the maximum delivery time is specified as 90 minutes or 300 revolutions of the mixer drum...
Foundations	33	CHAPTER 4
Formwork	41	CHAPTER 5

1 Exam Prep Tab	Page	Subjects Covered/Highlight

Placing Concrete in the Forms: Freshly mixed concrete must be properly consolidated after it is deposited into the form if it is to achieve its desired material properties…..The use of external form vibrators requires special form design to determine the power output and location of the vibrators because external vibration can destroy a form that is not designed for such loading.

Figure 5.22 - An internal vibrator causes the concrete within its field of action to act like a thick liquid and thus consolidate better…

Reinforcement 63 CHAPTER 6

Types of Reinforcement: Though most reinforcement for concrete is made of steel, today's concrete reinforcement can also be manufactured from plastic and other synthetic materials…..

The most commonly used types of reinforcement are deformed bars and welded wire reinforcement.

Deformed bars are round steel bars with lugs rolled into the surface of the bar. There are 11 ASTM standard bar sizes (See Table 6.1).

Another type of reinforcement is welded wire fabric…..Welded wire reinforcement is commonly (but incorrectly) called mesh". WWR is shipped in rolls or flat sheets

Other Types of Reinforced Concrete: Fibered-reinforced concrete has dispersed, randomly oriented fibers added to the concrete mix.

Storing and Handling Reinforcing Bars on the Job: Before reinforcing bars are placed, many inspectors require that the bar surface be free of any coatings that might reduce the bond between concrete and steel.

A thin film of rust or mill scale is normal and is not harmful, but loose rust or mill scale should be brushed off.

Concrete cover: Example: Number 5 and smaller 1 ½ inches. (Also See Fig. 6.12)

Placing of Reinforcement: Reinforcing bars must be held securely in position while the concrete is being placed… usually No. 16 gage black, soft annealed wire

74-75 There are many different types of rebar ties:
  Type A: Called a single tie, are the simplest and are normally used in flat horizontal work
  Type B: Called a wrap-and-snap tie, are for tying wall reinforcement
  Type C: Saddle or "U" ties, are more complicated and are used for tying footing bars or mats to hold hooked ends in bars in position; they are used also to secure column ties to vertical bars
  Type D: Called a wrap-and-saddle ties, are similar to the saddle tie and can be used to secure heavy mats that are lifted by cranes

- Type E: Figure eight ties, can be used in walls instead of the wrap-and-snap tie

Figure 6.14 -The most common ties.

Splicing Reinforcing Steel: The three types of splices are:
  Lap Splices: May be more economical than the other types of splices, depending on the amount of congestion and labor productivity. In lap splices, the bars are lapped next to each other a certain length and securely wired together with tie wire.
        Mechanical Splices: Use two basic splicing devices: couplers and end-bearing. Couplers are used to resist both tensile and compressive forces. End-bearing devices are used for splices capable of transferring compression forces only.
        Welded Splices: Are generally lap splices or butt splices, of which there are several types. Another process, called thermite welding, is used in making butt-welded joints in large size bars, particularly #43 and #57 bars.

CHAPTER 7

Three types of joints are used in concrete slabs and walls:
        Contraction Joints: Are made within a structural element or building to accommodate movements that are caused by temperature changes, drying, shrinkage, and creep…
-Isolation Joints: Are used at points of restraint, including the junction between the elements of a structure…..
        Construction Joints: Are joints that are introduced for the convenience or needs of the construction process…

Be familiar with: **Construction Joints for Supported Beams & Slabs**

Be familiar with: **Contraction Joints for Walls**

Isolation Joints for Walls

Construction Joints in Walls
        Horizontal Construction Joints
        Vertical Construction Joints

CHAPTER 8

Contraction (Control) Joints: Contraction joints are not intended to prevent cracks…..These planned cracks at the contraction joints are usually induced by cutting into the slab to a depth of one-fourth the slab thickness, or a minimum of 1 in. creating a weakened plane.

1 Exam Prep Tab	Page	Subjects Covered/Highlight

90   **Contraction Joint Spacing:** A common guideline for spacing contraction joints is to space them in feet approximately 2-½ times the slab depth in inches… under less than average conditions as little as two times the depth of the slab.

91   Isolation Joints (Expansion Joints): Isolation joints are used to separate the slab from any adjacent structure such as another slab, wall, column, adjacent building, or any appurtenance in the slab.
- Junction of slab and wall
- Columns

92   **Reinforcement in a Concrete Slab**: Reinforcement in a slab includes reinforcing bars, welded wire fabric, steel and synthetic fibers, smooth dowels, and tie bars…..Tie bars are used to prevent adjacent slabs from separating at warping joints or to tie the outside or perimeter lane in a large paved area to the adjacent lane

92   **Welded Wire Reinforcement**: To serve its purpose, the WWR should be placed 2 in. below the slab surface or within the upper one-third of the slab thickness, whichever is closer to the surface…..Hooks may be used to pull up low spots after screeding but before initial floating.

124   **Pumping Concrete:** Because the concrete pumping must be continuous, trucks scheduling is extremely important. A long delay may require having to break down the line, clean it out, and start again

125   **Finishing a Slab-on-Ground:** A checkrod follows screeding to fill in minor low spots or cut off high points and to embed coarse aggregate particles into the surface.

126   **Surface Finishes:** Properly done, a troweled surface will be hard, dense, and extremely wear-resistant…..This procedure avoids the problems caused by over-troweling or troweling overly-wet surfaces

126   **Figure 10.16** - Timely power floating…

Figure 10.18 - Hand troweling for the final finish…

Figure 10.19 - Applying a broomed finish for a uniform and skid-resistant surface

127   **Controlling Placement**: In wall and column placement, the distance of free fall of the concrete may have to be controlled. High slump, non-air-entrained mixes are most likely to segregate, possibly at heights of more than 5 or 6 ft. When segregation may be a problem, dropchutes (elephant trunks) may be used (Fig 10.21). Splashing can also be eliminated by use of dropchutes

Hot Weather Placement:

Cold Weather Placement: ACI 301 requires cold-weather concreting procedures when the mean daily temperature is less than 40° F. When the concrete materials are heated, the concrete temperature should be between 50° and 70° F at the time of placing. The concrete temperature should then be maintained at 50° F for five days or 70° F for three days.....

Curing to Maintain proper Moisture Content:

Fresh Concrete/Plastic Shrinkage Cracks: Plastic shrinkage cracks occur while the concrete is still plastic or workable, often before final finishing.....Other contributing factors are high concrete temperature in relation to air temperature and high slump mixes.

Surface Scaling: The scaling of concrete flatwork surfaces in areas of severe winter weather can be (but shouldn't be) a serious problem when deicing chemicals are used.....Without adequate air, even the best of construction practices won't prevent the concrete from scaling when exposed to deicers.

Figure 11.17 - Early scaling of the surface mortar of a non-air-entrained concrete slab.....

Hardened Concrete/Reported Low Cylinder Strengths:
The term "reported" is used to distinguish between what is reported and what may be the truth.....Most often violated is the requirement for keeping the fresh cylinders at a temperature between 60 and 80 °F during the 24 or 48 hours they are stored on the jobsite before being transported to the testing laboratory

Figure 11.21- Left in the sun for the first day of storage at the jobsite, these cylinders will not provide a valid test result.

1 Exam Prep

Gypsum Construction Handbook – 7th Edition
Tabs and Highlights

These 1 Exam Prep tabs are based on the *Gypsum Construction Handbook 7th Edition*.

Each 1 Exam Prep Tabs sheet has five rows of tabs. Start with the first tab at the first row at the top of the page; proceed down that row placing the tabs at the locations listed below. Place each tab in your book setting it down one notch until you get to the bottom of a page. Then start back at the top again.

1 Exam Prep Tab	Page #
Contents	v
Drywall & Veneer Products	1
Framing	69
Cladding	99
Backerboard Installation	141
Finishing Drywall System	159
Finishing Veneer	205
Conventional Plaster Products	227
Conventional Plaster Applications	249
Acoustical Ceiling Design & Application	285
System Design Considerations	322
Planning Execution & Inspection	349
Problems, Remedies, & Preventive Measures	369
Safety Considerations & Material Handling	403
Tools and Equipment	417
Building Sciences	441
Sustainability	467

*** *This concludes the tabs for this book. Please continue with the highlights below.* ***

Page #	Highlight

3   **Gypsum Panel Limitations**

1. Exposure to excessive or continuous moisture and extreme temperatures should be avoided. Not recommended for use in solar or other heating systems when board will be in direct contact with surfaces exceeding 125°F

3. Maximum spacing of frame members: ½ inch and ⅝ inch gypsum panels are designed for use on framing centers up to 24 inches; ⅜ inch panels designed for use on framing centers up to 16 inch….. ¼ inch SHEETROCK Brand are not recommended for single-layer applications on open framing.

5   **Products Available**

5-6   **USG Sheetrock Brand Ultralight Panels Firecode X:** A lightweight 5/8"-thick Type X panel that is up to 15% lighter … Available with tapered edges and 48" width.

6   **USG Sheetrock Brand Gypsum Panel, Firecode C Core:** Available in ½ inch and ⅝ inch thickness…..and column fire-protective assemblies using these special products provide 1-hr. to 4-hr. fire-resistance ratings

11   **Veneer Plaster Gypsum Base Products**

14   **Specifications – Gypsum Bases Table**

15   **Sheathing Limitations:** 6. Felt should be applied horizontally with 2" overlap and immediately anchored with metal lath, masonry ties or corrosion resistant screws or staples.

22   **Bead and Trim Accessories**

USG Sheetrock Brand and Beadex Brand … Corner Tape-On Bead (B1W, B1XW EL, Micro Bead, B1 Super Wide): For 90 degree outside corners. Suitable for use on any thickness of wallboard.

Page #	Highlight
31	**Z-Furring Channels:** used to mechanically attach … to interior side of monolithic concrete and masonry walls.
36	**Fasteners**
	Gypsum Board Screws
38-39	**Selector Guide for Screws Table**
40	**Basic Types of Screws**
42	**Screw Applications**
43	**Double Thread Screw Applications**
44	**Selector Guide for Gypsum Board Nails**
49	**USG Sheetrock Brand Powder Setting-Type Joint Compounds:** These setting-type powder products were developed to provide faster finishing of drywall interiors.
52	**Reinforcing Tapes**
	SHEETROCK Brand Joint Tape: A joint treatment system (reinforcing tape and joint compound) must provide joint as strong as the gypsum board itself. Otherwise, normal structural movement in a wall or ceiling assembly can result in the development or cracks over the finished joint.
70	**General Requirements**
	Deflection: For drywall assemblies it is desirable to limit deflection to L/240 (L = the length of the span in inches) and to never exceed L/120. The preferred limit for veneer assemblies L/360 and should not exceed L/240. Note: know formula
71	**Wood Framing** 1. Framework should meet the minimum requirements of applicable building codes
73	**Maximum Frame Spacing – Drywall Construction Table**
74	**Maximum Frame Spacing – Veneer Plaster Construction**
75	**Steel Framing**
77	**Stud Installation:** Insert floor to ceiling studs between runner, twisting them into position…..The recommended practice for most installations is to anchor only those studs adjacent to door and borrowed light frames.

Page #	Highlight

81
Gypsum Panel Installation: Attach gypsum panels to the suspension system's main runners …. 8" o.c. at the periphery of gypsum panels and located 3/8" in from panel edges and spaced 12" o.c. in the field.

83
Suspended Ceiling Grillage: Space 8-ga. Hanger wires 48" o.c. carrying channels and within 6" of ends of carrying-channel runs.

Install 1-1/2" carrying channels 48" o.c. … Position channels for proper ceiling height, level, and secure with hanger wire saddle tied along channels.

85
Wall Furring

87
Furring Channel Erection- Direct Attachment: For channels positioned horizontally, attach a furring channel not more than 4" from both the floor line and the ceiling line.

90
Wood Furring Erection: Wood furring over wood framing must be 2 inches x 2 inches minimum size for nail-on applications. Strips may be 1 inch x 3 inches if gypsum board is screw attached.

93
Steel Framing: For doors up to 2'8" wide and weighing 100 lb. or less and borrowed light openings use 25-ga. Steel studs and runners to frame the opening.

100
General Planning Procedures

101
Estimating Materials

Screws: for single-layer wall application to 16" o.c framing, approx.. 1,000 Type W screws …per 1,000 SF of gypsum board.

103
Environmental Conditions: In cold weather, controlled heat in the range of 55° to 70°F must be provided…..Minimum temperature of 50°F should be maintained during gypsum board application.

105
Gypsum Drywall and Plaster Base Application

General Recommendations
Apply ceiling boards first
Cut boards so that they slip easily into place
Butt all joints. Never force panels into position
4. Whenever possible, place tapered or wrapped edges next to one   another
Wherever possible, ….If butt joints do occur, stagger and locate them as far from the center of wall and ceilings as possible.
Support all ends and edges of gypsum board and framing,…and where ends joints are to be floated between members and back-blocked

Page #	Highlight

7. When fastening, apply hand pressure on panel net to fastener being   driven to insure panel is in tight contact with framing member

8. If metal or plastic trim is to be installed around edges, doors, or windows, determine if trim is to be installed before panel application

107   **Screw Application**

108   **Start Screw Straight:** Firm hand grip on electric screwgun is important for straight line of entry.....The electric screwgun technique is relatively simple and a proficiency with the tool can be developed layer assemblies

109   **Single-Nailing Application**

3. Drive nails at least ⅜ inch from ends or edges of gypsum board

110   **Maximum Fastener Spacing – Constructions Using Drywall, Gypsum Base and Similar Products Table**

111   **Adhesive application**

113   **Wood Frame Single-Layer Application:** All types of gypsum boards may be used in this assembly.

             Installation: Wood Studs and Joist

122   **Furred Framing Board Application**: Apply gypsum boards of maximum practical length with long dimension at right angles to furring channel.....Use 1 inch screw length for ½ inch or ⅝ inch thick boards

123   **Gypsum Sheathing Application**

131   **Floating Interior Angle Application**

135   **Curved Surfaces**

136-7   **Tables:**
- Minimum Bending Radii of Dry Gypsum Board[1]
- Minimum Radii of SHEETROCK Brand ¼" Flexible Gypsum Panels
- Minimum Bending Radii of Wetted Gypsum Board[1]

137   **Installation: Framing:** Bend the runners to a uniform curve of the desired radius (90 degree max arc).

139   **Soffits**

142   **Cement board sizes**

148   **Job Preparation and Design Considerations**

Page #	Highlight
148-9	**Control Joints:** Certain interior wall surface constructions should be isolate with surface control joints or other means where: (a) a wall abuts a structural element or dissimilar wall or ceiling (b) construction changes within the plane of the wall (c) tile and thin brick surfaces exceed 16' in either direction
161	**Finishing Level Definitions**
172	**Check Working Surfaces:** Open spaces between panels of ¼" or more should be filled with compound at least 24 hours prior to embedding tape or first-coat work.
179	**Setting –Type Joint Compounds- System Applications**
180	**Drying Time-Joint Compound Under Tape**
201	**Interior Patching and Repairing**
206	**Advances of Veneer Plaster:** Veneer plaster provides a monolithic surface with a durable finish that resist scuffs, gouges and impact damage. **Job Environment:** Maintain building temperature in a comfortable working range, at least 55 degrees F with a relative humidity between 20% and 50%.
208	**Corner Bead Application:** Apply No. 800 and No. 900 corner bead with nails through the board … spaced 12" o.c. through both flanges.
210	Control joints should be used in the face of gypsum partitions and ceilings when the size of the surface exceeds the following control joint spacings: (4 bullets).
215	**Veneer Plaster Finish Applications**
233	**Control Joints**
235	**Framing Components**
252	**Framing Installation**
254	**Steel Stud – ROCKLATH Base Furring**
256	**Frame Spacing and Attachment**: For joists spaced about 25" o.c. attachment of ¾ channels …place attachment at every joists.
287	**Grid System Types and Profiles**
295	**Acoustical Requirements**
314	**Installation of Suspended Acoustical Ceilings**
314-318	**Step-by-Step Installation:** Become familiar with steps 1 – 12.

Temperature: Temperature can have a dramatic effect on the performance of gypsum products…..Avoid sudden changes in temperature, which may cause cracking from thermal shock.

Humidity: High humidity resulting from atmospheric conditions or from on the job use of such wet materials as concrete, stucco, plaster and spray fireproofing often creates situations for possible problems…..Under hot. Dry conditions, handle gypsum board carefully to prevent cracking or core damage during erection

Moisture: Wind-blown rain and standing water on floors increases the humidity in a structure and may cause the problems previously described…..DUROCK Brand Cement Board is recommended for these uses.

Ventilation: Ventilation should be provided to remove excess moisture, permit proper drying of conventional gypsum plasters and joint compounds and prevent problems associated with high-humidity conditions…..Rapid drying also creates problems with joint compounds, gypsum plasters and finishes when then dry out before setting fully and, as a result, don't develop full strength

Sunlight: Strong sunlight for extended periods will discolor gypsum panel face paper and make decoration difficult…..Applying finishes containing alkali to this degraded base may result in bond failure unless the base is treated with an alum solution or bonding agent.

Relief Joints: Select gypsum assemblies to provide the best structural characteristics to resist stresses imposed on them…..The alternative solution is to provide control and relief joints to eliminate stress buildup and still maintain structural integrity of the assembly. To control external stresses, partitions and other gypsum construction must be relieved from the structural framework…..Relief joints for individual structures should be checked for adequacy by the design engineer to prevent cracking and other deformations.

Gypsum Systems Without Expansion Joints: Long partitions runs and large ceiling areas must have control joints to compensate for hygrometric and thermal expansion and contraction…..If corrective measures are effective, all involved will be rewarded with a satisfactory performance, and costly complaints will be avoided.

Description of Defect:

Fastener Imperfections: A common defect, which takes on many forms…..Usually caused by improper framing or fastener application.

Joint Defects: Generally occur in a straight-line pattern and appear as ridges, depressions or blisters at the joints,….Imperfections may result from incorrect framing or joint treatment application, or climatic condition.

Loose Panels:

Joint Cracking: Appears either directly over the long edge or butt ends of boards, or may appear along the edge of taped joints. Often caused by structural movement and/or hygrometric and thermal expansion and contraction, or by excessively fast drying of joint compounds.

Fielding Cracking:

Angle Cracking: Appears directly in the apex of wall-ceiling or interior angles where partitions intersect…..Can be caused by structural movement, improper application of joint compound in corner angle or excessive build-up of paint

Bead Cracking

Wavy Surfaces

Board Sag: Occurs in ceilings, usually under high-humidity conditions. Caused by insufficient framing support for board;…..or improperly fitted panels.

Surface Defects

Discoloration: Board surface has slight difference in color over joints, supports or fasteners. Caused by improper paint finishing, uneven soiling and darkening from aging or ultraviolet light.

Water Damage: Stains, paper bond failure, softness in board core or mildew growth are caused by sustained high humidity, standing water and improper protection from water leakage during transit and storage.

Drywall Panel Problems
1. Panels—Damaged Edges
2. Panels—Water-Damaged
3. Panels—Paper Delamination
4. Panels—Mold
5. Panels—Improperly Fitted
6. Panels—Surface Fractured After Application
7. Panels—Ceiling Sag after Installation
Note Cause & Prevention

Framing Problems
Framing—Members Out of Alignment
Framing—Members Twisted
Framing—Protrusions
Framing (Steel)—Panel Out of Alignment

1 Exam Prep
International Residential Code, 2012
Tabs and Highlights

These 1 Exam Prep Tabs are based on the *International Residential Code-2012 Edition.*

Each 1 Exam Prep tabs sheet has five rows of tabs. Start with the first tab at the first row at the top of the page; proceed down that row placing the tabs at the locations listed below. Place each tab in your book setting it down one notch until you get to the last tab (usually the index or glossary). Then start with the highlights.

1 Exam Prep Tab	Section
Table of Contents	Pg. xix
Scope & Administration	R100
Definitions	R200
Building Planning	R300
Protection of Openings	R301.2.1.2
Fire Resistant Construction	R302
Foundations	R400
Drainage	R401.3
Footings	R403
Under Floor Ventilation	R408.1
Floor Sheathing	R503
Spans and Loads (Wood)	Table R503.2.1.1(1)
Concrete Floors (On Ground)	R506
Drilling & Notching	R602.6
Masonry Construction	R606
Bed and Head Joints	R607.2.1
Wood Roof Framing	R802
Roof Assemblies	R900
Requirements for Masonry Fireplaces & Chimneys	Table R1001.1

1 Exam Prep Tab	Section
Energy Efficiency	R1100
Mechanical Administration	R1200
Mechanical System Req.	R1300
Heating & Cooling Equipment	R1400
Foundations and Supports	M1403.2
Exhaust Systems	R1500
Duct Systems	R1600
Combustion Air	R1700
Chimney/Vent Connector Clearances	Table M1803.3.4
Special Appliances, Systems, & Equipment	R1900
Water Heater Prohibited Locations	M2005.2
Hydronic Piping	R2100
Special Piping & Storage Systems	R2000
Solar Energy Systems	R2300
Fuel Gas	R2400
Plumbing Administration	R2500
Plumbing Requirements	R2600
Plumbing Fixtures	R2700
Water Heaters	R2800
Water Supply/Backflow Protection	P2902.3
Sanitary Drainage	R3000
Vents	R3100
Traps	R3200

1 Exam Prep Tab	**Section**
Storm Drainage	R3300
Electrical Requirements	E3400
Electrical Definitions	E3500
Services	E3600
Branch Circuit & Feeders	E3700
Wiring Methods	E3800
Power & Lighting	E3900
Devices & Luminaries	E4000
Appliance Installation	E4100
Swimming Pools	E4200
Remote Control & Power Limited Circuits	E4300
Referenced Standards	E4400
Appendices	Pg. 785
Index	Pg. 891

This concludes the tabs for this book. Please continue with the highlights on the following page.

3

Section #	Highlight
R100	**Chapter 1 – Scope and Administration**
R101.2	**Scope** ... shall apply to the construction, alteration, movement enlargement, replacement, repair, equipment, use and occupancy, location, removal and demolition of one and two family dwellings and multiple single family dwellings (townhouses) not more than 3 stories in height with a separate means of egress and their accessory structures.
R200	**Chapter 2 – Definitions**
R202	**Definitions**
R300	**Chapter 3 - Building Planning**
R301.1	**Application.** Building and structures, and all parts thereof, shall be constructed to safely support all loads ... to comply with the requirements of this section.
R301.1.3	**Engineered design.** When a building... contains structural elements exceeding the limit of...these elements shall be designed in accordance with accepted engineering practice.
R301.2.1.2	**Protection of Openings:** Glazed openings in windborne debris areas shall meet the requirements of the Large Missile Test of ASTM E 1996, SSTD 12 or TAS 201,202 and 203 or AAMA 506 referenced therein.
	Exception: 7/16 inch structural panels, 8' span permitted. Attachments per table 301.2.1.2)
Figure R301.2(3)	**Weathering Probability Map for Concrete**
Figure R302.2(4)A	**Basic Wind Speeds**
Figure R302.2(6)	**Termite Infestation probability Map**
Table R301.2.1.2	**Windborne Debris Protection Fastening Schedule for Wood Structural Panels**
R301.2.1.3	**Wind speed conversion.** When required ultimate design wind Speeds, V_{ult}, of Figure R301.2(4) shall be converted to nominal design wind speeds, V_{asd}, using Table R301.2.1.3.
Table R301.2.1.3	**Equivalent Basic Wind Speeds**
Table R301.6	**Minimum Roof Live Loads in Pounds-Force per Square Foot of Horizontal Projection**
R310	**Emergency Escape and Rescue Openings**
R310.1	**Emergency escape and rescue required:** Where emergency escape and rescue openings are provided they shall have a sill height of not more than 44 inches above the floor.
R310.1.1	**Minimum opening area:** All emergency escape and rescue opening s shall have a minimum net clear opening of 5.7 square feet.
R310.1.2	**Minimum opening height:** 24 inches

Section #	Highlight
R310.1.3	**Minimum opening width**: 20 inches
R310.2	**Window Wells:** The minimum horizontal area of the window well … 36 inches.
R400	**Chapter 4 – Foundations**
R401.3	**Drainage:** Surface drainage shall be diverted to a storm sewer conveyance or other approved point of collection that does not create a hazard. Lots shall be graded to drain surface water away from foundation walls. The grade shall fall a minimum of 6 inches within the first 10 feet.
R401.4	**Soil tests:** Where quantifiable data created by accepted soil science methodologies... thru the end of the paragraph.
Table R401.4.1	**Presumptive Load-Bearing Values of Foundation Materials**
R402	**Materials**
R402.1	**Wood Foundations**
R402.1.1	**Fasteners:** used below grade to attach plywood to the exterior side of exterior basement or crawl space wall studs, or fasteners used in knee wall construction shall be of Type 304 or 316 stainless steel... Electro-galvanized steel nails and galvanized (zinc coated) steel staples shall not be permitted.
R402.1.2	**Wood treatment:** Where lumber and/or plywood is cut or drilled after treatment … the wood absorbs no more preservative.
R402.2	**Concrete:** Concrete shall have a minimum specified compressive strength as shown in Table R402.2.... Materials used to produce concrete and testing thereof shall comply with the applicable standards listed in Chapter 3 of ACI 318 or ACI 332.
Table R402.2	**Minimum Specified Compressive Strength of Concrete**
R403.1.1	**Minimum size**: Minimum sizes for concrete and masonry footings shall be set forth in Table R403.1. and figure R403.1(1). Footing for wood foundations shall be in accordance with … and Figures R403.1(3).
Table R403.1(1)	**Concrete and Masonry Foundation Details**
Figure R403.1(2)	**Permanent Wood Foundation Basement Wall Section**
Figure R403.1(3)	**Permanent Wood Foundation Crawl Space Section**
R403.1.4	**Minimum depth**: All exterior footings shall be placed at least 12 inches below the undisturbed ground surface.
R403.1.7.3	**Foundation Elevation:** On graded sites, the top of any exterior foundation shall extend above the elevation of the street that are at point of discharge or the inlet of unapproved drainage device a minimum of 12 inches plus 2%.

Section #	Highlight

R404   **Foundation and Retaining Walls**

R404.1.5   **Foundation wall thickness on walls supported.**

R404.1.5.1 Masonry wall thickness. shall not be less than the thickness of the wall supported, except that 8 inches nominal thickness shall be permitted under brick veneered frame walls and under 10 inch wide cavity walls there the total height of the wall supported including gables is not more than 20 feet, provided Section R404.1.1 is met.

R404.1.6   **Height above finished grade:** minimum of 4 inches were masonry veneer is used and a minimum of 6 inches elsewhere

R404.1.8   **Rubble stone masonry:** shall have a minimum thickness 16 inches, shall not support an unbalanced backfill exceeding 8 feet in height or soil pressure >30 P. S. F.

R404.3   **Wood sill plates:** shall have a minimum of 2 x 4 anchored per R 404.2.7.1

R405   **Foundation Drainage**

R405.1   **Concrete or masonry foundations:** Drains shall be provided around all. .thru located below grade. Gravel or crushed store drains shall extend at least 1 foot beyond the outside edge of the footing and 6 inches above the top of the footing and covered with an approved filter membrane... .thru the end of the paragraph.

R406   **Foundation Waterproofing and Dampproofing**

R406.2   **Concrete and Masonry Foundation Waterproofing:** In areas where high water table or other severe soil water conditions are known to exist, ... thru end of paragraph: Include bullets numbered 1 thru 8 following the paragraph. Exception: Use of plastic roofing cements, acrylic coatings, mortars and pargings to seal ICF walls is permitted.

R407   **Columns**

R407.3   **Structural requirements:** Wood columns shall not be less in nominal size than 4 inches by 4 inches. Steel columns shall not be less than 3 inch diameter schedule 40 pipe manufactured in accordance with ASTM A 53 Grade B or equivalent.

R408   **Under-Floor Space**

R408.1   **Ventilation:** minimum net area one square-foot per 150 ft.^{2}. When a Class I vapor retarder material is used the minimum net area shall not be less than 1 sft for each 1,500 sft. One such ventilating opening shall be within 3 feet of each corner of the building.

R408.2   **Openings for under floor ventilation.** Ventilation openings shall be covered for their height and width with any op the following materials provided that the least dimension of the covering shall not exceed 1/4 inch — List allowed materials from 1 thru 6.

R408.4   **Access.** Access shall be provided for all under- floor spaces. Access openings through the floor shall be a minimum of 18 inches by 24 inches....Through wall access openings shall not be located under a door to the residence.

Section #	Highlight
R500	**Chapter 5 – Floors**
R502	**Wood Floor Framing**
R502.1.2	**Blocking and subflooring:** Blocking shall be … or No. 4 common grade boards.
R502.11	**Wood Trusses**
R502.11.1	**Design:** The truss design drawings shall be prepared … in accordance with Section R106.1.
R502.11.2	**Bracing:** Trusses shall be braced to prevent … on individual truss design drawings.
R502.11.3	**Alterations to trusses:** Alterations resulting in the addition of load that exceed the design load for the truss, shall not be permitted without verification that the truss is capable of supporting the additional load.
R502.1.3.4	**Truss design drawings:** Truss design drawings shall include, at a minimum the information specified below: (1 -12).
R502.13	**Fireblocking required**
R503	**Floor Sheathing**
R503.1	**Lumber sheathing:** as per tables R503.1, R503.2.1.1(1) & (2)
Table R503.1	**Minimum thickness of lumber floor sheathing.**
R503.2	**Wood structural panel sheathing**
Table R503.2.1.1(2)	**Allowable Spans for Sanded Plywood combination subfloor underlayment.**
R 503.2.2	**Allowable spans:** per table R 503.2.1.1(1) or ΛPΛ E30.
R 503.2.3	**Installation:** shall be attached to wood framing to cold formed steel framing in accordance with the standards used for the design of the building as specified in Section R301.2.1.1
Table R503.2.1.1(1)	**Allowable spans and loads for wood structural panels for roof and** **subfloor sheathing and** **combination subfloor underlayment.**
R504	**Pressure preservatively treated wood floors (on ground)**
R504.1.3	**Uplift and buckling:** where required resistance shall be provided by interior bearing walls or properly designed stub walls anchored in the supporting soil.
R504.2	**Site Preparation:** the area within the foundation walls shall have all vegetation, topsoil and foreign material removed. The fill shall be compacted
R504.2.1	**Base:** 4 inch minimum base gravel maximum size 3/4," or crushed stone 1/2", shall be placed on compacted earth.
R504.2.2	**Moisture barrier:** six mil thickness, joints lapped 6 inches unsealed

Section #	Highlight
R506	**Concrete floors (on ground)**
R506.1	**General:** minimum 3.5 inches per R403.1.8.
R506.2	**Site Preparation**
R506.2.1	**Fill:** free of vegetation and foreign material; filled depths shall not exceed 24 inches for clean sand or gravel and 8 inches for earth
R506.2.2	**Base:** a 4 inch base course consisting of clean grated sand, gravel, crushed stone, or blast furnace slag passing a 2 inch sieve shall be placed on the prepared subgrade when the slab is below grade. Exception: A base course is not required when the slab is installed on well drained soils classified as Group I.
R506.2.3	**Vapor retarder:** A six mil polyethylene with joints laps not less than 6 inches shall be placed between the concrete floor and the base course.
R600	**Chapter 6 - Wall Construction**
R602	**Wood Wall Framing**
Table R602.3(1)	**Fastener Schedule for Structural Members**
R602.6	**Drilling and notching of studs**
R602.6.1	**Drilling and Notching of top plate:** On exterior or interior load bearing walls when drilling or notching of the top plate by more than 50% of its width, a galvanized metal tie not less than 0.054 inch Thick and 1.5 inches wide shall be fastened across and to the plate on both side of the opening with not less than 8 10d diameter, 1.5 inches long. The metal tie must extend a minimum of 6 inches past the opening.
Figure R602.6(1)	**Notching and bored hole limitations for exterior walls and bearing walls.**
Figure R602.6(2)	**Notching and bored hole limitations for interior nonbearing walls.**
Figure R602.6.1	**Top plate framing to accommodate piping.**
R606	**General Masonry Construction**
R606.3	**Corbeled Masonry:** shall be in accordance with Sections R606.3.1 thru R606.3.3
R606.3.1	**Units:** units filled with mortar or grout shall be used for corbeling.
R606.3.2	**Corbel projection :** shall not exceed 0.5 the height of the unit or 0.3 the thickness at right angles to the wall. Maximum projection shall not exceed: (1) 0.5 of the wall thickness for multiwythe walls; (2) 0.5 the wythe thickness for single wythe walls.
R607	**Unit Masonry**
R607.2	**Placing mortar and masonry units**

Section #	Highlight
R607.2.1	**Bed and head joints:** Head and bed joints shall be 3/8 inch thick … shall not be less than ¼ inch and not more than ¾ inch.
R612	**Exterior Windows and Doors**
R613	**Structural Insulated Panel Wall Construction**
R613.3	**Materials**
R613.3.1	**Core:** The core material shall be foam plastic insulation meeting one of the following requirements: (1) – (3).
R613.3.2	**Facing :** Wood 7/16 inch
R613.3.3	**Adhesive:** Shall conform to ASTM D 2559
R613.3.4	**Lumber:** Number 2 Spruce pine fir
R613.3.5	**Screws:** Corrosion resistant and have a minimum shank diameter of 0.188 inch and head diameter of 0.620 inch.
R613.3.6	**Nails:** As per Section R613 common or galvanized box Gypsum
R700	**Chapter 7 - Wall Coverings**
R701.1	**Application:** Interior and Exterior wall coverings for all buildings
R702	**Interior Covering**
Table R702.1(1)	**Thickness of Plaster**
Table R702.3.5	**Minimum Thickness and Applications of Gypsum Board**
R702.1	**General:** Shall be in accordance with Tables R702.1(1), R702.1.(2), R702.1(3) and 702.3.5. Interior masonry veneer shall comply with Section R703.7.1 for support and R703.7.4 for anchorage, except an air space is not required. Interior finishes and materials shall conform to the flame spread and smoke development of Section R302.9
Table R702.1(2)	**Gypsum Plaster Proportions**
Table R702.1(3)	**Cement Plaster Proportions Parts by Volume**
R702.2	**Interior Plaster**
R702.2.3	**Support:** Support spacing for gypsum or metal lath on walls or ceilings shall not exceed 16 inches fir 3/8 inch thick or 24 inches fir 1/2 inch thick plain gypsum lath.
R702.3	**Gypsum Board**

Section #	Highlight

R702.3.6   **Fastening:** Screws for attaching gypsum board to wood framing ... not less than 5/8 inch.

R702.3.8   **Water resistant gypsum backing board:** Shall be permitted on ceilings where framing spacing does not exceed 12 inches on center for 1/2 inch thick or 16inches for 5/8 inch thick gypsum board. It should not be installed over a Class I or II vapor retarder in a shower or tub compartment.

R702.5   **Other finishes:** cold formed steel (16" o.c); Wood veneer 1/4" thickness; cold formed steel (1/4" thick with 3/8" gypsum board backer)

R703   **Exterior Covering**
R703.2   **Water-resistive barrier:** One layer No 15 lapped 2 inches, or 6" at joints.

R703.3   Wood, hardboard and wood structural panel siding

R703.3.1   Panel Siding — Vertical joints shall occur over framing members. Horizontal joints shall be lapped a minimum of 1 inch or shall be shiplapped or shall be flashed with Z flashing and occur over solid blocking.

R703.5   **Wood Shakes and Shingles**
Table
R703.5.2   **Maximum Weather Exposure for Wood Shakes and Shingles on Exterior Walls.**
Weather Resistant Siding Attachment and Minimum
Table R703.4 **Thickness**

R703.5.3   **Attachments:** Each Shake or Shingle...two hot dipped, zinc coated, stainless steel, or aluminum nails or staples.... penetrate 1/2 inch.

R703.7   **Stone and masonry veneer, general**
Flashing: Flashing shall be located beneath the first course
R703.7.5   of masonry above   finished ground
level above the foundation wall or slab.

R703.7.6   **Weepholes** : 33" o.c.; 3/16 " inch diameter, above flashing

R703.10   **Fiber cement siding**

R703.10.1   **Panel siding:** Panel siding shall be installed with the long dimension either parallel or perpendicular to framing, and shall be sealed with caulking covered with battens.

R703.10.2   **Lap Siding:** Fiber-cement lap siding having a maximum width of 12 inches shall comply with ASTM C1186. Shall be lapped a minimum of 1 1/4 inches and lap siding not having tongue and groove should have the ends sealed with caulking.

R800   **Chapter 8 — Roof-Ceiling Construction**

R802   **Wood Roof Framing**

R802.1.3.4   **Labeling:** The label shall contain: (8 items)

Section #	Highlight

R802.2   **Design and Construction:** The framing details … slope of 3 units vertical in 12 units horizontal or greater.

R802.3   **Framing Details:** Ridge board shall be at least 1-inch … …hip rafter not less than 2-inch nominal thickness.

R803
Table
R803.1   **Roof Sheathing**

Minimum Thickness of Lumber Roof Sheathing

R806   **Roof Ventilation**

R806.1   **Ventilation required:** Ventilation openings shall have a least dimension of 1/16 inch minimum and1/4 inch maximum. Openings larger than 1/4 inch shall be provided with corrosion resistant wire cloth screening or similar with openings having a least dimension of 1/16 inch and 1/4 inch maximum.

R806.2   **Minimum Vent Area:** The minimum net free ventilating area shall be 1/150 of the area of the vented space.

R807   **Attic Access**

R807.1   **Attic Access:** Buildings with combustible ceiling or roof shall have an opening to areas that exceed 30 square feet and have a vertical height of 30 inches or greater. The rough framed opening shall not be less than 22 inches by 30 inches and shall be located in a hallway or other readily accessible location.

R900   **Chapter 9 - Roof Assemblies**

R902   **Roof Classification**

R902.1   **Roofing Covering Materials:** A, B & C roofing defined (Fire Resistance, A is Most)

R903   **Weather Protection**

R903.2   **Flashing**

R903.2.1   **Locations:** Flashings shall be installed at wall and roof intersections, wherever there is a change in roof slope or direction and around roof openings.

R903.3   **Coping:** Parapet walls shall be properly coped with noncombustible, weatherproof materials of a width no less than the cross section of the parapet wall.

R903.4   **Roof drainage**

R903.4.1   **Secondary (emergency overflow) drains and scuppers:** Overflow drains having the same size as the roof drains …shall be installed in the adjacent parapet walls with the inlet flow located 2 inches above the low point of the roof served.

| R905 | Requirements for roof coverings. |
| Section # | Highlight |

R905.2   **Asphalt Shingles**

R905.2.2   **Slope:** Asphalt shingles shall be used only on roof slopes … double underlayment is required in accordance with section R905.2.7.

R905.2.5   **Fasteners:** Fasteners for asphalt shingles shall be galvanized, stainless, aluminum or copper, 12 gage, 3/8" diameter head, 3/4 inch penetration.

R905.2.6   **Attachment:** 4 fasteners per strip shingle, 2 per individual shingle

R905.2.7   **Underlayment application:** For roofs slopes from 2:12 to 4:12, two layers of underlayment: 19 inch at eave; 36" wide sheets with 19" overlap; end laps shall be offset by 6 feet; corrosion resistant fasteners are to be applied at a maximum spacing of 36 inches on center.

R905.2.8.2   **Valleys:** valley linings shall be permitted: 1 – 3.

R905.2.8.5   **Drip edge:** Adjacent pieces of drip edge shall be provided at eaves …a maximum of 12" o.c. with fasteners as specified in section R905.2.5.

R905.3   **Clay and Concrete Tile**

R905.3.5   **Concrete Tile**

R905.3.6   **Fasteners:** Shall be corrosion resistant and not less than 11 gage. 5/16 head... Penetrate deck minimum of 3/4".

R905.4   **Metal roof shingles**

R905.4.2   **Deck slope:** shall not be below 3:12

R905.4.6   **Flashing:** The valley flashing shall extend at least 8 inches from the center line each way and shall have a splash diverter rib not less than 3/4 inch high. Shall have an end lap of not less than 4 inches. The metal valley flashing shall have a 36-inch wide underlayment.

R905.6   **Slate and slate type shingles**

R905.6.3   **Underlayment:** Underlayment shall be installed in accordance with the manufacturer's installation instructions.

Table R905.6.5   **Slate Shingle Headlap**

R905.6.6   **Flashing:** Valley flashing shall be a minimum of 15 inches wide.

R905.7   **Wood Shingles**

R905.7.1   **Deck Requirements:** Where spaced sheathing is used, sheathing boards shall not be less than 1 inch by 4 inch nominal dimensions.

R905.7.2   **Deck Slope:** Wood shingles shall be installed on slopes of 3:12 or greater.

Section #	Highlight
R905.7.6	**Valley Flashing:** Roof flashing shall not be less than No. 26 gage … Sections of flashing shall have an end lap of not less than 4 inches.
Table R905.7.5	**Wood Shingle Weather Exposure and Roof Slope**
R905.8	**Wood shakes**
R905.8.1	**Deck requirements**: Wood shakes shall be used only on solid or spaced sheathing.
R905.8.2	**Deck slope**: Wood shakes shall only be used on slopes of 3:12 or greater
Table R905.8.6	**Wood Shake Weather Exposure and Roof Slope**
R905.9	**Built Up Roofs**
R905.9.1	**Slope**: Built-up roofs shall have a design slope of a minimum of 1/4:12 for drainage.
R905.9.2	**Material Standards:** As per Table R905.9.2
R905.9.3	**Application:** Built-up roofs shall be installed according to this chapter and the manufacturer's installation instructions.
Table R905.9.2	**Built-Up Roofing Material Standards**
R905.10	**Metal Roof Panels**
R905.10.1	**Deck Requirements:** Metal roof panel roof panels shall be applied on solid or spaced sheathing.
R905.10.2	**Slope:** shall comply with the following: 1) be 3:12; 2) lapped, non-soldered-seam shall be 1/2:12;3) minimum slope for standing seam roof systems shall be 1/4:12
R905.11	**Modified Bitumen Roofing**
TableR905.11.2	**Modified Bitumen Roofing materials Standard**
R905.12	**Thermoset single-ply roofing**
R905.12.1	**Slope:** Thermoset single-ply roofs shall have a design slope of a minimum of 1/4:12
R905.13	**Thermoplastic single-ply roofing**
R905.13.1	**Slope:** Thermoplastic single-ply roofs shall have a design slope of a minimum of minimum of 1/4:12
R905.14	**Sprayed polyurethane foam roofing**
R905.14.1	**Slope:** Sprayed polyurethane foam roofs shall have a design slope of a minimum of 1/4:12 for drainage.
R905.15	**Liquid applied roofing**

Section #	Highlight

R905.15.1 **Slope:** Liquid applied roofing shall have a design slope of a minimum of 1/4:12.

R906 **Roof Insulation**

R906.1 **General:** Such insulation is covered with an approved roof covering and passes FM 4450 or UL 1256.

Table R906.2 **Material Standards for Roof Insulation**

R1000 **Chapter 10 - Chimneys and Fireplaces**

R1001.2 **Footings and Foundations:** Footings for masonry fireplaces and their chimneys shall be constructed of concrete or solid masonry at least 12 inches thick and shall extend at least 6 inches beyond the face of the fireplace or foundation wall on all sides...footings shall be at least 12 inches below finish grade.

R1001.5 **Firebox walls:** Masonry fireboxes shall be constructed of solid masonry units, hollow masonry units grouted solid, stone or concrete.

When no lining is provided, the total minimum thickness of back and side walls shall be 10 inches of solid masonry.

R1001.7 **Lintel and throat.** Masonry over a fireplace Opening shall be supported by a lintel of noncombustible material. The minim am required bearing length on each end of the fireplace opening shall be 4 inches.

R1001.7.1 **Damper:** Masonry fireplaces shall be equipped with ferrous metal damper located at least 8" above fireplace opening.

Table
R1001.1 **Summary of Requirements for Masonry Fireplaces and Chimneys**

R1001.10 **Hearth extension dimensions:** Hearth connections shall extend at least 16 inches in front, 8" or each side.

R1001.11 **Fireplace clearance:** All wood beams, joists, studs and other combustible material shall have a clearance of not less than 2 inches from the front faces and sides of masonry fireplaces and not less than 4 inches from the back faces of masonry fireplaces.

R1003 **Masonry Chimneys**
Footings and foundations: Footings for
R1003.2 masonry chimneys   shall be constructed of concrete or solid masonry at least 12" thick and shall extend at least 6" beyond the face of the foundation or support wall on all sides.
Footings shall be at least 12" below finished grade.

R1003.5 **Corbeling:** Masonry chimneys shall not be corbelled more than 1/2 of the chimney's wall thickness from a wall or foundation.

R1003.10 **Wall thickness:** Masonry chimney … not less than 4 inch nominal thickness.

Section #	**Highlight**
Table R1003.14(1)	**Net Cross Sectional Area of Round Flue Sizes**
Table R1003.14(2)	**Net Cross Sectional Area of Square and Rectangular Flue Sizes**
R1003.17	**Masonry chimney cleanout openings**: Cleanout openings shall be provided within 6" of the base of the flue, 6" below lowest chimney inlet, 6" high.
R1003.18	**Chimney Clearances** ... air space clearance, 2 inches...
R1004	**Factory-Built Fireplaces**
N1100	**Chapter 11 — Energy Efficiency**
N1101.9	**Defined terms**
Table N1101.10	**Climate Zones**
R1200	**Chapter 12 - Mechanical Administration**
R1300	**Chapter 13 - General Mechanical System Requirements**
M1400	**Chapter 14 - Heating and Cooling Equipment and Appliances**
M1403	**Heat Pump Equipment**
M1403.2	**Foundations and supports**: Supports and foundations for the outdoor unit of a heat pump shall be raised at least 3 inches above the ground.
M1406	**Radiant Heating Systems**
M1406.2	**Clearances**: shall comply with Chapter 34 – 43 of this code.
M1408	**Vented floor furnaces**
M1408.3	**Location:** 1) Floor registers of floor furnaces shall be installed not less than 6 inches from a wall. 6) The floor furnace shall not be installed in concrete floor construction built on grade.
M1500	**Chapter 15 - Exhaust Systems**
M1502	**Clothes Dryer Exhaust**
M1502.3	**Duct Termination:** Exhaust ducts shall terminate on the outside of the building... the exhaust duct shall terminate not less than 3 feet in any direction from openings into buildings. Exhaust duct terminations shall be equipped with a backdraft damper.
M1502.4.3	**Transition duct**: shall be a single length ... maximum length of 8 feet.

Section #	Highlight

M1502.4.4.1   **Duct Length** : shall be determined by one of the methods in section M1502.4.4.1 or M1502.4.4.2.

M1505   **Overhead exhaust hoods**

M1505.1   **General:** Domestic open top broiler units ...28 gage with .25 inch clearance between the hood and the underside of combustible materials or cabinets.

Table M1507.4   **Minimum Required Exhaust Rates for One and Two Family Dwellings**

M1600   **Chapter 16 - Duct Systems**

M1700   **Chapter 17 - Combustion Air**

M1800   **Chapter 18 - Chimneys and Vents**

M1803   **Chimney and Vent Connectors**

M1803.3.1   **Floor, ceiling and wall penetrations**: A chimney hall not pass through any floor or ceiling... through wall...

Table M1803.3.4   **Chimney and Vent Connector Clearances to Combustible Materials**

M1900   **Chapter 19 - Special Appliances, Equipment & Systems**

M2000   **Chapter 20 - Boilers and Water Heaters**

M2005.2   **Prohibited Locations:** Fuel fired water heaters shall not be installed in .... a room used as a storage closet. Water heaters located in a bedroom or bathroom shall be installed ... ... will not be taken from the living space.

M2100   **Chapter 21 - Hydronic Piping**

M2200   **Chapter 22 - Special Piping and Storage Systems**

M2300   **Chapter 23 – Solar Energy Systems**

G2400   **Chapter 24 - Fuel Gas**

G2403   **General Definitions**

P2500   **Chapter 25 - Plumbing Administration**

P2600   **Chapter 26 - General Plumbing Requirements**

P2700   **Chapter 27 - Plumbing Fixtures**

P2800   **Chapter 28 - Water Heaters**

P2801.5   **Pan required.** The tank shall be installed ... 24 gage or other pans approved for such use.

Section #	**Highlight**
P2801.5.1	**Pan size and drain**: The pan shall not be less than 1.5 inch deep and of sufficient size to receive all dripping or condensate from the tank or water heater.
P2801.5.2	**Pan drain termination**: not less than 6" and not more than 24" above ground surface
P2803	**Relief valves**
P2803.3	**Pressure relief valves**: They shall be set to open at least 25 psi above the system pressure but not over 150 psi
P2803.4	**Temperature relief valves**: The valves shall be installed thin top 6 inches
P2900	**Chapter 29 - Water Supply and Distribution**
P2902.3	**Backflow protection**: A means of protection against backflow shall be provided in accordance with sections P2902.3.1 through P2902.3.6.
P3000	**Chapter 30 - Sanitary Drainage**
P3100	**Chapter 31 – Vents**
P3200	**Chapter 32 – Traps**
P3300	**Chapter 33 — Storm Drainage**
E3400	**Chapter 34 - Electrical General Requirements**
E3500	**Chapter 35 — Electrical Definitions**
R3600	**Chapter 36 — Services**
E3700	**Chapter 37 — Branch Circuit and Feeder Requirements**
E3800	**Chapter 38 - Wiring Methods**
E3900	**Chapter 39 - Power and Lighting Distribution**
E4000	**Chapter 40 - Devices and Luminaires**
R4100	**Chapter 41 - Appliances Installation**
R4200	**Chapter 42 - Swimming Pools**
R4300	**Chapter 43 – Remote Control Signaling and Power Limited Circuits**
R4400	**Chapter 44 – Referenced Standards**
Appendix A	**Sizing and Capacities of Gas Piping**

1 Exam Prep
Modern Masonry
Tabs and Highlights

These 1 Exam Prep Tabs and Highlights are based on *Modern Masonry, 8th Edition*.

Each 1 Exam Prep Tabs sheet has five rows of tabs. Start with the first tab at the first row at the top of the page; proceed down that row placing the tabs at the locations listed below. Place each tab in your book setting it down one notch until you get to the bottom of a page. Then start back at the top again.

*** *This concludes the tabs for this book. Please continue with the highlights on the following page.* ***

<u>Page</u>	<u>Highlight</u>
5	**Figure 1-5.** C- Sled runner half round. D – Sled runner V groove
17	**Masonry Saws:** Blades are made of very hard material, such as silicon carbide or industrial diamond.
37	**Figure 3-4.** Symbols commonly found on construction drawings.
82-85	Learn the different types of building bricks and their uses. Also the difference between modular and non-modular brick.
91	**Solid Masonry Units:** A solid masonry unit is "one whose cross-sectional area in every plane parallel to the bearing surface is 75% or more of its gross cross-sectional area measured in the same plane.
	Bricks are usually classified as solid masonry units because 75% of their area is solid material.
92	**Durability:** Several conditions affect weathering (durability) of a brick. These include heat, cold, and the action of soluble salts.
	Figure 5-20. Efflorescence on masonry walls is caused by soluble salts in wet brick being carried to the surface as water evaporates.
96-97	**Five Basic Bonds:** Become familiar with the five basic bonds. - Running bond - Common bond or American bond - Flemish bond - English bond - Block or stack bond
99	**Mortar Joints:** Concave joints V-shaped joints Because the two joints are compacted, they effectively prevent rain from penetrating into the joint … The concave joint is the most popular mortar joint.
104	(FTX) unglazed facing tile: - high degree of mechanical perfection
119	**Figure 6-3.** Note: A 8x8x16 CMU (sand and gravel) weighs 40 lbs.
122	**Sizes and Shapes:** Sizes are usually given in their nominal dimensions. A unit measuring 7 5/8" x 7 5/8" x 15 5/8" is known as a 8x8x16 unit.
125	The two-core design has the following advantages: (4 bullets)
133	Glass blocks are manufactured in three popular sizes … A ¼" mortar joint is required.

Page	Highlight
	Figure 6-31. Masonry glass block joints are typically ¼" on all sides.
143	**Stone Applications:** Limestone is an excellent sill material that can be used on exterior masonry walls. The fact that it is one piece ensures better protection against water leakage.
147	Mortar is general made up of cementitous materials together with sand and water.
148	**Cementitous Materials:** Cementitous materials include Portland cement (Type I, II, or III), masonry cements, and Hydrated Lime (Type S)
	Hydrated Lime: Hydrated lime is quicklime that has been slacked before packaging. Slacked means the quicklime has been formed into putty by combining it with water.
151	**Retempering Mortar:** Workability can be restored by adding the lost water and mixing briefly (retempering).
	Mortar should be used and placed within 2-1/2 hours after mixing.
152	**Properties of Hardened Mortar:** The compressive strength of mortar increases as the cement content is increased.
	Bond strength is the most significant property of hardened mortar, but it is also the most difficult to predict.
153	**Type M mortar**: It is useful for unreinforced masonry below grade and in contact with earth. Such structures include foundations, retaining walls, walks, sewers and manholes.
154	**Type S Mortar: Type S** is recommended for the following applications: - unreinforced masonry where maximum flexural (bending) strength is required
158	**Figure 8-10:** become familiar with the cubic feet of mortar reuired
166-167	**Types of Ties:** Become familiar with the three types of ties: - Corrugated - Rectangular - Z
169	**Figure 9-10:** Note: All reinforcing rods or bars used in masonry walls must have 5/8 of an inch mortar coverage.
173	**Figure 9-21**. A strap anchor being put into place connecting a partition wall into a bearing wall.
182-183	**Cutting Brick with a Brick Hammer:** This procedure produces a rough cut, but is acceptable for applications where the cut edge is hidden by mortar.

Page	Highlight
186	**Using a Corner Pole and Gauge Stick:** A corner pole, sometimes referred to as a story pole … used to measure the mortar joint heights of each course of masonry.
200	**The Placement/Joint Reinforcement:** The most important factors affecting performance of wall ties are as follows: - Full bedding of the bed joint and placing the edge of the wall tie in the mortar 5/8" from either edge of the masonry unit.
208	**Cleaning Brick:** A solution of hydrochloric acid is used extensively as a cleaning agent for new masonry.
209-210	**Abrasive Blasting:** For best results, use a very low pressure (60-100 psf).
214	**Cavity Walls:** Cavity walls usually consist of two walls separated by a continuous air space that is at least 2" wide.
216	**Veneered Walls:** metals ties are used in residential veneer construction to anchor the veneer to the frame or masony backing.
220	**Handling Concrete Blocks:** Position in a wall with the wide flange on the top to provide a wider space for the bed joint.
222	The twig is a thin piece of metal designed to hold the line between its metal fingers … to ensure that the final top edge of the block is at the same elevation as its corner leads. Stay a line width (1/16") away from the line so you … usefulness as a reference guide.
223	**Figure 11-20.** A full mortar bed is being furrowed with the trowel …ensure a good bond between the footing and bed course of masonry.
225	Note 9: A 5/8" diameter bar is usually used for a 3/8" concave mortar joint.
226	**Control Joints in a Concrete Block Wall:** They should be sealed with caulking compound after the mortar has been raked out to a depth of ¾".
268	Cover the wall from the footing to 6" above the finished grade.
278	**Four-Inch RBM Curtain and Panel Walls:** Curtain walls can be anchored to columns … These walls must support their own weight for the height of the wall.
282-283	**Expansion Joints:** It sis recommended that expansion joints be … where the walls are 50' in length.

<u>Page</u>	<u>Highlight</u>
286	**Lintels, Sills, and Jambs:** Become familiar with the materials used for lintels. Concrete, cast stone, stone, and steel.
300	**Jack Arch Construction:** The jack arch is relatively weak and should be supported by steel if the opening is over 2 feet wide.
348	**Figure 16-32:** Sheets of welded wire reinforcing are overlapped at least one full stay spacing plus 2".
392-393	**Exposed Aggregate:** Terrazzo toppings on outdoor slabs are generally ½" thick.
485	**Tuckpointing:** Filling in the cut or defective mortar joints in masonry with fresh mortar.

1 Exam Prep
Finish Carpenters Manual
Tabs and Highlights

These 1 Exam Prep tabs are based on *Finish Carpenters Manual, 1993 Edition*.

Each 1 Exam Prep tabs sheet has five rows of tabs. Start with the first tab at the first row at the top of the page; proceed down that row placing the tabs at the locations listed below. Place each tab in your book setting it down one notch until you get to the last tab (usually the index or glossary). Then start with the highlights.

This concludes the tabs for this book. Please continue with the highlights on the following below.

Page #	Highlight
5	The smooth, even surfaces we install have to fit right because they're always in full view. That means…. "A good finish carpenter is the conscience of the construction project.
7	The basic clothing and safety equipment needed by a professional finish carpenter include the following:

Workpants with built-in knee pads…
Workboots or shoes…
Hearing and eyesight protection…
Lung protection…
First aid kit…
Soap and shop towels…
Floor sweep and pan…

| 8 | Leather pouch tool bets are traditional. Some newer bels have pockets made of synethetics. These belts are lighter and may possibly last longer, but I still like the feel of a solid leather belt. It's stiff enough to maintain pocket shape but still flexible enough to bend in tight situations. |

Page #	Highlight

9   Here's a list of tolls typically found in the finish carpenter's belt- or overalls. (Highlight bulllets.)

13   This chapter describes the power tools commonly used by modern....
hand power tools and stationary power tools.

17   Pneumatic finish nailers- Like the compound miter... less common when driving namils near the edges and ends of boards.

19   Few finish carpenters lug their old 200-pound... 3-15 shows a setup with an after-market extension table and fence system.

21   A commercial-quality locking steel storage chest is essential if you have to leave your tools at the construction site... something permanently affixed to the site, like a metal soil pipe.

23   Sometimes power is available only at the drop pole. A good solution to this problem is to run a heavy feed line to a secondary power feed box set up in the work area.

26   There is much to be done, and often, much to be fixed, before you can get down... rough framing you might want to do before the arrival of the drywallers.

27   There are two phases to finish work:
1) The first stage I call the "prep work." You make corrections, additions...
2) The second stage is the actural cutting...

Make a list of all the things you're going to do in the second phase. Put them in order. In general, I like to work from... as fireplace surrounds and balustrades, I usually do at the very end.

28   I've found that it's more convenient to use the term running molding to refer to any tiem that can be ordered by the linear foot. This type of stock comes in random lengths for a specific application.

29   Figure 5-2 Bill of materials.

31   While the framers add a corner stud as a nailer for the drywall, it often doesn't extend out far enough to catch the ends o f cornice and base moldings.

Here are some other spots that need backing.
(Highlight the 3 bullets that follow)

34   Window height depends on the construction of... always check and follow the manufacturer's recommendations.

37   Stair Carriages
Figure 6-11 shows the parts of a typical open-sided stair carriage with a square laid in position for checking the risers, and a level laid in place for checking the treads.

Page #	Highlight
	Before securing the carriages, be sure there's... Without it, the first riser can't be nailed securely along its bottom edge.
39	The Four Rules of Door Swing (Highlight 1,2,3,and 4)
41	Place the dado so the inside legs of the jambs are long enough to accommodate: (Highlight the four bullets).
44	Figure 7-7 Sizing butt hinges.
45	The door may not have a back-bevel worked into the striker side edge. (See Figure 7-1). In that case you'll have to create one. Here's how: (Highlight 1,2,3)
46	(Highlight 1,2,3)
47	Figure 7-13 Shop –made hardwood jig for installing latch mechanisms
48	Sequence for installing a pocket door: (Highlight 1,2,3,4,5,6)
50	For the most part, installing exterior doors is much the same as installing interior passage doors, with these exceptions: (Highlight the 6 bullets).
55	Here are two other points to consider before you begin trimming out the doors: (Highlight 1,2)
62	Note that the line created by the pencil... Be sure to use a sharp pencil when marking this line. Figure 9-5 Window trim (plan view)
66	Figure 9-12 Marking a horn on a jambless window opening
68	Installing the Casings. Install the header casing first. Then fit the sides in between the head casing and the stool and mark the length of the side cases: (Highlight numbers 1-4)
70	Laying out the boards that make up the... Figure 9-19 shows the optimal layout for this particular radius of the arch.
73	Scaffolding should reach the perimeter of the room and be high enough so you can place your outstretched palm flat to the ceiling. Safety tip: Always inspect your scaffold thoroughly before using it. Be sure all diagonal struts are in place and that the connections.... Grains that's more than 20to 30 degrees out of alignment with the surface.

Page #	Highlight
78	Applied Beams, Posts and Corbels
	Let's begin by defining the basic parts (see Figure 10-9) (Highlight numbers 1-6)
85	Note in Figure 11-5 that the molding is placed in the chop box upside down. The saw fence is in the position of the wall surface and the base is in the position of the ceiling. What will become the bottom edge of the molding is facing up.
86	Figure 11-6 Angle settings for crown molding
91	It's better to start at that corner, even if you have to work right to left. Concentrate on fitting the wainscot board edge precisely against the uneven wall. The other side of that piece of wainscot- the open side- just needs to be plumb.
95	If someone is fabricating panels off site, make these suggestions to the fabricator: (Highlight numbers 1-4)
	Start at the wall at the left side by setting a panel in place. Use blocking to hold… With the panel on the sawhorses, make your cuts for outlet boxes and other openings.
97	Chair rails are often made from more than one molding. The cap may be supported from below with a bed molding (as in Figure 12-7) … Cut a miter on outside corners and cope the inside corners.
101	When you're working "top down" baseboard… leave the baseboard off until they're done installing, sanding, and finishing.
104	Attach the baseboard to the walls with a pair of finish nails driven into each… the upper nail goes into the backing.
105	In life, we learn to cope with these curves. With baseboard, we have to kerf… See Figure 13-8. You can also use a circular saw.
	These kerfs make it easy to bend the baseboard into what looks like an even curve, while not risking breaking the board.
117	Before you set the cabinets in place, draw reference lines on the walls to indicate the top of base cabinets and the bottom of wall cabinets. This tells you where to set the cabinets. Establishing these lines is a quick, easy job with a builder's sight level and leveling rod.
118	Figure 15-1 Cabinet installation checklist
122	Start wall cabinets at the corners. Set the bottom… insert shims between the back of the cabinet and the wall to get the face plumb.

Page #	Highlight
128	Cut the mantel to length. Then cut the width slightly wider than you need... Do whatever detailing is required.
130	You may not fabricate every mantel and surround, but you... Figure 16-6 shows the dimensions you'll have to know before ordering: (Highlight the four bullets).
132	The most common tongue and groove strips are ¾ inch thick by 2 inches... grooves to cut down on warpage and to ensure that the strips lay flat.
134	Moisture content- Laying wood flooring with a high moisture content is almost always a mistake. The wood will shrink as it dries, opening gaps... want you to go ahead with the job, have them sign a waiver of responsibility.
145	There's only one quick way to get a room of flooring flat and ready to... damage if run out of control. And they're right. Here are some tips for using a drum sander: (Highlight the four bullets).
151	Stair work is a big topic. A 500-page book couldn't cover every possible stair cutting and stair trim problem. Every stairway can be unique, with its own special challenges and special details. Building codes give us very specific guidance on... carriage and proposed design will meet current code requirements.
152	The Basic Stair Parts (Highlight numbers 1-3)
158	Some carpenters prefer to install treads and risers one step at a time, starting at the... stairs while you're not looking, mashing the unprotected top edge of the risers!
174	For those of us who seldom install anything but prehung doors, we may need a little extra coaching. Here are the steps to follow: (Highlight numbers 1-7)
177	When backing is missing at an inside corner, drive a long finish nail at 45 degrees into the corner. The joint here is probably a cope... Figure 19-9 shows a plan view of nailing molding at a corner.

1 Exam Prep

ASTM Standard Practice for Installation of Rigid Poly (Vinyl Chloride) Siding and Soffit

Tabs and Highlights

These 1 Exam Prep Tabs are based on ASTM D 4756-06 Standard Practice for Installation of Rigid Poly (Vinyl Chloride) (PVC) Siding and Soffit, 2006.

Each Tabs sheet has five rows of tabs. Start with the first tab at the first row at the top of the page; proceed down that row placing the tabs at the locations listed below. Place each tab in your book setting it down one notch until you get to the bottom of a page. Then start back at the top again. After each Tab, under "Reason" is a brief explanation of the purpose of the tab, and/or items to highlight in the section.

1 Exam Prep Tab	Page #	Reason/Highlight	
Definitions	1	3.2.1	Backerboard
		3.2.2	Buttock
		3.2.3	Crimp
		3.2.4	Crimper
		3.2.5	Face nail
		3.2.6	Fascia
		3.2.6.1	Fascia board
		3.2.6.2	Fascia cap or cover
		3.2.7	Flashing
	2	3.2.8	Furring/furring strip
		3.2.9	Nailslot punch
		3.2.10	Rake (roof)
		3.2.11	Rake (wall)
		3.2.12	snaplock ears
		3.2.13	snaplock punch
		3.2.14	soffit
		3.2.15	starter strip
		3.2.16	undersill trim
		3.2.17	zip tool
Protection of Materials	2	" Do not store in any location or in any manner where the temperature of the siding, soffit or accessories is likely to exceed 130F.	

1 Exam Prep Tab	Page #	Reason/Highlight
	3	5.2 "Store the cartons on a flat surface and support the entire length of the cartons."
		5.3 "Store the cartons away from areas where falling objects or other construction activity could impact the cartons. Keep the cartons dry."
		5.4 "Do not store the cartons in stacks more than 12 boxes high."
Fasteners	3	7.5 Fasteners
Substrate, Surface Preparation	3	8.1 "Weather-resistant barrier-Vinyl siding must be installed over a weather-resistant barrier system that includes (1)…(2)…"
	4	8.2 "Do not use caulk where it could restrict the normal expansion of the vinyl siding."
		8.3 "Do not apply vinyl siding directly to studs without sheathing."
		8.4 "Driving of fasteners directly into sheathing or existing siding is permitted in accordance with the siding manufacturer's instructions, where substantiated by windload testing…"
		8.7 " Furring- Masonry and uneven surfaces, as examples, require wood furring strips nominal 1 by 2 in. (25.4 by 50.8 mm) applied vertically and typically spaced 16 in (406 mm) on center…"
Application of Horizontal Siding	4	9.1.1 ""When applied, vinyl siding products must be attached "loosely", leaving approximately a 1/32-in (0.8-mm) space between the vinyl and the fastener head or crown to permit thermal movement."
		9.2.1 "Starter Strip- Determine the lowest point along the area to receive siding and install starter strips located so that the bottom edge of the initial course of siding which will be on a level…"
		9.2.2 " Corner posts- Outside and inside corner posts will start ¼ in. (6.4 mm) below the top, and end ¾ in. (19.1 mm) below the bottom edge of the first course of siding which will be…"
	5	9.3.3 "Lap the next panel over the first by approximately one-half of the factory cut notch, provided the overlap is at least ¾ in. (25.4 mm) but not greater than 1 ¼ in. (38.1 mm). Insert backerboard (if used) and fasten."

1 Exam Prep Tab	Page #	Reason/Highlight
	6	9.3.6 "If the top of the siding panel will extend above the bottom of the window, cut a section out of the panel to fit under the opening." "Allow ¼ in. (6.4 mm) clearance at the edges for insertion into each side of the J-channel."
	7	9.3.8.3 "Use furring behind the top of this panel if necessary to maintain the proper plane of the siding."
		9.3.8.4 "Nailing into the panel without pre-drilled hole has the potential to crack or kink the vinyl."
		9.3.9 "If more than one length of undersill trim is needed, splice by cutting out 1/1/4 in. (31.7 mm) inch from the back and nailing flange of one piece of trim."
Application of Vertical Siding	7	
		10.4 "trim around all windows and doors as described in 9.2.3, using J-channel at least as wide as the butt height of the vertical siding."
	8	10.9 "At windows and doors, cut the panels to fit the opening allowing ¼ in. (6.4 mm) for expansion."
	9	10.10.2 "If the panel is cut on the flat surface, place a piece of undersill trim, backed by furring, into the receiver of the corner post. Punch snap locks the cut edge of the panel at 6-in. (152-mm) intervals and snap it into the undersill trim."
Application of Soffits And Fascia	9	11.1 "Requirements for Proper Ventilation."
		11.2 "Installation of Soffit on an Open Rafter."
		11.3 "Installation of Soffit on an Enclosed Rafter."
		11.4 "Installation of Fascia."
		11.5 "Installation of Corner Cap."
	10	11.5.1 "Trim the fascia cover ends at the corners as in Fig. 37."
Shutter Installation	11	12.3 Shutter Installation:
		12.3.2 " Drill expansion holes through the siding (siding only) where attachment screws will be located, a minimum of ¼ in. (6.4 larger than the diameter of the screws."

1 Exam Prep Tab	Page #	Reason/Highlight
Keywords	11	13.1 "crimp; horizontal siding; installation practice…"

1 Exam Prep
ANSI ICC A117.1-2017: Accessible and Usable Buildings and Facilities Tabs and Highlights

These 1 Exam Prep tabs and highlights are based on *ANSI ICC A117.1-2017: Accessible and Usable Buildings and Facilities, 2017.*

Each 1 Exam Prep tabs sheet has five rows of tabs. Start with the first tab at the first row at the top of the page; proceed down that row placing the tabs at the locations listed below. Place each tab in your book setting it down one notch until you get to the last tab (usually the index or glossary). Then start with the highlights.

***This concludes the tabs for this book. Please proceed with the highlights below. ***

Section #	Highlight
106	**Definitions** - **Ramp:** A walking surface that has a running slope steeper than 1:20.
302	**Floor Surfaces**
302.3	**Openings:** Openings in floor surfaces shall be of a size that does not permit the passage of a ½ inch diameter sphere.
303	**Changes in Level**
303.1	**General:** Changes in level in floor surface shall comply with section 303.
303.2	**Vertical:** Changes of level of ¼ inch maximum height shall be permitted to be vertical.
303.3	**Beveled:** Changes in level greater than ¼ inch in height and nor more than ½ inch maximum height shall be beveled with a slope not steeper than 1:2.
304	**Turning Space**
304.3.1	**Circular Space**
304.3.1.1	**New Buildings and Facilities:** the turning space shall be a circular space with a 67-inch minimum diameter.

Section #	**Highlight**
306	**Knee and Toe Clearance**
306.2	**Toe Clearance**
306.2.2	**Maximum Depth:** Toe clearance shall be permitted to extend 25 inches maximum under an element.
306.3	**Knee Clearance**
306.3.2	**Maximum Depth:** Knee clearance shall be permitted to extend 25 inches maximum under an element at 9 inches above the floor.
307	**Protruding Objects**
307.2	**Protrusion Limits:** Objects with leading edges more than 27 inches and not more than 80 inches above the floor shall protrude 4 inches maximum into the circulation path. **Exception:** Handrails shall be permitted to protrude 4 ½ inches maximum.
Fig. 307.2	**Limits of Protruding Objects**
307.4	**Vertical Clearance:** The leading edge of such rails or barrier shall be located 27 inches maximum above floor.
308	**Reach Ranges**
308.2.2	**Obstructed High Reach:** The high forward reach shall be 48 inches maximum above floor where the reach depth is 20 inches maximum.
308.3	**Side Reach**
308.3.1	**Unobstructed:** The high side reach shall be 48 inches maximum and the low side reach shall be 15 inches minimum above the floor.
309	**Operable Parts**
309.4	**Operation:** Operable parts shall be operable with one hand and shall not require tight grasping, pinching, or twisting of the wrist. The force required to activate operable parts shall be 5.0 pounds.
402	**Accessible Routes**
402.3	**Revolving Doors, Revolving Gates, and Turnstiles:** Revolving doors, revolving gates, and turnstiles shall not be part of an accessible route.
403	**Walking Surfaces**
403.5	**Clear Width**

Section #	Highlight

403.5.1   **General:** The clear width of an accessible route shall be 36 inches minimum.

           Exception: Highlight # 1 and #2.

404   **Door and Doorways**

404.2.2   **Clear Width:** Doorways shall have a clear width of 32 inches minimum.

404.2.4   **Thresholds:** If provided, thresholds at doorways shall be ½ inch maximum in height.

404.2.6.1   **Hardware Height:** Operable parts of such hardware shall be 34 inches minimum and 48 inches maximum above the floor.

404.2.8   **Door and Gate Opening Force:** The force pushing or pulling open doors or gates (other than fire doors) shall be as follows:
1. Interior hinged door: 5.0 pounds maximum.
2. Sliding or folding door: 5.0 pounds maximum.

405   **Ramps**

405.2   **Slope:** Ramp runs shall have a running slope greater than 1:20 and not steeper than 1:12.

405.5   **Clear Width:** The clear width of a ramp run shall be 36 minimum.

405.6   **Rise:** The rise for any ramp run shall be 30 inches maximum.

405.7   **Landings**

405.7.2   **Width:** Clear width of landings shall be at least as wide as the widest ramp run leading to the landing.

405.7.3   **Length:** Landings shall have a clear length of 60 inches minimum.

405.8   **Handrails:** Ramp runs with a rise greater than 6 inches shall have handrails complying with Section 505.

406   **Curb Ramps and blended Transitions**

406.5.1   **Width:** The clear width of curb ramps runs (excluding any flared sides) and blended transitions shall be 48 inches.

407   **Elevators**

407.2.1.2   **Size:** Call buttons shall be ¾ inch minimum in the smallest dimension.

407.4.6   **Elevator Car Controls**

407.4.6.4   **Emergency Controls**: Emergency controls shall comply with Section 407.4.6.4.

Section #	Highlight
407.4.6.4.1	**Height:** Emergency control buttons shall have their centerlines 35 inches minimum above the floor.
409	**Private Residence Elevators**
409.4.5	**Illumination:** The level of illumination at the car controls … shall be 5-foot candles minimum.
502	**Parking Spaces**
502.2	**Vehicle Space Size:** Car parking spaces shall be 96 inches minimum in width. Van parking spaces shall be 132 inches minimum in width.
	Exception: Van parking spaces shall be permitted to be 96 inches minimum width where the adjacent access aisle is 96 inches minimum in width.
502.4	**Access Aisle**
502.4.2	**Width:** Access aisles serving car and van parking spaces shall be 60 inches minimum width.
502.5	**Floor Surfaces:** Parking spaces and access aisles shall comply with Section 302 and have surface slopes not steeper than 1:48
502.7	**Identification:** Where accessible parking spaces are required to be identified with signs … signs shall be 60 inches minimum above the floor of the parking space, measured to the bottom of the sign.
505	**Handrails**
505.4	**Height:** Top of gripping surfaces of handrails shall be 34 inches minimum and 38 inches minimum and 38 inches maximum vertically above stair nosing, ramp surfaces and walking surfaces.
505.5	**Clearance:** Clearance between handrail gripping surface and adjacent surfaces shall be 1 ½ inches minimum.
505.7	**Cross Section**
505.7.1	**Circular Cross Section:** Handrails with a circular cross section shall have an outside diameter of 1 ¼ inches minimum and 2 inches maximum.
505.7.2	**Noncircular Cross Sections:** Handrails with noncircular cross section shall have a perimeter dimension of 4 inches minimum … and a cross-section dimension of 2 ¼ maximum.
505.10	**Handrail Extensions**
505.10.1	**Top and Bottom Extension at Ramps:** Ramp handrails shall extend horizontally above the landing 12 inches minimum.

Section #	Highlight
Fig. 505.10.2	**Top Handrail Extensions at Stairs**
602	**Drinking Fountains and Bottle Filling Stations**
602.2.3	**Spout Outlet Height:** Spout outlets of drinking fountains shall be 36 inches maximum above the floor.
603	**Toilet and Bathing Rooms**
604	**Water Closets and Toilet Compartments**
604.2	**Location:** The centerline of the water closet shall be 16 inches minimum and 18 inches maximum from the side wall or partition.
Fig. 604.2	**Water Closet Location**
604.3	**Clearance**
604.3.2	**Clearance Depth:** Clearance around the water closet shall be 56 inches minimum in depth, measured perpendicular from the rear wall.
604.4	**Height:** The height of the water closet seats shall be 17 inches minimum and 19 inches maximum above the floor, measured from the top of the seat.
604.5	**Grab Bars**
604.5.1.1	**Horizontal Grab Bars:** A horizontal grab bar 42 inches minimum in length shall be located 12 inches maximum from the rear wall extending 54 inches minimum from the rear wall.
604.5.2	**Rear Wall Grab Bars:** The fixed rear-wall grab bars shall Highlight #1, #2, and #3.
604.9	**Wheelchair Accessible Compartments**
604.9.2.1	**Minimum Area:** The minimum area of a wheelchair accessible compartment shall be 60 inches … and 56 inches minimum in depth for wall hung water closets.
604.9.3	**Doors** **Exceptions**: Highlight #1.
604.9.3.1	**Door Opening Location:** The farthest edge of a toilet compartment door opening shall be … as required by Table 604.9.3.1.
Tb 604.9.3.1	**Door Opening Location**
609	**Grab Bars**

Section #	Highlight
Section #	**Highlight**

609.3   **Spacing**: The space between the wall and the grab bar shall be 1 ½ inches.

609.4   **Position of Grab Bars**

609.4.1   **General:** Grab bars shall be installed in a horizontal position, 33 inches minimum and 36 inches maximum above the floor measured to top of the gripping surface or shall be installed as required by items 1 through 3.

609.8   **Structural Strength:** Allowable stresses shall not be exceeded for materials used where a vertical or horizontal force of 250 pounds is applied at any point on the grab bar, fastener mounting device, or supporting structure.

611   **Washing Machines and Clothes Dryers**

611.2   **Clear Floor Space:** A clear floor space complying with section 305 … The centerline of the clear floor space shall be offset 24 inches maximum from the centerline of the door opening.

703   **Signs**

703.2.9   **Height Above Floor:** Visual characters shall be 40 inches minimum above the floor of the viewing position, measured to the baseline of the character.

707   **Automatic Teller Machines (ATM) and Fare Machines**

Tb 707.6.1   **Raised Symbols**

1103.12   **Kitchens**

1103.12.4   **Sink**

1103.12.4.2   **Height:** The front of the sink shall be 34 inches maximum above the floor, measured to be higher of the rim or counter surface.

1106   **Units with Accessible Communication Features**

1006.2   **Unit Smoke Detection:** Where provided, unit smoke detection shall include audible notification complying with NFPA 72 listed in Section 106.2.4.

1 Exam Prep
OSHA 29 CFR 1926
Tabs and Highlights

These 1 Exam Prep Tabs are based on the *29 CFR 1926 OSHA Construction Industry Regulations*.

Each Tabs sheet has five rows of tabs. Start with the first tab at the first row at the top of the page; proceed down that row placing the tabs at the locations listed below. Place each tab in your book setting it down one notch until you get to the last tab (usually the index or glossary). Then start with the highlights.

*Note: In the July 2014 and January 2015 Edition, Section 1910 is located at the front of the book, in numerical order. In the July 2015 Edition, Section 1910 is located throughout the book and is *not* in numerical order. You will need to use the index and/or table of contents in the book to locate the page numbers for the highlights and/or tabs for Section 1910. This is excellent practice for your exam.

*Note: Section 1926 is located in all OSHA editions in numerical order. Page numbers are not provided since the edition changes every six (6) months.

1 Exam Prep Tab	Section #
Table of Contents	i
1903: Inspections	1903.3
Citations/Penalties	1903.14
1904: Recordkeeping	1904.0
Fatalities	1904.39
1910: General	1910.12
Escape Only Respirators	1910.134
QLFT	1910.134
*Permit Required Spaces	1910.146
Lockout Tagout	1910.147
Access to Records	1910.1020
Noise Exposure	1926.52
Hazard Communications	1910.1200
Personal & Life Saving Equipment	Subpart E
Fire Protection & Prevention	Subpart F

This Tab only appears in editions prior to July 2015

New Tab 04/27/16. If you have purchased pre-printed tabs please write this one in.

1 Exam Prep Tab	Section #
Yard Storage	1926.151(C) *New Tab 04/27/16. If you have purchased pre-printed tabs please write this one in.*
Signs, Signals & Barricades	Subpart G
Material Handling, Storage Use & Disposal	Subpart H
Tools - Hand & Power	Subpart I
Compressed Air	1926.302(b)(4)
Welding & Cutting "Cracking"	Subpart J
Electrical	Subpart K
Scaffolds	Subpart L
Fall Protection	Subpart M
Roof Widths	1926.501 (b)(10)
Personal Fall Systems	1926.502(d)
Positioning Device Systems	1926.502(e)
Sample Fall Protection	1926.502(k)
Cranes, Derricks & Hoists	Subpart N
Motor Vehicles	Subpart O
Excavations	Subpart P
Soil Classifications	Appendix A
Sloping & Benching	Appendix B
Demolition	Subpart T
Power & Distribution	Subpart V
Rollover & Overhead Protection	Subpart W
Stairways & Ladders	Subpart X
Diving	Subpart Y

1 Exam Prep Tab	**Section #**
Toxic & Hazardous Substances	Subpart Z
Index	Index

This concludes the tabs for this document. Please continue with the highlights on the following page.

Section #	**Highlight**
1903	**Inspections, Citations, and Proposed Penalties**
1904.1	**Recording and Reporting Occupational Injuries and Illnesses**
1904.1(a)(1)	**Basic Requirement:** If your company had ten (10) or fewer employees at all times during the last calendar year, you do not need to keep OSHA illness and injury records.
1904.39	**Reporting fatalities and multiple hospitalization incidents to OSHA**
1910	**General Industry Standards**
1910.134(b)	Escape only respirators means a respirator intended to be used only for emergency exist.
1910.134(f)(6)	QLFT may only be used to fit test negative pressure air purifying respirators that must achieve a fit factor of 100 or less.
1910.146	**Permit required confined spaces**
1910.147	**The control of hazardous energy (lockout/tagout)**
1910.1020	**Access to employee exposure and medical records**
1910.1020(e)(1)(i)	Whenever an employee requests access to records (15 days)
1910.1200	**Hazard Communications**
Subpart A	**General**
1926.1	**Purpose and scope**
1926.3	**Right of Entry, right to accompany**
Subpart B	**General Interpretations**
1926.12	Reconciles various documents and Acts
1926.13	**Interpretation of Statutory Terms**

Section #	Highlight
1926.15(b)	Federal Contracts over $10,000: Nothing can be bought from violating manufacturer's; no services from violating contractors
Subpart C	**General Safety and Health provisions**
1926.20 (a)(1)	**General safety and health provisions**. No one works in unsafe environment
	1926.21(b)(2) Employer responsibility: instruct each employee in the recognition and avoidance of unsafe conditions
1926.21-31	First aid, fire, housekeeping, illumination, sanitation, personal protective equipment, these are all general areas of employer responsibility. Specific details are not elaborated in the remainder of 1926
1926.32(d)	Definition of an authorized person
1926.32(m)	Definition of a qualified person
1926.32(j)	Definition of an employee
Subpart D	**Occupational Health and Environmental Controls** – minimum site conditions
1926.50	**First Aid Kits (Non-Mandatory)**
1926.51	**Sanitation.** Potable water available. See Table D-1 for number of employees and minimum # of facilities
1926.52	**Occupational noise exposure.** Table D-2 Permissible noise exposures. The info from the table is used to complete the formula under it. If after the calculation is done, the answer exceeds 1 (unity) it means that the cumulative effect of long term exposure equals to lower levels of noise or exceeds the limit of exposure and therefore has the effect of injury.
1926.55	**Vapors, fumes, dusts, and mists. Appendix A-1970 American Conference of Governmental Hygienists' Threshold Limit Values of Airborne Contaminants**
1926.56	**Illumination: Table D-3 Minimum Illumination Intensities in Foot Candles**
1926.57	**Ventilation.** This section covers grinding or dust and particle producing activities, such as abrasive blasting grinding, polishing equipment.
1926.60	**Methylenedianiline.** Practices and procedures for Methylenedianiline.
1926.62	**Lead.** References Appendix A-D; Begins section on lead, Lead paint reduction, protection esp. PEL 50 micrograms per cubic meter of air.
1926.62(f)	**Respiratory Protection**

Section #	Highlight
1926.62(j)(2)	**Biological monitoring**
1926.64	**Process safety management of highly hazardous chemicals.**
Subpart E	**Personal & Life Saving Equipment**
1926.95	**Criteria for personal protective equipment.** Section starts identifying and prescribing head, hearing, eye and face protection measures. Shall be provided; employer responsible that equipment is safe design and use head protection whenever necessary
1926.100	**Head Protection**
1926.102	**Eye and Face Protection**
1926.104	**Safety belts, lifelines, and lanyards.** Safety belts, minimum 5,400 dead weight, 1/2 inch thick nylon, hardware cadmium plated type 1 class b plating, tensile loading 4,000 lbs
1926.105	**Safety Nets.** Safety nets, needed over 25', 6" x 6" mesh, 17500 foot points minimum resistance; edge ropes 5000
1926.106	**Working over or near water.** Over water: Ring buoys 90 feet line, 200 max distance.
Subpart F	**Fire Protection and Prevention**
1926.150	**Fire protection. Table F-1 Fire Extinguishers Data**
1926.151	**Fire prevention**
1926.151(C)	**Open Yard Storage**
1926.152	**Flammable liquids**
1926.153	**Liquefied Petroleum Gas (LP-Gas).** Includes handling and storage as well as container. Specifications, Table F-3 & F-31 Storage of LP-gas.
1926.154	Table F-4 minimum clearance for heating equipment.
Subpart G	**Signs, Signals and Barricades**
1926.200	**Accident prevention signs and tags.** Accident prevention, danger and caution defined. Specific coloring; exit, safety instruction, directional traffic signs defined, accident prevention tags demonstrated
Subpart H	**Material Handling, Storage Use & Disposal**
1926.250	**Requirements for storage**

Section #	Highlight
1926.250(b)	**Material storage.** (1) "Material stored inside buildings under construction shall not be placed within 6 feet of any hoist way or inside floor openings …"(4) "Bagged materials shall be stacked by stepping back the layers and cross keying the bags at least every 10 bags high."(6) "Brick stacks not more than 7' in height. When a loose brick reaches a height of 4', it shall be tapered back 2" per ft. the above 4' level." (7) When masonry blocks are stacked higher than 6', the stack shall be tapered back ½ block per tier above the 6' level." (8) Lumber.
1926.251	**Rigging equipment and material handling.**
1926.251(c)	(4)(iv) Wire rope shall not be used if any length of eight diameters, 10% strands broken (13) Minimum sling lengths 10 times component rope diameter (14) Safe operating temperatures
1926.251(d)	Natural ropes and synthetic fiber. (2)(i) In manila rope, eye splices shall contain at least three full tucks. (2)(iii) strand end tails various minimums (6) Removal from service
	Tables H-1 through H-2. Series of tables for capacities for various slings
1926.252	**Disposal of Waste Materials**
Subpart I	**Tools -Hand & Power**
1926.300	**General Requirements.** Various rules about specific tools and machines.
1926.300(b)(4)(iv).	"The following are some machines which usually require point of operation guarding: (Note [a]-[i])."
1926.300(d)	**Switches**
1926.301	**Hand Tools.** Various rules of operation for powerhand tools
1926.302	**Power-operated Hand Tools**
1926.302(b)(4)	"Compressed air should not be used for cleaning purposes except where reduced to less than 30 psi and then only with effective chip guarding and personal protective equipment which meets the requirements the requirements of subpart E of this part…"
1926.303	**Abrasive wheels and tools**
1926.303(b)(1)	**Guarding.** Grinding machines shall be equipped with safety guards.
1926.304	**Woodworking Tools**
1926.305	**Jacks – lever and ratchet, screw, and hydraulic**. Blocking required for firm foundation
Subpart J	**Welding & Cutting**

Section #	Highlight
1926.350	**Gas welding and cutting**
1926.350(a)	**Transporting, moving, and storing compressed gas cylinders.**
1926.350(a)(10)	Oxygen cylinders in storage shall be separated from fuel-gas cylinders ... having a fire resistance rating of at least one-half hour.
1926.350(d)	**Use of Fuel Gas.** The employer shall thoroughly instruct employees in the safe use of fuel gas, as follows:
1926.350(d)(1)	Before a regulator to a cylinder valve is connected ... This action is general termed "cracking" and is intended to clear the valve of dust or dirt that might otherwise enter the regulator.)
1926.351	**Arc Welding and Cutting**
1926.351(d)	**Operating Instructions.** Employers shall instruct employees in the safe means of arc welding and cutting as follows:
1926.351(d)(1)	When electrode holders are left unattended ... with employees or conducting objects.
1926.354	**Welding, cutting, and heating in way of preservative coatings.** (a) "Before welding cutting or heating is commenced on any surface covered by a preservative coating whose flammability is unknown, a test shall be made by a competent person to determine its flammability."
Subpart K	**Electrical**
1926.400	**Installation Safety Requirements Introduction**
1926.403	**General Requirements: Tables K-1 Working Clearances, K-2: Minimum Depth of Clear Working Space, K-3 Elevation of Unguarded Energized Parts**
1926.404	**Wiring design and protection.**
1926.404(b)	**Branch Circuits**
1926.404(b)(1)	Ground-fault protection
1926.404(b)(1)(ii)	Ground-fault circuit interrupters. All 120-volt, single-phase, 15- and 20-ampere receptacle outlets ... need not be protected with ground-fault circuit interrupters. [C] Each chord set, attachment cap, plug and receptacle ... Equipment fund damaged or defective shall not be used until repaired. [D] The following tests shall be performed on all cord sets ... [1] – [2].
1926.404(b)(2)	**Table K-4: Receptacle Ratings for Various Size Circuits**

Section #	Highlight
1926.405	**Wiring Methods, Components, and Equipment for General Use**
1926.407	**Hazardous locations.** Section deals with classification of locations from Class I – III
1926.408	**Special Systems**
Subpart L	**Scaffolds**
1926.450	**Scope, application, and definitions applicable to this subpart.**
1926.450(b)	**Definitions**
1926.451	**General Requirements**
1926.451(a)	**Capacity.** (1) scaffold component shall be capable of supporting, without failure, its own weight and at least support 4 times the maximum intended load. (2) Direct connections to roofs and floors, and counterweights … at least 4 times the tipping moment.(3) Each suspension rope … at least 6 times the maximum intended load.(4) Each suspension rope … 6 times intended load … or 2 (minimum) times the stall load of the hoist, whichever is greater. (5) Stall load not exceed 3 times rated load (6) Scaffolds shall be designed by a qualified person … Non-mandatory Appendix A to this subpart contains examples of criteria that will enable the employer to comply with paragraph (a) of this section.
1926.451(b)	**Scaffold platform construction.** (1)Each platform on all working levels of scaffolds shall be fully planked or decked between the front uprights and guardrail supports as follows: (i) Each platform unit … uprights is no more than 1 inch wide (ii) Where the employer makes demonstration …remaining open space between the platform and the uprights shall not exceed 9 1/2 inches (2) Except provided in paragraphs … at least 18 inches wide (i) Each ladder jack scaffold… at least 12 inches wide (ii) Where scaffolds must be used … 18 inches wide… personal fall arrest systems. (3) Except as provided …the front edge of all platforms shall not be more than 14" from the face of the work … of this section to protect an employee from falling. (i) The maximum distance from the face for outrigger scaffolds shall be 3 inches. (ii) The maximum distance from the face for plastering and lathing operations shall be 18 inches. (4) Each end of a platform…extend over the centerline of its support at least 6 inches. (5)(i) Each end of a platform 10 feet or less in length shall not extend over its support more than 12 inches … or has guardrails which block employee access. (ii) Each platform greater than 10 feet in length shall not extend more than 18 inches … or has guardrails which block employee access to cantilevered ends.
1926.451(c)	**Criteria for supported scaffolds.** (1) "Supported scaffolds with height to base width ratio of more than four to one (4:1) shall be restrained…"
1926.451(d)	**Criteria for Suspension Scaffolds**

Section #	Highlight

1926.451(e)

Access. This paragraph applies to …. (1) "When scaffold platforms are more than 2 feet above or below a point of access, portable ladders, hook-on ladders, attachable ladders, stair towers, stairway-type ladders, ramps, walkways, integral prefabricated scaffold access, or direct access from another scaffold ,,, shall be used." (3)"Stairway-type ladders shall: (i) - (iii)." (4) "Stair towers shall be positioned such that their bottom step is not more than 23 inches above the scaffold supporting level."

1926.451 (g)

Fall protection. (1) Each employee on a scaffold more than 10 feet above a lower level shall be protected from falling to that lower level. (iii) Each employee on a crawling board … minimum 200 lb top rail capacity … handhold securely fastened beside each crawling board. (3) In addition to meeting the requirements of … adjustable suspension scaffold. (ii) When horizontal lifelines are used, they shall be secured to two or more structural members of the scaffold … Horizontal lifelines shall not be attached only to suspension ropes. (4) Guardrail systems installed … meet the requirements of paragraphs (g)(4) (vii), (viii), and (ix) of this section. (vii) Each top rail or equivalent …100 pounds for guard-rail systems installed on single-point … or two-point adjustable … at least 200 pounds for guardrail systems installed on other scaffolds. (viii) When loads specified … shall not drop below the height above the platform surface … of this section.

1926.451(h)

Falling object protection.(2)Where there is danger of tools … the following provisions apply: (ii) A toe board shall be erected along the edge of platforms more than 10 feet above lower levels … wood or equivalent may be used in lieu of toeboards. (4) Where used, toeboards shall be:(ii) At least three and one-half inches high from the top edge of the toe board to the level of the working surface … Toeboads shall be solid or with openings not over one inch in the greatest dimension.

1926.452

Additional Requirements for specific types of scaffolding
(a) Pole Scaffolding
(b) Tube and coupler scaffolds
(c) Fabricated frame scaffolds
(6)Scaffolds over 125 feet in height above their base shall be designed by a registered engineer
(d) Plasterer's scaffolding
(e) Bricklayer's square scaffolds
(f) Horse scaffolds
(g) Form and carpenter's bracket
(h) Roof bracket scaffolds
(j) Pump jack scaffold
(k) Ladder jack scaffold
(1) Window jack scaffold
(m) Crawling boards (chicken ladders)
(n) Step platform and trestle ladder
(o) Single point adjustable suspension
(p) Two point adjustable suspension
(q) Multi point adjustable
(r) Catenary
(s) Float (ship)

Section #	**Highlight**
	(t) Interior hung (u) Needle beam (v) Multi-level suspended (w) Mobile (x) Repair bracket scaffolds (y) Stilts
1926.453	**Aerial Lifts**
1926.454	**Training Requirements**
Appendix A	**Scaffold Specifications (Non-mandatory). Index to Appendix A for Subpart L.** Note: This is indicating where more detail can be found for scaffolding which was defined above. Two tables, first maximum intended nominal load (this table correlates load with thickness for dressed and undressed lumber rated capacity).
Appendix E	Pictorial of types of scaffolding components and basic rules identified.
Subpart M	**Fall Protection**
1926.500	**Scope, application, and definitions applicable to this subpart.**
1926.500(b)	**Definitions**
1926.501(b)(10)	Determining Roof Widths
1926.501	**Duty to have fall protection**
1926.501(b)	(1) Unprotected sides above 6' must have guard rail (2) Leading edge above 6 feet guardrail, or safety net, or personal protection required (above 6' is key) (10) Roofing work on low slope system requires warning line or guard rail, or safety net, or personal fall arrest system: exception width 50' or less can use safety monitoring system
1926.501(c)	**Protection from falling objects**: "when an employee is exposed to falling objects, the employer shall have each employee wear a hard hat and shall implement one of the following measures: 1. Erect toe boards; 2. Erect a canopy structure; 3. Barricade
1926.502	**Fall protection systems criteria and practices**
1926.502(b)	**Guardrail systems.** (1) Top edge height 42 inches plus or minus 3"(2) Midrails, screens, mesh...installed between the top edge of the guardrail system and the walking surface... when there is no wall or parapet wall at least 21 inches high (iv) ...no openings in the guardrail system that are more than 19 inches wide (4) Guardrail systems capable... 200 lbs applied within 2 inches of the top edge (9) Top rails and midrails shall be at least 1/4" nominal diameter or thickness to prevent cuts
1926.502(c)	**Safety net systems.** (1) Safety nets.... no case more than 30 feet below such level(2) Safety nets shall extend outward

Section #	Highlight
1926.502(d)	**Personal fall arrest systems.** Body belts not acceptable (9) Lanyards a vertical lifelines shall have a minimum breaking strength of 5,000lbs (12) Self retracting lifelines... limit free fall distance to 2 ft. with minimum tensile load of 3,000lbs (15) Anchorages used for...personal fall arrest equipment.... 5,000lbs (16) (system) shall: (i) limit arresting force on employee to 900lbs with body belt (ii) 1,800 lbs with body harness (iii) employee can neither free fall more than 6', (iv) deceleration distance limited to 3.5 feet (v) Have sufficient strength to withstand twice the potential impact energy of an employee free falling a distance of 6'.
1926.502(e)	**Positioning device system** (1) Positioning device systems...shall be rigged such that an employee cannot free fall more than 2' (2) Positioning devices....load...3,000 lbs (5)Connecting assemblies 5,000lbs (6) dee rings, snaphooks,3600 lbs
1926.502(f)	**Warning line systems.** (2)(i) Flagged at 6' intervals (2)(ii) Lowest point 34", highest 39" (2)(iii) Tipping 16 lbs (iv) Rope, 500lbs
1926.502(g)	**Controlled access zones** This section defines storage areas, cover controls and stacking materials. Fall protection plan defined as option.
1926.502(k)	Sample Fall Protection Plan
1926.503	**Training Requirements**
Subpart N	**Cranes, Derricks & Hoists**
1926.551	**Helicopters**
1926.552	**Material Hoists, Personnel elevators**
1926.552(b)	**Material hoists.** (2) Entryways protected by 2x4 bars 2' from hoistway line, not less than 36 nor more than 42 inches above floor.
1926.552(c)	**Personnel hoists.** (3) Towers shall be anchored ...not exceeding 25'(14) Note the table titled, **Minimum Factors of Safety for Suspension Wire Ropes**
1926.553	**Base Mounted drum hoists**
1926.554	**Overhead Hoists**
1926.555	**Conveyors**
Subpart O	**Motor Vehicles and Marine Operations**
1926.600	**Equipment**
1926.602	**Material Handling Equipment**

Section #	Highlight
1926.603	**Pile driving equipment**
1926.605	**Marine Operations and Equipment**
Subpart P	**Excavations**
1926.650	**Scope application, and definitions applicable to this subpart**. (For additional reference see Walkers Builder's Estimators Reference Table B4 if your exam calls for this book.)
1926.651	**Specific excavation requirements**
1926.651(c)	**Access and egress.** (2)Means of egress needed at depth 4' or over
1926.651(g)	**Hazardous atmospheres.** (1)(i) *"Where oxygen deficiency* (atmospheres containing less than 19.5 percent oxygen) or a hazardous atmosphere exists or could reasonably be expected to exist, such as in excavations in landfill areas or excavations in areas where hazardous substances are stored nearby, the excavations greater than 4 feet in depth."
1926.651(i)	**Stability of adjacent structures.**
1926.651(j)	**Protection of employees from loose rock or soil.** (2) *"Employees shall be protected from excavated or other materials* or equipment that could pose a hazard by falling or rolling into excavations. Protection shall be3 provided by placing and keeping such materials or equipment at least 2 feet from the edge of excavations, or by the use of retaining devices that are sufficient to prevent materials or equipment from falling ..."
1926.652	**Requirements for protective systems**
1926.652(b)	**Design of sloping and benching systems.** (1) Option 1 allowable configurations and slopes (2) Option 2 determination of slopes and configurations using appendices A and B (3) Designs using other tabulated data (4) Design by a registered professional engineer
Subpart P	**Appendix A: Soil Classification.** This section provides definitions, including types A, B & C soil *"Type A* means cohesive soils with an unconfined compressive strength of 1.5 ton per square foot (tsf) or greater. Examples of cohesive soils are: clay, silty clay, sandy clay, clay loam ..." *"Type B* means: (i) *Cohesive soil with an unconfined* compressive strength greater than .05 tsf but less than 1.5 tsf ..." *"Type C* means: (i) *Cohesive soil with an unconfined* compressive strength of 0.5 tsf or less ..."

Section #	**Highlight**
Subpart P	**Appendix B: Sloping and Benching.** This section provides pictorial descriptions of run to rise calculations. Also Figure B-1 which relates the types of soil to the required run to rise (horizontal to vertical) ratio to determine the amount of slope.
	(b) **Definitions**. "*Distress* means that the soil is in a condition where a cave-in is imminent or is likely to occur. Distress is evidenced by such phenomena as the development of fissures in the face of adjacent to an open excavation; the subsidence of the edge of an excavation; the slumping of material from the face or the bulging or heaving of material …"
	(3) *Actual Slope*. (ii) "*The actual slope shall be less* steep than the maximum allowable slope, when there are signs of distress. If that situation occurs, the slope shall be cut back to an actual slope which is at least 1/2 horizontal to one vertical (1/2 H:1V) less steep than the maximum allowable slope."
	(4)"*Configurations.*" Configurations of sloping and benching systems shall be in accordance with Figure B-1." Note: **Figure B-1** and number 3 in the notes.
Subpart P	**Appendix C:** Tables **C-1.1** through **C-2.3**
	Appendix D: Tables **D-1.1** through **D-1.4** These are aluminum shoring components flow charts.
Subpart Q	**Concrete and Masonry Construction**
1926.700	**Scope, application, and definitions applicable to this subpart**.
1926.700(b)	**Definitions** 1 – 9.
1926.702(b)	**Concrete mixers.** Concrete mixers with 1 c.y. or more shall be equipped with: (1) Mechanical device to clear the skip; (2) Guardrails installed
1926.702(c)	**Power concrete trowels.** Shall be equipped with a control switch that will automatically shut off the power whenever the hands of the operator are removed … handles.
1926.702(j)	**Lockout / tag out procedures**
1926.703	**Requirements for cast in place concrete**
1926.703(b)	**Shoring and Reshoring**
1926.704	**Requirements for precast concrete**
1926.706	**Requirements for masonry construction**
1926.706 (a)	**A limited access zone shall be established** … shall conform to the following:

Section #	Highlight
1926.706(b)	**All masonry walls over 8 ft. in height** shall be adequately braced to prevent overturning … elements of the structure are in place.
Subpart R	**Steel Erection**
1926.751	**Definitions**
1926.754	**Structural steel assembly**
1926.754 (b)	**The following additional requirements** shall apply for multi-story structures. (2) At no time shall there be more than four floors or 48 feet of unfinished bolting ... result of the design.
Subpart S	**Underground Construction, Caissons, Cofferdams and Compressed Air**
1926.800	**Underground Construction**
1926.802	**Cofferdams**
1926.803	**Compressed air**
Subpart T	**Demolition**
1926.850	**Preparatory operations**
1926.851	**Stairs, passageways and ladders**
1926.852	**Chutes**
1926.852(b)	"The openings shall not exceed 48 inches in height measured along the wall of the chute."
1926.859	**Mechanical demolition**
1926.859(b)	"**The weight of the ball** shall not exceed 50 % or the cranes rated load…"
Subpart U	**Blasting and Use of Explosives**
Subpart V	**Power Transmissions and Distribution**
1926.965	**Underground Electrical Installations**
1926.968	**Definitions:** barrier and barricade
Subpart W	**Rollover Protective Structures; Overhead Protection**
Subpart X	**Stairways and Ladders**

Section #	Highlight
1926.1050	**Scope, application, and definitions applicable to this subpart**
1926.1050(b)	**Definitions**
1926.1051	**General Requirements**
1926.1051(a)	Needed break in elevation of 19 inches (1) No spiral staircases unless permanent ones (2) Double cleated ladder or two or more separate ladders provided... 25 employees or more
1926.1052	**Stairways**
1926.1052(a)	(1) Landings not less than 30 inches and extend 22 inches (3) Variations in riser height and tread depth not over 1/4"
1926.1052(c)	**Stair-rails and handrails**
	(1) Stairways having four or more risers, or rising more than 30 inches … shall be equipped with (i) At least one handrail (ii) One stairrail system along each unprotected side or edge
	(4)(11) Handrails that will not be permanent … minimum clearance of 3 inches … and other objects.
1926.1053	**Ladders**
1926.1053(a)	(1) Ladders shall be capable of supporting the following loads without failure: (i) Each self-supporting potable ladder ... sustain at least 3.3 times the max. intended load … appendix A of this subpart will be deemed to meet this requirement. (ii) Each portable ladder that is not self-supporting: At least four times the maximum intended load … appendix A will be deemed to meet this requirement. (iii) Each fixed ladder: At least two loads of 250 pounds each ... appendix A will be deemed to meet this requirement (3)(i) Rungs, cleats and steps of portable ladders and fixed shall be spaced not less than 10 inches nor more than 14 inches apart. (3)(ii) Rungs, cleats and steps of step stools not less than 8 inches apart, nor more than 12 inches … as measured between center lines of the rungs, cleats, and steps. (3)(iii) Rungs, cleats and steps of … trestle ladders not less than 8 inches nor more than 18 inches …as measured between center lines of the rungs, cleats, and steps. (4)(i) The minimum clear distance between sides of individual ladders... shall be 16 inches. (6)(i) The rungs of fixed metal ladders … treated to minimize slipping. (7) Ladders shall not be tied or fastened together … unless they are specifically designed for such use. (8) A metal spreader or locking device shall be provided on each step ladder … when the ladder is being used.

Section #	Highlight
	(13) The minimum perpendicular clearance fixed ladder rungs, cleats, and steps 4.5 … inches where required. (19)Where the total length of a climb equals or exceeds 24 feet the following applies: (i-iii) (21) Wells for fixed ladders shall conform to all of the following: (i-v) (22) Ladder safety devices … shall conform to all of the following: (i-iv) (24) The side rails of a through or side step fixed ladder shall extend 42 inches above the top of the access level … the top of the parpet.
1926.1053(b)	**Use.** (1)"When portable ladders are used for access to an upper landing surface, the ladder side rails shall extend at least 3'...(5)(i) Non Self supporting ....used at an angle such that horizontal distance from the top support to the foot of the ladder is approx. 1/4 the working length of the ladder (5)(ii) Wood job made ladders with spliced side rails shall be used at an angle ...1/8 working length
Subpart Y	**Diving**
1926.1091	Record Keeping Requirements
Subpart Z	**Toxic and Hazardous Substances**
1926.1101	**Asbestos**
1926.1101(b)	**Definitions**
1926.1101(c)	**Permissible exposure limits (PELS).** (1) *Time-weighted average limit (TWA).* The employer shall ensure that no employee is exposed to an airborne concentration of asbestos in excess of 0.1 fiber per cubic centimeter of air as an eight hour time-weighted average … or by an equivalent method."
1926.1101(g)	**Methods of compliance.** (8) *Additional Controls for Class II work.* (i) "*For removing vinyl and asphalt flooring materials* … these practices pursuant to paragraph (k)(9)" (ii) "*For removing roofing materials* … the following work practices are followed" (iii) "*When removing cementitious asbestos-containing* siding and shingles … the following work practices are followed" (iv) "*When removing gaskets containing ACM* … the following work practices are followed" (v) "*When performing any other Class II removal* of asbestos containing material for which specific controls have not been listed … the following work practices are complied with." (vi) "*Alternative Work Practices and Controls* … the following provisions are complied with.*"
1926.1101(h)	**Respirator protection.** (ii) Employers must provide an employee with … PAPR and it provides adequate protection to the employee. (iii) Employers must provide employees with an air-purifying half mask … whenever employees perform:

Section #	Highlight
1926.1101(j)	**Hygiene facilities and practices for employees.** (1) Requirements for employees performing Class I … surfacing ACM and PACM.(i) *"Decontamination areas … regulated through the decontamination area.* [A] Equipment room [B] Shower area [C] Clean change room.
Subpart CC	**Cranes and Derricks in Construction**
1926.1400	**Scope**
1926.1401	**Definitions**
1926.1412	**Inspections**
1926.1415	**Safety devices**
1926.1417	**Operation**
1926.1419	**Signals - general requirements**
1926.1423	**Fall protection**
1926.1431	**Hoisting personnel**
1926.1435	**Tower cranes**
1926.1436	**Derricks**
1926.1437	**Floating cranes/derricks and land cranes/derricks on barges**
1926.1438	**Overhead & gantry cranes**
Index	**Index**
Inside back cover	Examples of OSHA reporting forms 300 and 300a, how to fill them out and summary of when required.

29 CFR 1926 OSHA
Questions and Answers

1. Forms and shores in concrete shall not be removed until:

A. directed by the architect or engineer
B. the removal time stated in the specifications has elapsed
C. the concrete has attained the specified compressive strength
D. the concrete has gained sufficient strength to support its weight and superimposed loads

2. When ropes are used to define control access areas the rope shall have a minimum breaking strength of:

A. 75 lbs.
B. 100 lbs.
C. 200 lbs.
D. 300 lbs.

3. Exposure to impulse or impact noise should not exceed:

A. 92 dB peak sound pressure level
B. 110 dB peak sound pressure level
C. 140 dB peak sound pressure level
D. 188 dB peak sound pressure level

4. Excavations 8' or less in depth which have unsupported, vertically-sided lower portions, shall have a maximum vertical side of _____ feet.

3
3.5
4
5

Employees must use a safety belt or equivalent fall protection when on the face of formwork or reinforcing steel at height of more than:

A. 4 feet
B. 6 feet
C. 8 feet
D. 10 feet

6. What is the maximum number of employees you can have on a job site with only one toilet facility?

10
15
20
50

What is the maximum permissible span for 2" x 10" full thickness undressed lumber with a working load of psf?

6'
8'
10'
12'

8. All the following are true concerning OSHA regulations about employees working over or near water except:

A. ring buoys with at least 90 feet of line shall be provided and readily available
B. at least one lifesaving skiff shall be immediately available
C. where the danger of drowning exists, provide employees with life jackets or buoyant work vests
D. at least one person certified in lifesaving swimming courses shall be employed at all times

9. According to OSHA, prior to excavation, the contractor should locate the:

A. dump site
B. site entrances
C. underground installations
D. adjacent property elevations

The maximum intended load for a metal tubular frame scaffold including its components is 1,000 pounds. According to OSHA, the scaffold as described shall be designed to support a minimum of:

A. 1.0 ton
B. 1.5 tons
C. 2.0 tons
D. 2.5 tons

11. Storing masonry blocks in stacks higher than 6' is permissible provided that:

A. bracing is installed at the 6' level
B. containment is provided every 4'
C. the stack is tapered back one-half block per tier above the 6' level
D. the stack is on a concrete floor

Lifelines shall be secured above the point of operation to an anchorage or structural member capable of supporting a minimum dead weight of:

A. 4,200 pounds
B. 4,800 pounds
C. 5,400 pounds
D. 6,000 pounds

If hazardous waste cleanup and removal operations at any site take longer than_____ months to complete, the employer must provide showers and changing rooms for employees exposed to such conditions.

3
6
9
12

14. No employee should be exposed to lead at concentrations greater than <u>micrograms pe</u>r cubic meter of air in an 8 hour period.

A. 30
B. 40
C. 50
D. 60

15. Training for Class II asbestos removal work requires hands-on-training and shall take at least:

A.4 hrs
B. 8 hrs
C. 12 hrs
D. 16 hrs

Where oxygen deficiency (atmospheres containing less than 19.5 percent oxygen) or a hazardous atmosphere exists or could reasonably be expected to exist, such as in excavations in landfill areas or excavations in areas where hazardous substances are stored nearby, excavations deeper than _____ must be tested before employees are allowed enter the excavation site?

A. 3'
B. 4'
C. 5'
D. 6'

Whenever a masonry wall is being constructed, a limited access zone shall be established. The access zone shall run the entire length of the wall, on the side of the wall that is not scaffolded, and extend to the height of the wall to be:

A.constructed
B.constructed plus two feet
C.constructed plus four feet
D.constructed plus six feet

A scaffold platform to be used by workers is 8' high and 41" wide. What is the approximate height of the required guardrails for this platform?

36"
42"
48"
54"

What is the OSHA requirement for the permissible span of full thickness 2" x 10" undressed scaffolding lumber with a 50 psf work load?

4'
5'
6'
8'

The short-term maximum allowable slope for excavations greater than 12' and less than 20' in Type A soil shall be:

A. 1/4 horizontal to 1 vertical
B. 1/2 horizontal to 1 vertical
C. 3/4 horizontal to 1 vertical
D. 1 horizontal to 1 vertical

Employees must use a safety belt of equivalent fall protection when placing or tying reinforcing steel at a height above any adjacent working surface of more than:

4'
6'
8'
10'

The Code of Federal Regulations, 1926.1060, requires an employer to provide a training program for each employee:

A. using ladders and stairways
B. working with toxic substances
C. working in excavations
D. using scaffolding

An employer shall ensure that no employee is exposed to an airborne concentration of asbestos in excess of per cubic centimeter of air as averaged over a 30-minute sampling period.

A. 1.0 fiber
B. 2.0 fibers
C. 10.0 fibers
D. 20.0 fiber

24. How many times its maximum intended load must scaffolding withstand without breaking?

2
4
6
10

When a safety net is required on a construction site, the net shall meet the minimum performance standard of:

15,000 foot-pounds impact
17,500 foot-pounds impact
20,000 foot-pounds impact
22,500 foot-pounds impact

A wire core manila rope is used as a lifeline where it may be subjected to cutting or abrasion. What is the required minimum size of the rope?

A. 1/2 inch
B. 3/4 inch
C. 7/8 inch
D. 1 inch

27. Routine inspection of open excavations shall be conducted by a competent person:

daily
weekly C.every
two days D.every
three days

Haulage vehicles, whose payload is loaded by means of cranes, power shovels, loaders, or similar equipment, shall have:

A. pneumatic tires capable of supporting 1-1/2 times the payload capacity
B.automatic dumping mechanisms capable of payload leveling
C.an automatic transmission and a cab shield on the load side of the operator station
D.a cab shield and/or canopy adequate to protect the operator from shifting or falling materials

29. Barricades for protection of employees shall:

A. be approved by OSHA
B. be constructed of wood laminated framing and conform to 489.134
C. be constructed of laminated steel and conform to 489.134
D. conform to the Manual of Uniform Traffic Control Devices

When removing hazardous waste materials, personal protection equipment is divided into four categories based upon protection required. Which category has the highest level of respiratory protection but a lesser level of skin protection?

A. Level A
B. Level B
C. Level C
D. Level D

31. Fuel gas and oxygen manifolds shall NOT be placed where?

A. indirect sunlight
B. no closer than 15' of main electric
C.elevated at least 6' off of a dirt floor
D. they shall not be located within enclosed areas

32. What is the maximum permissible noise exposure that a worker may be subjected to for an 8-hour duration?

A. 90 dB
B. 95 dB
C. 100 dB
D. 105 dB

33. What does the term "point of operation" refer to?

A. the starting point of a project
B. the specific operation of a project being performed
C. the area of a project where work is underway
D. the area on a machine where work is actually performed

What is the minimum, above the top of the vertical side, must the support shield systems at the vertically sided lower portion of an excavation extend?

20"
18"
16"
14"

35. What is the highest stack allowed when bricks are being stored?

A. 5 feet
B. 7 feet
C. 9 feet
D. 10 feet

Employees shall be provided with anti-laser eye protection devices when working in areas in which a potential exposure to reflected laser light is greater than:

A. 5 miliwatts
B. 4 miliwatts
C. 3 miliwatts
D. 2 miliwatts

37. The minimum illumination required for first aid stations is:

A. 30 foot candles
B. 20 foot candles
C. 5 foot candles
D. 3 foot candles

A job site having 90 employees with temporary rest rooms is required to have a minimum of how many of toilets and urinals?

A. one toilet and one urinal
B. two toilets and two urinals
C. three toilets and three urinals
D. four toilets and four urinals

39. The minimum illumination required for general construction area lighting is:

A. 3 foot candles
B. 5 foot candles
C. 10 foot candles
D. 30 foot candles

Employees shall be protected from excavated or other materials or equipment that could pose a hazard by falling or rolling into excavations. What is the minimum distance required from the edge of excavations for placing and keeping such materials or equipment?

A. 2'
B. 3'
C. 4'
D. 5'

41. The indoor storage of flammable and combustible liquids requires that no more than _____ gallons to be stored in a room outside of an approved storage cabinet.

A. 10
B. 15
C. 25
D. 60

42. Flammable and combustible liquids in excess of _____ gallons shall be stored in an acceptable or approved cabinet meeting the requirements of OSHA.

A. 60
B. 25
C. 15
D. 10

43. Not more than _____ gallons of combustible liquids shall be stored in any one storage cabinet.

25
60
80
120

44. A hand-held grinder with a 2-1/8" diameter wheel shall be equipped with only a:

A. constant pressure switch
B. momentary contact on/off switch
C. positive percussion switch
D. positive on/off switch

45. Which of the following is not accepted?

A. a 1-1/2" diameter grinder with a positive on/off control switch
B. a hand-held powered drill with a momentary contact on/off control switch
C. a circular saw with a constant pressure switch
D. a drift pin with a mushroom head

Each end of a scaffold platform, unless cleated or otherwise restrained, shall extend over the centerline of its support at least:

2"
4"
6"
12"

Where platforms are overlapped to create a long platform, platforms shall be secured from movement or overlapped at least:

2"
4"
6"
12"

When lifting concrete slabs, operation of jacks shall be synchronized in such a manner as to insure even and uniform lifting of the slab. All points of the slab support shall be kept level within:

1/2"
1"
1-1/2"
2"

A "Controlled Access Zone" is implemented to protect employees from access to an area where the erection of precast concrete members is being performed. The control lines in a "Controlled Access Zone" shall be erected not more than_____ feet from the unprotected or leading edge or half of the length of the member being erected, whichever is less.

6
15
25
60

Toeboards, when used as a protection against falling objects, shall have a minimum vertical height of:

3-1/2"
4"
5-1/2"
6"

51. Shoring for concrete shall be designed by a:

contractor
carpenter
qualified designer
lumber supplier

All masonry walls over in height shall be adequately braced to prevent overturning and to prevent collapse unless the wall is adequately supported so that it will not overturn or collapse.

A. 8'
B. 12'
C. 16'
D. 20'

53. Self-supporting portable ladders shall be capable of supporting without failure at least times the maximum intended load.

A. 3
B. 4
C. 5
D. 6

Non-self-supporting ladders shall be used at an angle such that the horizontal distance from the top support to the foot of the ladder is approximately:

A. one-third the working length of the ladder
B. one-quarter the working length of the ladder
C. one-fifth the working length of the ladder
D. one-eighth the working length of the ladder

A non-self-supporting ladder has a working length of 20'. According to OSHA, the horizontal distance from the top support to the foot of the ladder is approximately:

A. 1/4 of a foot
B. four feet
C. five feet
D. six feet

Job-made wooden ladders with spliced side rails shall be used at an angle such that the horizontal distance from the top support to the foot of the ladder is:

A. one-third the working length of the ladder
B. one-quarter the working length of the ladder
C. one-fifth the working length of the ladder
D. one-eighth the working length of the ladder

57. During asbestos removal, how many separate chambers shall the asbestos disposal contractor erect?

2
3
4
5

58. All pneumatic nailers, staplers and other similar equipment provided with automatic fastener feed shall have a safety device to prevent the tool from ejecting fasteners when operation pressures exceed _____ .

A. 75 psi.
B. 100 psi.
C. 125 psi.
D. 150 psi.

59. A portable ladder that is NOT self-supporting must be capable of supports at least <u>times the</u> maximum intended load.

A. 2
B. 4
C. 6
D. 8

60. When portable ladders are used to access a roof or upper landing surface, the ladder side rails shall extend at least _____ above the roof or upper landing surface to which the ladder is used to gain access.

1'
2'.
3'
4'

61. The common drinking cup is _____ .

prohibited
not prohibited.
prohibited in areas where more than 3 workmen will use the cup.
prohibited in hazardous areas.

62. Whenever materials are dropped more than _____ to any point lying outside the exterior walls of the building, an enclosed chute of wood, or equivalent material, shall be used.

10'
15'
20'
25'

63. Eye protection near dangerous working conditions _____ .

A. is required at the employee's cost.
B. is required at the employer's cost.
C. can only be required by union regulations.
D. is not required.

64. The use of electrical cords for hoisting or lowering shall

A. be permitted.
B. not be permitted.
C. only be permitted during daylight hours
D. not be permitted during dusk or evening hours

65. A project with 200 men and 20 women would require _____ toilets.

A.4 toilets and 4 urinals
B.4.4 toilets and 4.4 urinals
C. 5 toilets and 5 urinals
D. 5.5 toilets and 5.5 urinals

66. An employee is exposed to the following noise levels:

- 1. 90 dba at 2 hours
- 2. 100 dba at 1/2 hour
- 3. 110 dba at 1/4 hour

According to OSHA, the noise exposure factor is? (Round up to the nearest whole number)

A. 1.00, not allowed
B. 10.00, allowed
C. 10.00, not allowed
D. 1.00, allowed

67. During construction the minimum illumination required for an indoor warehouse is _____ foot-candles.

A.3
B.5
   10
   30

68. What is the minimum illumination required for shops in construction areas?

   3 foot-candles
   5 foot-candles
   10 foot-candles
   30 foot-candles

69. Safety belt lanyard shall be a minimum of 1/2-inch nylon, or equivalent, with a maximum length to provide for a fall of no greater than_____ feet.

A. 6
B. 8
C. 10
D. 12

70. Safety nets, where required, shall be provided when workplaces are more than <u>feet above</u> the ground or water surface.

A. 100
B. 75
C. 50
D. 25

71. When safety nets are required to be provided, such nets shall extend _____ feet beyond the edge of the work's surface.

A. 4
B. 6
C. 8
D. 10

72. The mesh size of safety nets shall not exceed:

A. 12" x 12"
B. 10" x 10"
C. 8" x 8"
D. 6" x 6"

73. When masonry blocks are stacked higher than _____ feet, the stack shall be tapered back one-half block per tier above the six-foot level.

A. 4
   6
C. 8 D.
10

74. Lumber that is handled manually shall not be stacked more than _____ feet high.

   14
   16
   18
   20

75. The components of a scaffold loaded with 500 pounds shall be capable of supporting its own weight and a load of at least _____ without failure.

A. 1 ton
B. 2 tons
C. 2.5 tons
D. 4 tons

76. Each employee working on the face of formwork or reinforcing steel shall be protected from falling or more to lower levels by personal fall arrest systems, safety net systems, or positioning device systems.

   6'
   8'
   10'
   25'

77. All site clearing equipment shall be equipped with an overhead and rear canopy guard of at least 1/8" steel plate or _____ woven wire mesh with openings no greater than one inch, or equivalent.

    1/8"
    1/4"
    3/8"
    1/2"

78. A stairway, ladder, ramp or other safe means of egress shall be located in trench excavations that are 4' or more in depth so as to require no more than _____ feet of lateral travel for employees.

    15'
    20'
    25'
    30'

79. A trench 100' long by 10' wide and 5' deep will require a minimum of _____ ladders:

    2
    3
    4
    5

    Cohesive soil packed with an unconfined compressive strength of less than 1.5 tons per square foot but greater than .5 tons per square foot is defined as:

A. Type A
B. Type B
C. Type C
D. Type D

81. A six-foot deep trench excavated in Type C soil shall have the sides sloped at a maximum of:

A. 3/4' vertical to 1' horizontal
B. 1' vertical to 1' horizontal
    1-1/2' vertical to 1' horizontal
    1' vertical to 1-1/2' horizontal

    Sloping or benching of excavations shall be designed by a registered engineer when depth of excavations is:

A. more than 10'
B. more than 15'
C. at least 20'
D. more than 20'

83. A simple slope excavation with a depth of 10 feet and which will be open for 20 hours shall have a maximum allowable slope of _____ in Type A soil.

A. 1' horizontal to 3/4' vertical
B. 3/4' horizontal to 1' vertical
C. 1' horizontal to 1/2' vertical
D. 1/2' horizontal to 1' vertical

    When Type C soil is excavated over Type A soil, Type A soil shall be excavated to a maximum slope of in layered soils.

A. 1' horizontal to 3/4' vertical
B. 1' horizontal to 1' vertical
C. 3/4' horizontal to 1' vertical
D. 1-1/2' horizontal to 1' vertical

    Lifting inserts that are embedded, or otherwise attached to precast concrete members, other than the tilt-up members, shall be capable of supporting at least how many times the intended maximum load?

    2
    3
    4
    5

86. The maximum number of manually-controlled jacks allowed for lift-slab construction operations shall be limited to _____ on one slab.

    8
    10
    12
    14

    At no time during steel erection shall there be more than four floors or feet of unfinished bolting or welding above the foundation or uppermost permanently secured floor.

    32
    48
    58
    66

88. The approximate angle of repose for sloping the sides of an excavation, less than 20' deep, in sand is:

    90°
    53°
    45°
    34°

89. When excavating in the proximity of adjoining buildings, a general contractor must _____ for the safety and protection of workers.

A. remove all loose soils and rocks
B. compact adjacent soils and slope walls
C. provide adequate shoring and bracing systems
D. request a variance to move excavation farther away

90. When single post shores are tiered, they must:

A. never be spliced
B. be vertically aligned
C. be designed by a licensed engineer
D. be adequately braced at top and bottom

91. The maximum allowable slope for excavations less than 20' deep in Type B soil or rock is:

A. 34°
B. 45°
C. 53°
D. 90°

When erecting systems-engineered metal buildings, during placing of rigid frame members, the load is not to be released from the hoisting equipment until:

A. the crane operator signals that is safe to proceed
B. all bolts have been installed and tightened to the specified torque
C. the members are secured with not less than 50% of the required bolts at each connection
D. drift pins have driven into at least two bolt holes at each connection for the member

93. Prior to site layout, the contractor should:

A. obtain a certificate of occupancy and provide proof of occupancy
B. alert subcontractors to the requirements of their scope
C. start erecting structural steel and roof support members
D. locate surface encumbrances that may pose a hazard to employees

Drawings or plans, including all revisions, for concrete formwork (including shoring equipment) shall be available at the:

A. jobsite
B. owner's office
C. contractor's main office
D. building department's office

95. Shoring for supported concrete slabs shall be removed only when the contractor:

A. has had it inspected by the building inspector
B. makes sure the concrete is dry to the touch
C. determines that the concrete has gained sufficient strength to support its weight and superimposed loads
D. has been told by the concrete supervisor that it is safe to strip the shoring

1 Exam Prep
29 CFR 1926 OSHA
Questions and Answers

D1926.703 (e) (2)

C1926.502 (g) (3) (iii)

C1926.52 (e)

B1926.652 Appendix B Figure B-1

B1926.501 (b) (5)

C1926.51 Table D-1

C1926.454 Subpart L, Appendix A

8.   D   1926.106

C1926.651 (b) (1)

C1926.451 (a) (1)

        1,000 x 4/2000 = 2 tons

C1926.250 (b) (7)

C1926.104 (b)

B1926.65 (n) (7)

C1926.62 (c) (1)

B1926.1101 (k) (9) (iv) [A]

B1926.651 (g) (1) (i)

C1926.706 (a) (2)

B1926.451 (g) (4) (ii)

D1926.454 (1)(b)(i) Subpart L, Appendix A

C1926.652 Subpart P, Appendix B Table B-1 (Footnote 2)

B1926.501(b)(5)

A1926.1060 (a)

A1926.1101(c) (2)

B1926.451 (a) (1)

B1926.105 (d)

C1926.104 (c)

A1926.651 (k)(1)

D1926.601 (b) (6)

D1926.202

B1926.65 Appendix B, Part A, II

D1926.350 (e) (2)

A1926.52(d)(1) Table D-2

D1926.300 (b) (4) (i)

B1926.652 Subpart P Appendix B Figure B-1.3

B1926.250 (b) (6)

A1926.54 (c)

A1926.56 Table D-3

C1926.51 Table D-1

B1926.56 Table D-3

A1926.651 (j) (2)

C1926.152 (b) (1)

B1926.152 (b) (2)

D1926 .152 (b)(3)

B1926 .300 (d)(2)

D1926.300(d)(2) and 1926.301(c)

C1926.451 (b) (4)

D1926.451 (b) (7)
A1926.705 (g)
D1926.502 (g) (1) (ii)
A1926.502 (j) (3)
C1926.703 (b) (8) (i)
A1926.706 (b)
B1926.1053 (a) (1) (i)
B1926.1053 (b) (5) (i)
C1926.1053 (b) (5) (i) Solution:
$$20'/4 = 5'$$
D1926.1053 (b) (5) (ii)
B1926.1101, (j)(1)(i)
B1926.302 (b) (3)
B1926.1053 (a) (1) (ii)
C1926.1053 (b) (1)
A1926.51(a) (4)
C1926.252 (a)
B1926.102 (a) (1)
B1926.302 (a) (2)
C1926.51 Table D-1
D1926.52 Table D-2
B1926.56 Table D-3
C1926.56 Table D-3
A1926.104 (d)
D1926.105 (a)
C1926.105 (c)
D1926.105 (d)
B1926.250 (b) (7)
B1926.250 (b) (8) (iv)
A1926.451 (a) (1)

A1926.501 (b) (5)
B1926.604 (a) (2) (i)
C1926.651 (c) (2)
A1926.651 (c) (2)

B1926.652 Subpart P, Appendix A (b)
D1926.652 Subpart P, Appendix B Table B-1
D1926.652 Subpart P, Appendix B Table B-1, Note # 3
D1926.652 Subpart P, Appendix B Figure B-1.1
C1926.652 Subpart P, Appendix B Figure B-1.4
C1926.704 (c)
D1926.705 (j)
B1926.754 (b) (2)
D1926.652 Subpart P, Appendix A (b) [Type C](ii) and Appendix B Table B-1 "sand" is
        classified as Type C soil
C1926.651 (i)
B1926.703 (b) (8) (ii)
B1926.652 Subpart P, Appendix B Table B-1
C1926.758 (c)
D1926.651 (a)

A1926.703 (a) (2)
C1926.703 (e) (1)

1 Exam Prep
Carpentry and Building Construction
Questions and Answers

Questions Set #1

1. _____

      A. Career pathways
      B. Career clusters
      C. Occupation set
      D. Career set
are groups of related occupations.

2. The purpose of _____ is/are to ensure that building are structurally sound and safe from fire and other hazards.

      OSHA
      Stock plans
      Surveys
      Building codes

3. A _____ is a scale drawing showing the size and location of rooms on a given floor.

      A. Stock plan
      Blueprint
      Floor plan
      Schedule

4. Bulkhead is more commonly known as _____?

      Soffit
      Chase
      Cornice
      Eave

In concrete walls how does a cold joint occur?

      Concrete batches are mixed differently
      Fresh concrete poured on top of or next to concrete that has already begun to cure
      Too much air is in the concrete
      D. There is too much moisture in the concrete and the temperature is below 30□F

What is the measuring system used by the United States?

      Customary
      Metric
      Standard
      Both A and C

7. A scale of _____is the most often used for drawing houses.

      A. 1/8" = 1'0"
      B. ¼" = 1'0"
      C. ½" = 1'0"
      D. 1/2" = 2'0"

8. A _____ is a large landing at the top of steps.

      Stoop
      Porch
      Deck
      Large –scale landing

What is a tile without glaze called?

      Unglazed
      Unfinished
      Matte
      Bisque

In dealing with wood basics, what is a cambium?

      The rings of the tree that make give it its grain appearance
      Layer of living tissue that produces sapwood
      The fibers of the tree that gives it its hardness
      None of the above

Which of the following is not identified by a softwood board's grade stamp?

      Species
      Moisture content
      Price per lineal ft.
      Mill number

12. The two basic categories of plywood are structural plywood and _____ plywood?

       Hardwood
       Softwood
       Construction
       Engineered

What does OSB stand for?

       Occupational Safety Board
       Optimal-strand board
       Oriented-strand board
       Open-steel beam

14. The _____ is the part of a window that holds the glazing.

       Muntin
       Sash
       Casing
       Mounting flange

15. The _____ is the overall size of the window, including casings.

       A. Nominal dimension
       B. Total window dimension (TWD)
       C. Actual dimension
       D. Unit dimension

16. _____ are written notes that may be arranged in list form.

       Schedules
       Specifications
       Engineering renderings
       Site details

What does the abbreviation MH stand for in estimating?

       Man hours
       Middle-hand
       Materials holding
       Monetary holding

What is another name for overhead?

    Fixed costs
    Indirect costs
    Static costs
    None of the above

In concrete, what is crazing?

    Another name for moist-curing the concrete.
    Whitest crystalline deposits that sometimes appears on the surface of the concrete.
    Appearance of fine cracks that appear in irregular patterns over the surface of the concrete.
    The formation of loose powder on the surface of hardening concrete.

20. A _____ is a test to measure the consistency of concrete.

    A. Slump test
    B. Moisture test
    C. Cube test
    D. Viscosity test

What type of footings are often used on a lot that slopes?

    Pier footings
    Rabbeted footings
    Monolithic footing
    Stepped footings

22. A _____ is a transit that reads horizontal and vertical angles electronically.

    A. Vernier scale
    Theodolite
    Electronic transit level
    Electronic layout device

23. _____ is the process of spreading mortar or cement plaster over the block wall.

    Troweling
    Leveling
    Parging
    Grading

24. A glue laminated beam is often called a _____ .

      Camber
      Spline
      Glulam
      Gambrel

25. The _____ of a door refers to the direction in which a door will swing.

I. Lock face
   Hinge face
III. Hand

      III
      II
      I
      I and II

26. What does 3 ½" represent on a ¼" scale?

      A. 10 feet
      B. 12 feet
      C. 14 feet
      D. 16 feet

27. On a blueprint, lines that terminate with arrows are_____.

      A. Dimension lines
      Centerlines
      Leader lines
      Break lines

Which blueprint page shows the building with boundaries?

      Foundation plan
      Plot or site plan
      Floor plan
      Framing plan

Which blueprint page shows window and door placement?

      Foundation plan
      Plot or site plan
      Framing plan
      Floor plan

Which page of the blueprint shows the external views of the structure?

Elevation
Plot or site plan
Foundation plan
Framing plan

When precise information is needed about a small or complex portion of the building, what would you look for on a plan?

Section views
A detail drawing
Engineering drawings
Mechanical plan

What part of the blueprint designates the brand and model number of a window?

Section views
A detail drawing
Window schedule
Elevation

33. Concrete mixture is made of _____?

Cement
II. Sand III.
Gravel IV.
Water

II and IV
II and III
II, III, & IV
I, II, III & IV

What material impacts the weight of concrete the most?

Silt
Aggregate
Water
None of the above

What is added to concrete to make it set up at a slower rate?

Air-Entraining admixture
Super-Plasticizing admixtures
Retarding admixture
Water-reducing Admixtures

36. Concrete gains most of its strength in the _____ day period after it has been placed.

    28
    14
    7
    30

In a slump test, the greater the slump the wetter the concrete.

    True
    False

38. To remove air pockets from concrete _____ is performed.

    A. A slump test
    Moist-curing
    Crazing
    Consolidation

How thick is a #5 rebar?

    3/8"
    5/8"
    1/8"
    None of the above

Which tool measures horizontal angles only?

    Level
    Builder's square
    Protractor
    Transit

When laying out a building, what is the starting point from which measurements can be made?

I. Bench mark
   Point of reference
III. Station mark

    II
    I and III
    I and II
    III

If you are laying out a building and all of the diagonals are square, the building is square.

      True
      False

43. A _____ is a board fastened horizontally to stakes placed to the outside where the corners of the building will be located.

    A. Corner board
    B. Batter board
    C. Starter strip
    D. Foundation board

44. _____ is a measure of how well the soil can support the weight of a house.

    A. Load capacity
    B. Bearing capacity
    C. Load resistance
    D. None of the above

What is the minimum distance from the point of excavation that batter boards can be placed?

    2'
    3'
    4'
    5'

46. In surveying, if rod "A" reads 4' and rod "B" reads 4'6", then _____ .

    A. The ground point of "B" is 6" higher than the ground point of "A".
    The ground point of "A" is 6" lower than the ground point of "B".
    The ground point of "A" is 6" higher than the ground point of "B".
    None of the above

What is the formula for estimating concrete in cubic yards?

    L X W X D / 12
    L X W X D / 27
    L X W X D / 26
    L X W X D / 24

48. The sides of footings are molded by boards referred to as _____.

    A. Batter boards
    B. Backer board
    C. Haunch boards
    D. Form boards

What type of clip is used to hold foundation wall forms together?

    Snap ties
    Bracket
    6d nails
    Wales

In constructing a stack bond pattern block wall, what additional step is required that is NOT needed with a common bond wall?

    Joints should be tooled smooth to seal them against water seepage
    Joint reinforcement must be added to every third course
    Joint reinforcement must be added to every second course
    Full bedding should be performed

What type of support is used over window and door openings in a concrete block wall?

    Lintel
    Girder
    Collar beam
    Bond beam

52. A standard mortar joint when using concrete block is how wide"?

    1/8"
    ¼"
    3/8"
    5/8"

What is the nominal size of a standard block? Choose the closest answer.

    6" x 6" x 14"
    7" x 8 x 16"
    7" x 7" x 15"
    8" x 8" x 16"

54. Mortar should be used within what time period, when the air temperature is 80 □F or higher?

    A. 1.5 hours
    B. 2 hours
    C. 2 1/2 hours
    D. 3 ½ hours

55. A _____
window.
is a horizontal member placed at the bottom of a window opening to support the

    A. Trimmer stud
    B. Rough sill
    C. Cripple stud
      Stool

   The curve or camber on glulam beams should be installed with the curve oriented _____.

    A. Up, toward the ceiling
    B. Underneath, toward the floor
    C. In the direction opposite the fastener
    D. None of the above

57. Lumber shrinks, but, is most troublesome when shrinkage occurs across the _____ of a board.

    Length
    Width
    Height
    None of the above

58. A common defect in lumber where a lengthwise grain separation occurs through the growth ring is known as _____.

    Knot
    Pitch
    Ring Shake
    Torn grain

   The type of wood with lowest resistance to decay?

    Redwood
    Heartwood of bald cypress
    Cedar
    Sapwood of all common native wood

If a sheet of plywood has a 32/16 panel identification index, it may be used as a floor decking with a maximum span of?

    32"
    16"
    2'
    None of the above

Plywood that is used for concrete forms must be what minimum grade?

    C-D
    A-C
    B-B
    A-B

62. Horizontal members that carry the heaviest load of attached horizontal members are called _____.

    Girders
    Floor joist
    Collar beam
    Lally columns

When laying plywood subfloor, what is the spacing between each of the panels?

    1/8" on ends and sides
    1/4" on ends and sides
    5/6" on ends and sides
    3/6" on ends and sides

64. The main support under a wood deck is called a _____.

    Post
    Sill plate
    Floor joist
    Girder

A built-up girder should have how many inches clearance between the end of the girder and the masonry in a masonry pocket?

    1/8"

    ¼"
    1/16"

66. If the run of the standard rafter is 12', what is the run of the king hip? Select closest answer.

    15'
    16'
    17'
    18'

What type of door consists of stiles and rails?

    Flat-panel doors
    Raised panel doors
    Solid-core construction doors
    Sliding doors

What is the standard height of an interior door?

    6'8" or 7'0"
    6'6" or 6'8"
    6'4" or 6'6"
    7'0" or 7'2"

69. The proper war to hang a bifold door is _____.

    A. Install the top track, install the door, the install the bottom track B.
    Install the bottom track first, then fasten the top track to the ceiling
    C. Install the top track first, then fasten the lower track to the floor directly under the top rack.
    D. None of the above

What is the door hinge size for a 1- 3/8" interior door?

    3" x 3 ½"
    2 ½ x 2 ½"
    3" x 3"
    3 ½" x 3 ½"

When installing a door stop, nail the stop on which side first?

    Hinge side first
    Lock side first
    It does not matter which side
    Depends if it is a right or left hand door

When installing plywood soffit to the ledger strip, nails should be installed how far apart?

    2" apart
    4" apart
    6" apart
    8" apart

One square of 235 lb shingles will cover how many square feet and weigh how many lbs?

    100 sq ft, 235 lbs.
    50 sq. ft., 100 lbs
    175 sq. ft., 235 lbs
    200 sq. ft., 200 lbs.

The typical exposure while using roll roofing is how many inches?

    15"
    16"
    17"
    19"

Roll roofing endlaps should be offset by how many inches?

    4"
    6"
    7"
    8"

When using roll roofing, the strip should be nailed so that it overhangs the edge by a minimum of _____ .

    ¼"
    ½"
    1/8"
    3/16"

77. The proper installation of drip edge call for it to be installed _____ .

A. It is applied to the fascia and under the underlayment at the eaves, but over the underlayment at the rake

B. It is applied to the sheathing and under the underlayment at the rake, but over the underlayment at the eaves

C. It is applied to the sheathing and under the underlayment at the eaves, but over the underlayment at the rake

D. None of the above

How many bundles of shingles are there in a square of roofing?

    Two
    Three
    Four
    Five

When installing shingles, no nails should be placed within how many inches of a valley?

    2"
    4"
    6"
    8"

80. Gutters are fastened to the _____ of a house.

    Soffit
    Roof eave
    Gable end
    Fascia

Splash blocks at the bottom of drain spouts should be at least how long?

    3'
    2'
    1'
    None of the above

What is the minimum overlap for 6" beveled lap siding ?

    1"
    1.25"
    1.5"
    1.75"

83. The ends of siding boards cut during installation should be coated with _____.

    A. Same color paint as the siding
    B. Water repellant
       Rustoleum
       Termite shield

What is the strip nailed to the end of the rafter?

Starter strip
Fascia
Frieze
Ventilator

What is used at the brick course below the bottom of the sheathing and framing?

Girders
Floor joists
Flashing
Brick veneer

86. Radiating stair treads are also known as _____.

Landings
Newels
Risers
Winders

What is the horizontal length of a stairway called?

Total run
Total rise
Unit rise
Unit run

The total rise for a stairway is 8'-11". What is the total amount of risers in the stairway?

13
14
15
16

A stair stringer must have how many inches remaining after it has been notched?

2"
2 ½"
3"
3 ½"

A third stair stringer should be installed in the middle of the stairs when the stair width exceeds what width?

> 2'0"
> 2'4"
> 2'6"
> 2' 8"

How tall is a standard kitchen base cabinet, not including the counter top?

> 34"
> 34 ½"
> 36"
> 38"

How deep is a standard kitchen wall cabinet?

> 10"
> 12"
> 14"
> 18"

How deep is a standard kitchen base cabinet?

> 18"
> 20"
> 24"
> 28"

94. When installing ¾" thick cabinets to studs covered with ½" drywall, how long should the screws be to fasten the cabinets to the wall?

> A. 2 ¼" or long enough to go through the ¾ backrail and wall covering and extend at least 2" into the studs
> B. 2 ¼" or long enough to go through the ¾ backrail and wall covering and extend at least 1" into the studs
> C. 2 1/2" or long enough to go through the ¼ backrail and wall covering and extend at least 1" into the studs
> D. None of the above

A contractor is installing wall cabinets in a new home built with 2 x 6 studs. Some of the cabinets span only a single stud. How are the cabinets attached?

    With two #10 screws into the single stud and at least two 3/16" x 3 ½" toggle bolts through the drywall.

    With four #10 screws into the single stud and at least two 3/16" x 3 ½" toggle bolts through the drywall.

    With two #10 screws into the single stud and at least two 5/16" x 3 ½" toggle bolts through the drywall.

    None of the above

How long should wood flooring be stored in the building in which it is going to be installed in to allow for acclimation?

A. At least 3 days
B. At least 4 days
C. At least 7 days
D. 14 days

The first board of tongue and groove flooring should be installed how many inches from the frame wall and which side of the board should face the wall?

    1/4" to 5/8", tongue end
    1/2" to 5/8", tongue end
    1/2" to 5/8", grooved end
    1/2" to 3/8", grooved end

What type of product is used as a base for tile and in shower stalls?

    Backerboard
    Sheathing
    Plywood
    Fiberglass

Which of the following is NOT a common unit of measure?

    Length
    Liquid
    Volume
    Weight

Cracks in lumber that run parallel to and between the annular rings are called _____

    crooks
    cracks
    shakes
    splits

A board measures 6' long, 10" wide and 2" thick. How many board feet of lumber are contained in this board?

    0
    10
    1.3
    15

Which of the following statements are not true of plywood?

    Face and cross band is in the same direction.
    There are always an odd number of piles.
    Grain in outside layers runs in the same direction.
    Grain in successive plies runs at right angles.

The best appearing face veneer' of a softwood plywood panel is indicated by the letter _____

    A
    B
    E
    N

Panels made from reconstituted wood bonded with adhesive under heat and pressure are known as

_____

    Wafer board
    OSB
    Hard board
    All of the above

Engineered lumber products are designed as replacements or substitutes for: _____

    Solid lumber
    Second growth lumber
    Steel framing
    Structural lumber

Laminated veneer lumber is manufactured in lengths up to _____

    30 feet.
    40 feet.
    50 feet.
    66 feet

The tool most commonly used to lay out or test angles other than those laid out with squares is called _____

    a sliding T-bevel
    a compass
    a protractor
    a caliper

The saw commonly used with a miter box is called a _____.

    Cross-saw
    Rip-saw
    Back-saw
    Hack-saw

The size of a claw hammer is determined by _____.

    Length of the claw.
    Overall dimension
    Weight of the entire hammer
    Weight of the head

To bore holes over one inch in diameter, the carpenter uses a (an) _____

    Auger bit
    Bit brace
    Expansion bit
    Hole saw

A _____ cut, is a type of mitre cut that is made through the thickness of a board

    Bevel
    Mitre
    Coping
    Chamfer

A level transit differs from a builders level in that it _____

    A. can traverse a 360□ horizontal angle
    B. can measure vertical angles
    C. has a vernier scale
    D. has four leveling screws

A _____ is a mark on a permanent fixed object from which measurements and elevations are taken.

       turning point
       station
       reference
       bench mark

The point of reference where the builder's level is located is called the _____

       Degree mark
       Bench mark
       Elevation mark
       Station mark

Batter boards should be set a minimum of _____ the building lines and in such a manner that they will not be disturbed during excavation and construction.

       4' outside.
       4 ' inside.
       5' outside
       10' outside

One of the advantages of the balloon frame is that _____

       The bottom plates act as fire stops
       There is little shrinkage in the frame
       The second floor joists rest on a ribbon instead of a plate
       It is stronger, stiffer and more resistant to lateral pressures

A system of framing where the floor joists of each story rest on the top of the plates of the story below _____ is called framing.

       stud
       balloon
       platform
       post and beam

In what type of construction would you usually find "ribbons"?

       Post and beam
       Balloon framing
       Platform Framing
       Any of the above

A large horizontal beam that supports the inner ends of floor joists is called a _____

Pier
Girder
Stud
Sill

Which of the following is not a commonly available wood beam or girder?

Solid Wood beam
Laminate beam
Glue Laminate
Built up

121. Ten 2'L x 12"W X 16H" board contain _____ board feet of lumber.

240
320
267
400

The top and bottom horizontal members of a wall frame are called _____

headers
plates
trimmers
sills

The horizontal wall member supporting the load over an opening is called a _____

header
rough sill
plate
truss

When framing a pre-hung door unit that has a 36" door, what would the width of the rough opening be?

38"
40"
the width of the unit plus 1/2"
the width of the unit plus 1"

A birds mouth is a notch cut in a rafter to fit it to the _____

> fascia
> ridge
> soffit
> plate

A member of the cornice generally fastened to the rafter tails is called the?

> Drip
> Fascia
> Plancher
> Soffit

A window that consists of an upper and lower sash that slides vertically is called a _____

> casement window
> double-hung window
> hopper window
> sliding window

Stairways in residential construction should have a minimum width of _____

> thirty inches
> thirty-two inches
> thirty six inches
> forty inches

Most building codes specify a minimum headroom clearance of _____

> 6'6"
> 6' 8"
> 7'0"
> 7'6"

The horizontal part of a step upon which the foot is placed is called the _____

> riser
> nosing
> tread
> baluster

Questions Set #2

1 .Which of the following methods would allow you to determine the location of a proposed building?

      A. Using an instrument such as bench mark
      B. Measuring from an established reference line
      C. Using an optical level
      D. Both B and C

2. _____drying lumber is stacked in an oven and dried with steam and heat?

      Air
      Oven
      Seasoning
      Kiln

3. A_____ is a metal guide attached to a flat bar, which slips into slots in the front of the saw's shoe?

      Guard
      Baseplate
      Fence
      Motor

What are some patterns of decking or planking in contemporary architecture?

      V-joint
      Eased joint
      Double tongue and groove
      All of the above

The three basic types of ladders are?

      Folding
      Extension
      Straight
      All of the above

There are several careers related to construction. Landscape design, architect and interior design are all opportunities that require knowledge of _____building construction?

      Craft
      Professional
      Technical
      None of the Above

7. _____ is generally 3/4" thick?

    A. Wood siding
    B. Board siding
    C. Drop Siding
    D. Bevel siding

8. Flakes of wood that are randomly aligned throughout a panel describe _____?

    A. Waferboard
    B. Fiberboard
    C. OSB
    D. Hardboard

9. The standard-size for T & G panels measure on the face _____, with additional allowance for the tongue?

    A. 2' x 6'
    B. 4' x 8'
    C. 5' x 10'
    D. 8' x 8'

    What is difference between a hip rafter and a valley rafter?

    Hip rafters extend vertically from the corners formed by plates; valley rafter from the plate
    Hip rafters extend from the corners formed by plates; valley rafters extend from the plate
    Hip rafters extend from the corners formed by plates; valley rafters extend parallel from the plate
    Both B and C

11. There are _____ type(s) of scheduling needed in building a home?

    Two
    Three
    Four
    Five

12. Survey, deed, and abstract of title are considered _____ documents?

    Government
    Loan
    Shipping
    Legal

13. Plastic films, aluminum foil, and asphalt-laminated papers are _____ among the effective materials?

    A. Radiant barriers
    B. Vapor barriers
    C. Insulation barriers
    D. Insulating values

14. On slopes 4 in 12 or steeper, applying an additional course of _____ No. 30 forms

    A. Side locks
       Underlayment
       Eaves flashing
       Center rotation

The best time to provide protection against termites is after construction is complete?

    True
    False

A proportion between two sets of dimensions, as between those of a drawing and its original is defined as a _____ .

    A. Scale
    B. Drawing
    C. Symbol
    D. Blueprint

17. When laying out ceiling joists, the distance between the first two joists will be less than _____ , depending on the center space used?

    A. 2" or 6"
    B. 16" or 24"
    C. 18" or 24"
    D. 20" or 24"

18. A rectangular opening cut with the grain of wood is called a _____ .

    A. Fence
    B. Miter
    C. Bevel
    D. None of the above

19. The most common framing connector is _____ .

    A. Glulam beam
    B. Post base
    C. Joist hanger
    D. Hurricane clips

20. The metal bracket used to attach a shed roof to a building is called a _____ .

    A. Collar tie
    B. Ceiling joist
    C. Saddle brace
    D. Ridge strap

21. The standard size for a single garage door is _____ .

    A. 9' x 61/4' or 7'
    B. 9'/2' x 61/4' or 7'
    C. 9' x 71/4' or 81/4'
    D. 8' x 91/4' or 10'

22. Make sure panel is supported, hold saw at low angle, when cutting on table saw, always place good side face up, and store by laying sheets flat are precautions that must be taken when working with _____ .

    Cedarwood
    Softwoods
    Plywood
    Picea mariana

What type of flashing is used to install a skylight in a tile roof?

    Flexible lead step
    Fiberboard
    Eave
    Metal

What two handsaws are used for cutting irregular curves?

    Back saw and Miter box saw
    Coping saw and Dovetail saw
    Compass saw and Coping saw
    None of the above

How many cuts are necessary to make a rabbet on a table saw with a single saw blade?

    1
    2
    3
    4

26. The run of valley cripple No.13 is _____ the spacing of jacks on center?

    Two-third
    One-fourth
    Half
    Twice

27. The extension of a gable roof beyond the end wall is called the _____.

    A. Fascia runner
    Soffit
    Fly rafter
    Rake section

What is the purpose of the exterior sidewall in a structure?

    To support the ceiling load
    To support the roof load
    To support floor framing
    To serve as room dividers

29. There are three types of jambs: the two side jambs and _____.

    A. The wood jamb across the center
    B. The head jamb across the top
    C. The metal jamb across the bottom
    D. The one side jamb

Why is building paper applied between sheathing and siding?

    It prevents the passage of water through the walls
    It prevents the passage of heat through the walls
    It prevents the passage of air through the walls
    It prevents the passage of termites through the walls

31. The total vertical distance from one floor to the next is called _____ .

    A. Total Rise
    B. Total run
       Newel
       Platform

Why is it best to erect the ridge board in its proper position before beginning the installation of the rafters?

       Adjustments cannot be made
       To prevent the roof from swaying
       It will be easier to make adjustments
       None of the above

Corner, sidewall, and roofing are considered scaffold brackets?

       True
       False

Why isn't let-in corner bracing required when plywood wall sheathing is used?

       Plywood-sheathed walls are twice as strong and rigid as a wall sheathed with diagonal boards
       Plywood-sheathed walls are three times as strong and rigid as a wall sheathed with horizontal boards
       Plywood-sheathed walls are twice as strong and rigid as a wall sheathed with parallel boards
       Plywood-sheathed walls are four times as strong and rigid as a wall sheathed with diagonal boards

35. When wood I-beams are used as floor joists, the rim joists can be _____ .

    A. Solid lumber
       Plywood or laminated-veneer
       Wood I-beams
       All of the above

Below what moisture content is wood safe from decay?

    40%
    30%
    20%
    10%

What jobs will carpenters complete while mechanical subcontractors are doing their rough-in work?

    Install exterior doors
    Install exterior windows
    Complete special framing
    All of the above

38. The horizontal face of one step is called the _____ .

    Baluster
    Nosing
    Tread
    Riser

39. A carpenter needs a _____ to determine the kind of rafters that are needed?

    A. Mansard roof
    Pitch
    Roof framing plan
    Slope

Why doesn't the excavator remove the soil for the footing at the same time the soil is removed for the basement?

    Soil is stockpiled for future use
    Soil is not stable enough to prevent caving
    Soil becomes soft when exposed to air or water
    Soil conditions must be tested by checking existing homes constructed nearby

How deep is a kitchen wall cabinet?

    12 inches
    14 inches
    16 inches
    24 inches

The crown on canmber on a glulam must be placed _____ .

    no crown or cambers on glulams
    on bottom
    on its edge
    on top

The actual size of a 2 x 4 is _____.

    1-1/2 x 3-9/16
    1-1/2 x 3-1/2
    1-9/16 x 3-9/16
    2 x 4

A _____ is the vertical board used to enclose the spaces between trends.

    stringer
    nosing
    riser
    trend

Using ¼ inch scale; what does 3-3/4 inches represent?

    14 feet
    15 feet
    16 feet
    3-3/4 inches

How long must screws be to properly fasten a cabinet with a ¾ inch backrail to ½ inch drywall?

    2 inches
    2-1/4 inches
    2-1/2 inches
    3 inches

A cut made across the grain of a board is known as a _____.

    cut-back
    Back-cut
    rip-cut
    cross-cut

The measure of the effectiveness of vapor barrier is known as the _____.

    perm value
    R-value
    MSR rating
    R rating

Plain bevel siding must overlap at least _____ inches.

2-1/2
2
1-1/2
1

When placing WWM in a concrete slab what location should it be used in?

in the bottom
in the middle
top third
none of the above

How many board feet are in (48) 2 x 6 x 8's?

8
384
96
1152

A 32 inch door should have a rough opening of _____.

34-1/2"
32-1/2"
36"
34"

An 8d common nail is _____ inches long.

1-1/2
2
2-1/2
3

A stile is most likely found in which type of door?

Metal
Solid core
Hollow core
Raised panel

_____ is a condition that occurs when wood's moisture content is equal to the inside of the building the product is installed in.

acclimation
galvanization
fiber saturation point
incorporation

Spacing for plywood used as a sheathing should be _____ inches between each sheet.

1/8
1/16
¼
½

Kitchen base cabinet height is typically _____ inches.

36
34-1/2
35-1/2
34

A contractor is installing wall cabinets in a home built with 2 x 6 studs, one of the cabinets span only one single stud. How are the cabinets properly attached?

Two #10 screws into the stud and two 3/16" x 3-1/2" toggle bolts through the sheetrock
Four #10 screws into each corner
Four 3/16" x 3-1/2" toggle bolts into each corner with a 3/16" fender washer on each bolt
Four #10 screws into adjoining cabinets

On which of the following plans would you be able to find the footprint of the building on the lot?

Framing plan
Landscape plan
Site plan
Roofing plan

How far from the foundation walls are batter boards set?

2'
3'
6'
4'

What lumber defect is known as a lengthwise grain separation between or through the growth rings?

Cull
Shake
Knot
Check

The fink truss is also known as a _____.

W-truss
K-truss
S-truss
none of the above

What door consists of stiles, panels, and rails?

Bi-fold door
Neither 1, 3 or 4
Raised panel door
Flush panel door

Which of the following panels will provide an excellent base for tile?

EIFS
½ inch CDX
OSB
Backer board

When wood beams are placed inside masonry or concrete pocket, how much clearance is required on top, sides and end of the beam?

3/8"
½"
¾"
1"

Fireblocking is required in walls over _____ feet high.

10
12
14
16

What are the four basic ingredients of Portland concrete?

> Portland mortar, fine aggregate, coarse aggregate and water
> Gravel, lime, sand and water
> Portland cement, fine aggregate, coarse aggregate and water
> Portland cement, lime, sand and gravel

The typical exposure while using roll roofing products is _____ inches.

> 17
> 34
> 30
> 18

A _____ is used to support a header over a window or door.

> King
> Trimmer
> Cripple
> Joist

What board is nailed to the end of a rafter tail?

> Gutter work
> Fire-blocking
> Sheetrock
> Fascia

Questions Set #3

The following questions are trade questions not found in the book.

1. To screw gypsum panels to 18 gage steel studs, you should use what type of screw?

2. A mil gage is _____ .

3. A contractor is building a 40' x 24' single story house with a 6/12 straight gable roof and 96" from sole plate to top plate. How many 4' x 8' sheets of wall sheathing are required? Do not deduct openings or add waste.

4. What item is not part of an exterior frame wall?

   Where is the base flashing installed when using brick veneer for the outside finish over wood frame walls?

   When installing insulation, how should the vapor barrier be installed?

   What angle does the valley rafter form with the main ridge board in a roof of uniform pitch?

   What is the rafter run for a straight gable roof with a span of 36'?

.

1 Exam Prep
Carpentry and Building Construction
Answers

Set #1

1.	B	Page 6
2.	D	Page 34
3.	C	Page 37
4.	A	Page 460
5.	B	Page 266
6.	D	Page 42
7.	B	Page 44
8.	A	Page 1018
9.	D	Page 990
10.	B	Page 318
11.	C	Page 324
12.	A	Page 338
13.	C	Page 349
14.	B	Page 577
15.	D	Page 586
16.	B	Page 56
17.	A	Table 2-2 page 61
18.	B	Page 64
19.	C	Page 222
20.	A	Page 226
21.	D	Page 259
22.	B	Page 238
23.	C	Page 287
24.	C	Page 360
25.	A	Page 601
26.	C	Page 44

27. A   Page 45

28. B   Page 50

29. D   Page 51

30. A   Page 53

31. B   Page 55

32. C   Page 56

33. D   Page 218

34. B   Page 220

35. C   Page 221

36. A   Page 223

37. A   Page 227

38. D   Page 227

39. B   Page 230

40. A   Page 237

41. C   Page 239

42. A   Page 244

43. B   Page 244

44. B   Page 247

45. C   Page 244/245

46. C   Page 246

47. B   Page 250/266

48. C   Page 258

49. A   Page 265

50. C   Page 277

51. A   Page 287

52. C   Page 275

53. D   Page 275

54. C   Page 279

55. B   Page 434

56. A   Page 361

57. B   Page 323

58. C   Page 326

59. D   Page 329

60. B   Page 341

61. C   Page 341

62. A   Page 396

63. A   Page 421/423

64. D   Page 396

65. B   Page 401

66. C   Page 506

67. B   Page 597

68. A   Page 615

69. C   Page 616

70. D   Page 619

71. B   Page 620

72. C   Page 557

73. A   Page 626

74. C   Page 629

75. B   Page 629

76. A   Page 629

77. C   Page 634

78. B   Page 637

79. C   Page 641

80. D   Page 651

81. A   Page 653

82. A   Page 663

83. B   Page 663

84. B   Page 552

85. C   Page 698

86. D   Page 730

87. A   Page 732

88. C   Page 734, Step- by-

step application

89. D   Page 737

90. C   Page 736

91. B   Page 784

92. B   Page 783

93. C   Page 784

94. B   Page 796

95. A   Page 797

96. B   Page 975

97. C   Page 979

98. A   Page 993

99. B   Page 42

100. C   Page 326

101. B   Page 63

102. A   Page 338

103. A   Page 340

104. B   Page 349

105. A   Page 352

106. D   Page 353

107. A   Page 110

108. C   Page 113

109. D   Page 118

110. A   Page 166

111. A	Page 136	121. B	Page 63
112. B	Page 238	122. B	Page 432
113. D	Page 239	123. A	Page 432
114. D	Page 239	124. A	Page 432
115. A	Page 244	125. D	Page 481
116. B	Page 370	126. B	Page 552
117. B	Page 370	127. B	Page 578
118. B	Page 370	128. C	Page 730
119. B	Page 396	129. B	Page 730
120. A	Page 398	130. C	Page 725

Set #2

1. D	21. B
2. D	22. C
3. C	23. A
4. D	24. C
5. D	25. B
6. B	26. D
7. C	27. D
8. A	28. B
9. B	29. B
10. B	30. C
11. A	31. A
12. D	32. C
13. B	33. A
14. C	34. A
15. B	35. D
16. A	36. B
17. B	37. D
18. D	38. C
19. C	39. C
20. C	40. C

41. A	57. B
42. D	58. A
43. B	59. C
44. C	60. D
45. B	61. B
46. B	62. A
47. D	63. C
48. A	64. D
49. D	65. B
50. B	66. A
51. B	67. C
52. D	68. A
53. C	69. B
54. D	70. D
55. A	
56. A	

Set #3

S-12

Used to verify coating thickness.

How they figure it: 40+40+24+24=128 128 LF / 4LF = 32 pieces Then for the gables:
The 6/12 pitch would give us a gable peak of 72", or 6'.

6' x 24' = 144 sq ft.

144 sq ft / 32 sq ft is 4.5 pieces.

Bridging

Between the sheathing paper and the wood sheathing, extending into the mortar joint at the brick course below the bottom of the sheathing.

To the warm side of the house.

45

18'

1 Exam Prep

The Contractors Guide to Quality Concrete Construction

Questions and Answers

1. The most common type of cement is Type _____ .

   I
   II
   III
   IV

2. High early strength cement is Type _____ .

   II
   III
   IV
   V

3. Low heat hydration cement is Type _____ .

   II
   III
   IV
   V

Test cylinders stored on the job would ideally be stored under what conditions?

   Controlled moisture
   Controlled temperature
   Controlled conditions
   All of the above

What is not an example of a pozzolan?

   Microsilica
   Class C Fly Ash
   Class F Fly Ash
   Granulated slag

6. A _____ is used to extend the setting time of concrete.

   Accelerator
   Retarder
   Extending agents
   Setting inhibitor

7. _____ accelerates the setting of concrete but is prohibited in pre-stressed concrete designs.

    Calcium chloride
    Fly ash
    Calcium hypochlorite
    Sodium bicarbonate

8. For hot-weather concreting, a maximum temperature of _____ F is often specified.

    80
    85
    90
    95

9. You can increase the slump of concrete 5 to 7 inches by adding a/an _____ .

    Retarder
    Superplasticizer
    Accelerator
    Aggregate

10. You must discharge truck-mixed concrete before _____ revolutions of the mixer.

    200
    300
    500
    600

What is/are the fiber material(s) in fiber-reinforced concrete?

    Glass
    Steel
    Polypropylene
    All of the above

12. In _____ splice, the bars are lapped next to each other at a certain length and securely wired together with tie wire.

    A.   Lap
    B.   Welded
    C.   Mechanical
    D.   None of the above

13. For concrete cast against and permanently exposed to earth, minimum cover for bundled bars is _____.

    1 inch
    2 inches
    3 inches
    4 inches

What type of wire is used to tie rebars?

     No. 16 gage black soft-annealed wire
     No. 14 gage soft-annealed wire
     No. 16 gage green annealed wire
     No. 12 gage annealed wire

What type of tie is used to secure heavy mats of rebars to be lifted in place by a crane?

     Type A
     Type B
     Type C
     Type D

What is the maximum distance for placing control joints in a wall?

     18 feet
     20 feet
     24 feet
     25 feet

17.   Contraction joints in floors are designed _____ .

     To control random cracking
     So a crack forms at a pre-selected location
     To provide a deliberately weakened plane
     All of the above

18.   Control joints in slabs on grade are made by cutting into the slab to a depth of _____ times the slab thickness on the first cut.

     A.   1/8
     B.   1/4
     C.   1/2
     D.   3/4

19.   In an eight (8") slab, control _____ joints should be placed every feet.

     16
     18
     20
     24

What is an isolation joint?

     A joint made to accommodate movements cause by temperature changes
     A joint used at a point of restraint, including the junction between the elements of a structure
     A joint located where one placement ends and the next one begins
     Both A and B

What is the purpose of wire mesh placed in slabs on grade?

 To prevent the cracks that will occur between the joints from opening
 To control crack widths
 Both A and B
 None of the above

22. Reinforcing wire in slabs should be placed _____ inche(s) from the top of the slab.

 1
 1.5
 2
 2.5

What procedure is used to prevent excessive absorption of water from concrete slabs on grade?

 Before concreting, moisten the subgrade
 Before, concreting saturate the subgrade
 Use of a high-range water reducer
 None of the above

Running concrete over a rough surface in a concrete buggy could cause segregation of the mix.

 True
 False

When pumping concrete the flow must continuous.

 True
 False

When floating air-entrained concrete the bullfloat should be made of what material?

 Aluminum
 Magnesium
 Zinc

 I and II
 II and III
 I only
 II only

What is used to embed course aggregate particles into the slab?

 Checkrod
 Vibratory screed
 Power float
 Wood Float

28.   After non-air-entrained concrete is screeded it should be floated with a _____ .

        Wood float
        Aluminum float
        Magnesium float
        None of the above

        When should finish trowelling begin?

        Just before the water sheen disappears
        After the water sheen has disappeared
        Immediately after screeding
        None of the above

        When can you start the power floating operation?

        When the operator's footprints will appear on the surface without indenting the concrete
        The concrete is just firm enough to support the load
        Both A and B
        None of the above

31.   The maximum height for dropping concrete without an segregation is _____ feet.

        12
        10
        8
        4

        Spreading rocks on the surface of a slab and pressing them into the surface is which technique of creating an exposed aggregate finish?

        Monolithic technique
        Seeding technique
        Exposing Technique
        None of the above

33.   Cold weather concreting procedures are required if the average temperature falls below _____ degrees F.

        60
        50
        40
        30

34.   Cold weather concreting requires a curing temperature of degrees _____ F for at three days.

        50
        60
        70
        75

35.   A non-skid surface on outdoor slabs is created with a _____ .

       Stiff broom
       Texture trowel
       Soft broom
       None of the above

    Low humidity and wind are the primary causes of rapidly evaporating surface moisture that causes the surface tension resulting in _____ .

       Shrinkage cracks
       Crazing
       Plastic shrinkage cracks
       Blistering

37.   Sealing the surface of the concrete before it is fully compacted causes_____ .

       Shrinkage cracks
       Crazing
       Plastic shrinkage cracks
       Blistering

    Test cylinders stored on the job site should be protected from drying and maintained at a temperature _____ range.

       50 to 70 F
       55 to 75 F
       60 to 80 F
       65 to 85 F

    What procedure is used to prevent segregation of concrete components when pouring a slab?

       The concrete should be spread as it is deposited
       Deposit the concrete in a pile and then spread with a vibrator
       Addition of an admixture
       None of the above

40.   When performing a slump test, each layer is rodded _____ times.

       10
       15
       25
       50

41.   The normal curing time for formed concrete is _____ .

       12 to 48 hours
       12 to 72 hours
       48 to 72 hours
       None of the above

42. Excessive bleeding can be caused by _____?

    Insufficient fines in mix
    Excess mix water
    Vapor retarded directly under slab
    All of the above

43. Sawcutting joints should be done within _____ hours of concrete placement?

    1 to 2
    2 to 6
    4 to 10
    4 to 12

44. The maximum delivery time for ready-mixed concrete is _____ minutes.

    30
    60
    90
    120

45. 1 gallon of water added to a cubic yard of concrete will increase slump _____ inch.

    ¼
    ½
    1
    2

46. What are concrete cylinder tests used for?

    To estimate concrete strength at a given time
    To determine the workability if the mix
    To see if the mix segregates
    To see how much the concrete expands

When you need concrete to set quickly, what type of concrete should be used to produce high early strength?

    Type I
    Type II
    Type III
    Type IV

48. What chemical reaction takes place when portland cement is hardening?

    Permeability
    Hydration
    Dehydration
    None of the above

What is the effect of adding too much water to concrete?

Lower slump, higher strength
Lower slump, lower strength
Higher slump, lower strength
Higher slump, higher strength

What is the difference between fine & coarse aggregate?

The coarse stone will not pass through a 1/4" sieve
The coarse stone will not pass through a 1/8" sieve
The coarse stone will not pass through a 1/16" sieve
None of the above

What should be added to concrete in cold weather?

Calcium hypochlorite
Calcium chloride
Sodium bicarbonate
Fly ash

Which of the following is NOT a reason to use an admixture?

To increase early strength
To increase permeability
To increase ultimate strength
To increase workability

What is the not true of air-entrained concrete?

Increased workability
Segregation is reduced
Makes concrete more durable
Reduces bleeding

What is the effect of adding too much water to a concrete mix?

Higher slump and lower strength
Higher slump, higher strength
Lower slump, lower strength
Lower slump, higher strength

Can fly ash be introduced into a concrete mix specifying a minimum cement content?

No
Yes, if called for by the specifier

The maximum delivery time for ready mix concrete after water has been added to the cement is _____ .

    30 minutes or 200 revolutions of the mixer drum
    60 minutes or 250 revolutions of the mixer drum
    90 minutes or 350 revolutions of the mixer drum
    90 minutes or 300 revolutions of the mixer drum

57.   Mat, raft or floating foundations are specified when _____ .

    Budget does not allow for additional cost
    When builder is looking for a more economical choice
    The allowable bearing capacity of the soil is very low to great depths
    None of the above

What type of forms are used to place concrete by extrusion?

    Slip-forms
    Jump forms
    Stay-in-place forms
    All of the above

What is the minimal quality plywood that can be used when building concrete forms?

    A-B
    B-B
    A-A
    A-C

What is the best type of nail to use for nailing bracing and forms when the nails must be removed when the pour is completed?

    Double headed
    Duplex nails
    Both A and B
    Small-head (PTL)

Which of the following is the most economical wood to use for formwork?

    Cedar
    Kiln-dried pine
    Mahogany
    Oak

62.   The working load of new ties used in formwork should have a safety factor of _____ .

    2:1
    2:2
    3:1
    1:2

63. The purpose for form liners is to provide_____ on concrete surfaces.

        Designs
        Patterns
        Textures
        All of the above

How much does concrete weigh per cubic foot?

        100 lbs.
        125 lbs.
        150 lbs.
        200 lbs.

What is the best way to reduce lateral pressure on concrete forms when placing concrete?

        Slower placement or rate of pour
        Faster placement or rate of pour
        Distributing concrete as it pours out
        None of the above

When an engineer's specifications for removal of concrete forms is not available, the ACI has recommendations for the length of time concrete should remain in the forms when the
air temperature is above_____.

        45 degrees F
        50 degrees F
        60 degrees F
        65 degrees F

What is the main reason for steel reinforcement in a concrete member?

        To increase compressive strength
        To reduce cracking over time
        To resist tensile forces
        None of the above

68. Placing drawings show details for fabrication and_____.

        Formwork
        Placing concrete
        Placing of reinforcing steel
        None of the above

What are the characteristics of a #5 bar?

        A.
        B.
        C.
        D.
.325" diameter .20% area 1.022 lbs. per lineal foot
.425" diameter .21% area 1.033 lbs. per lineal foot
.525" diameter .31% area 1.032 lbs. per lineal foot
.625" diameter .31% area 1.043 lbs. per lineal foot

What do the markings on rebar represent?

Producers mill
Type of steel and grade of steel
Bar size
All of the above

Lowering the top bars or raising the bottom bars by 1/2" more than specified in a 6" concrete slab could reduce its load carrying capacity <u>by</u>_____.

Approximately 10%
Approximately 20%
Approximately 15%
Approximately 25%

What is the maximum variation of stirrup location in a floor slab?

+/- .5"
+/- 1"
+/- 1.5"
+/- 2"

Which of the following is not a type of rebar splice?

Mechanical
Bundled
Welded
Lap

What is the minimum length of lap in a lapped splice for reinforcing bars?

8"
10"
12"
14"

75.   The most effective water stops used to stop the seepage of water are <u>made of</u>_____.

Aluminum
Magnesium
PVC (Polyvinylchloride)
None of the above

To what depth should a control joint be cut into a concrete slab?

One-eight the slab thickness
One-fourth the slab thickness
10% of the slab thickness
up to 60% of the slab thickness

Joints in concrete should be sawcut within how many hours?

> Within 2 to 8 hours
> Within 4 to 10 hours
> Within 4 to 12 hours12
> Within 6 to 18 hours12

When concrete placement is interrupted, what type of joint must be provided?

> A construction joint
> A warping joint
> An isolation joint
> None of the above

What is the sole purpose for installing welded wire mesh in a concrete slab?

> To prevent cracks from opening
> To increase-load carrying capacity
> To add flexural strength
> None of the above

What is the proper location of welded wire mesh in a concrete slab?

> 1" below the slab surface, in the upper half of the slab
> 1.5" below the slab surface, in the upper third of the slab
> 2" below the slab surface, in the upper third of the slab
> 2" below the slab surface, in the upper half of the slab

Most specifications allow only one addition of water as long as you do not exceed what?

> Specified slump
> The water to cement ratio
> Admixture to cement ratio
> 20 mixer revolutions

What is the best shape of aggregate to use when pumping concrete?

> Rounded
> Angular
> Crushed stone
> None of the above

When using a 5" diameter pump line, what is the ideal mix to pump?

> 4" slump with air entrainment containing no fly ash
> 2" slump with air entrainment containing no fly ash
> 3" slump with air entrainment containing some fly ash
> 4" slump with air entrainment containing some fly ash

A concrete containing a lightweight aggregate should be presoaked to 70 to 80 % total absorption. If not, it will _____ .

    Segregate
    Crack when it dries
    Make pumping more difficult
    Lose moisture quickly

85.   When using a vibrator on concrete, it should not be kept in one location more than ____ .

    1 minute
    10 to 15 seconds
    20 to 30 seconds
    30 to 45 seconds

What type of concrete finish creates a skid-resistant surface?

    Broom finish
    Power floating
    Hand troweled
    None of the above

Air-entrained concrete is most vulnerable to what type of problem?

    Blistering
    Crazing
    Shrinkage
    Plastic shrinkage cracks

What temperature should concrete cylinders be maintained at during the first 48 hours prior to testing concrete?

    50-70 degrees
    60-80 degrees
    65-88 degrees
    70-80 degrees

89.   According to *The Contractor's Guide for Quality Concrete Construction*, _____ test is not used for quality control.

    A.   Nuclear density ASTM C 231
    B.   Air content ASTM C 231 and C 173
    C.   Compressive strength ASTM C 31 and C39
    D.   Slump ASTM C143

90.   _____ are strips of material placed across a joint to obstruct water seepage.

    Water retarders
    Isolation joints
    Construction joints
    Waterstops

91. _____ are concrete test that may be specified in a projects specifications.

> Compressive strength, slump, air, and temperature
> Compressive strength, slump, and temperature
> Compressive strength, slump, and air
> Compressive strength and slump

The most common way to determine concrete consistency is determined by one of the following:

> ASTM D75
> Soil compression and density
> Slump
> With a sodium hydroxide solution

Air-entrained concrete, among other benefits, increases the chance of damage due to freezing and thawing.

> True
> False

94. Two methods for testing air content in freshly mixed concrete is, _____ .

> pressure and temperature
> temperature and volumetric
> volume and pressure
> temperature and slump

Compressive strength lab tests use concrete cylinders usually 6" in diameter and 12" high.

> True
> False

96. _____ from a known quantity of ingredients.

> batch
> strength
> yield
> mix

Concrete test cylinder molds are filled with fresh concrete in layers. Each layer will be "rodded" _____ times.

> 15
> 20
> 25
> 30

98.   Concrete test cylinders are filled with fresh concrete in _____ equal layers.

      1
      2
      3
      4

The chemical and physical changes that occur when Portland cement cures is known as:

      leaching
      hydration
      lactation
      absorption

The **basic raw** materials of Portland cement are:

      limestone, clay or shale
      calcium, silica, iron
      alumina, limestone, clay
      alumina, calcium, shale

101.   Type _____ cement is used in massive concrete structures such as dams for low heat of hydration.

      I
      II
      III
      IV

The primary benefit of microsilica, a pazzolan, is:

      it's a binder
      its durability
      corrosion protection
      permeability

According to *The Contractor's Guide to Quality Concrete Construction*, many specified cements for projects are_____.

      color control cement
      blended cement
      masonry cement
      expansive cement

Type V Portland cement is a high sulfate resistance cement.

      True
      False

Fly ash is a by-product of:

    coal-burning
    coak-burning
    charcoal-burning
    wood-burning

A higher water/cementitious ratio in a workable concrete batch will decrease its:

    strength
    color set
    cure time
    slump rock

107.   The _____ inch sieve is the dividing point between course and fine grade aggregates.

    #200
    1/8"
    #4
    1/4"

According to *The Contractor's Guide to Quality Concrete Construction*, non-porous concrete is best achieved by which of the following?

    low water-to-cement ratio
    increased moist curing period
    non-air-entrained concrete and mortar
    permeability of the paste

109.   Concrete aggregates should contain no _____ material or highly porous particles that would prove harmful to the concrete mix.
    A.   deleterious
    B.   organic
    C.   chemical
    D.   degrading

110.   A high-range water reducer, or super plasticizers _____.

I. Requires less water for higher slump
II. Requires less water for lower slump

    I only
    II only
    Either I or II
    Neither I nor II

Super plasticizers in a concrete batch may reduce the amount of water in a batch by as much as _____%.

       10
       20
       30
       40

This additive can increase the set-up time and accelerate early strength development of concrete.

       pozzolans
       calcium hydrate
       calcium chloride
       sodium chloride

113.   Aggregates of a maximum of_____ inch or less is recommended for high strength concrete.

       1/2
       1
       3/4
       3/8

According to The According to *The Contractor's Guide to Quality Concrete Construction*, a mix using the largest allowable size aggregate will be the most economical, although a maximum size of ____ inch or less is recommended for high-strength concrete.

    A.   1/4
    B.   3/8
    C.   1/2
    D.   3/4

115.   Calcium chloride ushould be used in concrete as _____.

       a retarder
       an accelerator
       a hardener
       none of these

116.   The addition of a superplasticizer typically turns a 2" slump into a _____inch slump.

       2 - 4
       4 - 6
       7 - 9
       10- 13

According to *The Contractor's Guide to Quality Concrete Construction*, microscopic air bubbles from air-entraining agents _____.

       makes the concrete more workable
       allows reduction in water content
       makes a more uniform mix
       all of the above

118.   Maximum aggregate size is limited by _____.

    I. Section dimension
    II. Reinforcement spacing

       I only
       II only
       Both I and II
       Neither I nor II

According to *The Contractor's Guide to Quality Concrete Construction*, when a water reducer is used in the mix, the same slump can be retained with about _____% less water.

       6 - 8
       8 - 10
       10- 12
       12 - 14

Air entrainment in a concrete mix without adjusting the mix will reduce the strength of the batch.

       True
       False

"Standard Specifications for Structural Concrete" is also known as:

       American Concrete Institute Standard 301
       American Concrete Institute Standard 302
       American Concrete Institute Standard 318
       American Concrete Institute Standard 319

The American Society for Testing And Materials, ASTM, provides standards and specifications for cement materials, concrete aggregates and admixtures. Specifications for cement is under the jurisdiction of committee:

       C 1
       C 5
       C 7
       C 9

When pozzolans are used, the water-to-cementitious material ratio (*w/c*) is computed as a water-cementitious material ratio using which of the following formulas?

> (c + m)/w
> (c + w)/m
> w/(c + m)
> m/(c + w)

Determine the water-to-cementitious material ratio (*w/c*) with the following data:

1. 450 pounds of cement
2. 270 pounds of water
3. 125 pounds of flyash

> .495
> .479
> .469
> .457

According to *The Contractor's Guide to Quality Concrete Construction*, concrete exposed to severe conditions should be air entrained within what percentage range in mixes with 3/4" to 1" maximum size aggregate?

> 4%
> 5% - 8%
> 9% - 12%
> 15%

The purpose of a slump test is to measure:

> uniformity
> consistency
> strength
> durability

According to *The Contractor's Guide to Quality Concrete Construction*, after 300 drum revolutions _____ or minutes, structural concrete shall be rejected.

> 30
> 60
> 90
> 120

128.   For hot weather concreting, a maximum concrete temperature of _____ degrees F is often specified.

> 85
> 87
> 90
> 92

The most common type of shallow foundations are:

I. Continuous spread footings for walls
II. Non-continuous spread footings for walls

      I only
      II only
      both I and II
      neither I nor II

130.   A _____ type of foundation, utilizing heavily reinforced concrete over the entire area of the building, is used when the allowable bearing capacity of the soil is very low to great depths, making pile foundations uneconomical.

    A.   raft
    B.   mat
    C.   floating
    D.   all of the above

131.   According to *The Contractor's Guide to Quality Concrete Construction*, the _____ usually designs the forms for cast-in-place concrete.

      Architect
      Owner
      Engineer
      Concrete Contractor

Just prior to placing concrete into the forms, you would:

      check to insure that wall-ties are correctly installed
      install stiffeners
      check to insure that connection hardware is installed correctly
      A and C are correct

Concrete should be placed at or near as possible to its final position in its forms.

      True
      False

Freshly deposited concrete creates pressure against the forms in much the same manner as:

      gravity
      electrostatic pressure
      hydrostatic pressure
      harmonic wave pressure

135. Generally, new concrete shrinks as it hydrates, approximately _____ inches in 100 feet under field conditions.

    1/2
    3/4
    1
    1 1/4

Concrete will expand in rainy conditions and shrink in sunny and dry conditions.

    True
    False

Internal stress relief in concrete can he evidenced by:

    spelling
    crazing
    dusting
    cracking

138. An isolation joint permits _____ of various parts of the structure.

    differential movement
    isolation
    contraction
    warping

What is the maximum distance for placing control joints in a wall?

    18 feet
    20 feet
    24 feet
    25 feet

When concrete placement is interrupted, what type of joint must be provided?

    A construction joint
    A warping joint
    An isolation joint
    None of the above

141. Water stops are used to _____.

    obstruct the flow of water
    increase the flow of water
    reduce the flow of water

According to *The Contractor's Guide to Quality Concrete Construction*, construction, or control joints in concrete slabs are planned cracks induced by cutting into the slab to a depth of _____ the slab thickness, or a minimum of 1 inch, creating a weakened plane.

    A.   1/4
    B.   1/5
    C.   1/6
    D.   15/16

143.   Wherever there is a change in cross-sectional area of a slab, there should be _____.

    A. a joint
    B. a construction joint .
    C. a contraction joint
    D. an isolation joint

Columns and bases of columns should be separated from the slab by the use of:

    spray on curing compound
    construction joint
    isolation joint
    expansion joint material

145.   The term_____ is often used to describe the use of fibers in a concrete mix.

    secondary reinforcement
    fibrous reinforcement
    structural reinforcement
    primary reinforcement

Proportions for a concrete mix should be submitted by the hatch plant to the specifier. The procedure is simplest when there is a record of field performance on the batch. This field performance record should include _____ successive tests within the last 12 months.

    1
    15
    30
    90

Almost any natural water that is drinkable and has no pronounced odor or taste can be used for making concrete.

    True
    False

A method of measuring the penetration resistance of newly placed and cured concrete is the:

    nuclear probe
    Windsor probe
    MRI
    Blue stone dye test

Bucket and crane placement of concrete is a very flexible method of concrete placement on large buildings because of:

the ease with which a crane can maneuver for placement
the capacity of modern day concrete placement buckets
the ranee of horizontal and vertical distances available from one position
none of the above

The most common method of starting concrete pumping through a line is to start with approximately one cubic yard of a cement-sand slurry.

True
False

151. Vibratory screeds should have the proper balance of _____ to properly consolidate the concrete.

Freque
ncy II.
Amplitud
e

I only
II only
both I and II
neither I nor II

A darby or bullfloat is used to:

Fill in low spots/cut of high points
Remove excess bleed water

I only
II only
both I and II
neither I nor II

According to *The Contractor's Guide to Quality Concrete Construction*, a properly troweled surface will have all of the following characteristics EXCEPT:

hard
even
dense
wear-resistant

According to *The According to The Contractor's Guide to Quality Concrete Construction*, hot weather introduces all of the following problems EXCEPT:

lower strength
longer set up time
rapid drying of the surface
shorter set up time

155. Coarse aggregates are usually in the range of _____ inches.

    1/2 " to 2"
    3/8" to 2"
    3/8" to 1 /2"
    1/2" to 1 1/2"

According to *The Contractor's Guide to Quality Concrete Construction*, concrete segregation is caused by which of the following?

    placed at a fairly rapid rate
    excessive water to cement ratio
    not enough water, to much cement
    adding superplasticizers

157. A concrete pad is showing signs of dusting. This defect could be the result of _____ during finishing.

    under troweling the surface
    over troweling the surface
    NOT floating the surface
    poor concrete curing

Adequate curing is nearly always a preventative measure against almost every common quality problem.

    True
    False

According to *The Contractors Guide to Quality Concrete Construction*, sprayed-on membrane provides:

    temporary protection against drying
    prevents discoloration due to uneven drying
    efficiency in curing
    all of the above

160. 1 gallon of water added to a cubic yard of concrete will increase slump _____ inch.

    ¼
    ½
    1
    2

Type _____ cement is a general purpose cement that is used in the vast majority of concrete.

    I
    II
    III
    IV

Increase in strength of concrete stops after _____.

        7 days
        28 days
        there is no moisture present
        90 days

What form creates voids inside the concrete?

        Flatwork forms
        Slip forms
        Internal forms
        Jump forms

Concrete must be poured before mixing drum turns _____ revolutions.

        25
        300
        350
        400

_____ is way to obtain a non-slip finish on unhardened concrete surfaces.

        Brooming
        Floating
        Fogging
        None of the above

The maximum temperature for placing concrete is _____ degrees Fahrenheit.

        80
        85
        90
        95

Which of the following is a result of too much water in a concrete mix?

        Lower slump and lower strength
        High slump and higher strength
        Lower slump and lower strength
        Higher slump and lower strength

The most commonly used accelerating admixture is _____.

        Sugar
        Calcium chloride
        Sucrose
        Lime

The slump test is used to measure the _____ of concrete.

     Volume
     Consistency
     Cement-water ratio
     Strength

A tremmie is used to place concrete _____.

     Under bedrock
     Both 1 and 3
     Underwater
     Never

Which type of Portand cement is used if you need high-early strength?

     I
     II
     III
     IV

Concrete is approximately _____ pounds per cubic foot.

     75
     100
     125
     150

A vibrator should not be held in one location in concrete for more than _____ seconds.

     5 to 15
     3 to 15
     10 to 10
     A vibrator must never be used in concrete.

The type of concrete joint that permits both vertical and horizontal movement is the _____ joint.

     Control
     Construction
     Isolation
     Cover

Which of the following is used to slow down the hydration process and extend the setting time for concrete.

     Alumanite
     Retarder
     Admixture
     Air-entrainment

When removing your forms as soon as possible is required, what type of cement should be used to make the concrete?

I
II
III
IV

If a #5 rebar is lapped 30 times it diameter, how long would the lap be?

18.75"
18.65"
30"
15"

A load of concrete arrives on the jobsite 30 minutes after batching. How muc time remains to complete the discharge of all the concrete?

90 minutes
30 minutes
2-1/2 hours
1 hour

When placing concrete in heavily reinforced concrete members, what admixture can be used without weakening the concrete mix to improve the flow of the concrete?

S-lime
Super plasticizer
Calcium chloride
Sucrose

What is the purpose of using a vibrator in freshly placed concrete?

To segregate it
To increase hydrostatic pressure
To consolidate it
To pre-wet it

The design element in a form that allows for settlement and deflection is _____.

Camber
Pre-loading
Compression
Tension

The quality of cement depends primarily on the _____.

cement-lime ratio
Size of the aggregate
Admixture use
cement-water ratio

The cut of a control joint in a slab must be approximately _____ the thickness.

      ¼

      ½

      1/3

      1 inch

Moderate slump for most work is _____.

      2-4 inches

      3-4 inches

      4-6 inches

      5-8 inches

Which of the following will make concrete resistant to damage from the decing chemicals and the freeze and thaw cycle.

      Retarder

      Tri-calcium alumanite

      Air-entrainment

      Sugar

Over-vibration of a concrete mixture will cause _____.

      Consolidation

      Segregation

      Both 1 and 4

      Bleeding

Concrete will reach approximately _____ to _____ percent of its design strength in 7 days.

      25,50

      55,85

      65,70

      70,75

Within how many hours after concrete is placed on a jobsite should concrete joints be sawn?

      4 to 12

      2 to 8

      2 to 4

      24

How many gallons of water do you add to 8 cubic yards of concrete to increase the slump from 2" to 3"?

      20

      15

      40

      None of the above

190. Air-entrained concrete will not _____.

       A. Increase the water ratio
       B. Decrease the durability
       C. Improve the workability
       D. Increase the water tightness

1 Exam Prep

The Contractors Guide to Quality Concrete Construction

Answers

1.	A	17		39.	A	123
2.	B	17		40.	C	14
3.	C	17		41.	B	13
4.	D	16		42.	D	143
5.	D	17		43.	D	89
6.	B	20		44.	B	30
7.	A	20		45.	C	98
8.	C	31		46.	A	15
9.	B	20		47.	C	17
10.	B	24		48.	B	18
11.	D	68		49.	C	18
12.	A	76		50.	A	18
13.	C	73		51.	B	20
14.	A	74		52.	B	20
15.	D	74		53.	C	21
16.	C	80		54.	A	24
17.	D	87		55.	B	29
18.	B	89		56.	D	30
19.	C	90		57.	C	36
20.	B	79		58.	A	47
21.	C	92		59.	B	48
22.	C	92		60.	C	48
23.	A	98/99		61.	B	48
24.	A	122		62.	A	49
25.	A	124		63.	D	50
26.	A	126		64.	C	52
27.	A	125/126		65.	A	55
28.	A	126		66.	B	58
29.	B	127Fig. 10.18		67.	C	63
30.	C	126		68.	C	66
31.	D	134		69.	D	66
32.	B	127		70.	D	68
33.	C	129		71.	B	73
34.	C	129		72.	B	74
35.	A	126		73.	B	76
36.	C	135		74.	C	76
37.	D	138		75.	C	83
38.	C	140				

76.	B	88		120.	A	21
77.	C	89		121.	A	26
78.	A	90		122.	C	
79.	A	92		123.	C	18
80.	C	93		124.	D	18
81.	B	121		125.	B	30
82.	A	123		126.	B	23
83.	D	124		127.	B	30
84.	C	124		128.	C	31
85.	B	124		129.	A	34
86.	A	127		130.	C	36
87.	A	138		131.	D	51
88.	B	140		132.	D	53
89.	A	13		133.	A	54
90.	D	83		134.	C	54
91.	C	13/14		135.	B	78
92.	C	13		136.	A	78
93.	B	21		138.	A	81
94.	C	14		139.	C	80
95.	A	14		140.	A	90
96.	C	16		141.	D	83
97.	C	15		142.	A	89
98.	C	15		143.	C	80
99.	B	18		144.	D	91
100.	A	17		145.	A	94
101.	D	17		146.	C	95
102.	C	18		147.	A	18
103.	B	16/17		148.	B	98
104.	A	17		149.	C	123
105.	A	17		150.	A	123
106.	A	18		151.	C	125
107.	D	18		152.	A	126
108.	A	18		153.	B	126
109.	B	18		154.	B	127
110.	A	20		155.	C	18/19
111.	C	20		156.	B	133
112.	C	20		157.	B	137
113.	C	19		158.	A	130
114.	D	19		159.	C	132
115.	B	20		160.	C	98
116.	C	20		161.	A	
117.	D	21		162.	C	
118.	C	19		163.	C	
119.	B	20		164.	B	

165.	A		178.	D
166.	C		179.	B
167.	D		180.	C
168.	B		181.	A
169	B		182.	D
170.	C		183.	A
171.	C		184.	B
172.	D		185.	C
173.	A		186.	B
174.	C		187.	C
175.	B		188.	A
176.	C		189.	D
177.	A		190.	D

1 Exam Prep
Gypsum Construction Handbook
Questions and Answers

Question Set #1

Where 1¼ inch Type W bugle head screw is used, attach _____ gypsum panels to wood framing?

⅜ inch
½ inch
⅝ inch
All of the above

_____ are warning signs of fastener imperfections?

Darkening
Localized cracking
Protrusion of the fasteners
All of the above

Extended periods of _____ will discolor panel face paper?

High humidity
Low humidity
Cold weather
Strong sunlight

⅜-inch panels are designed for framing centers up to 16 inches?

24 inches
16 inches
20 inches
12 inches

_____ is often caused by excessively fast drying of joint compounds?

Loose panels
Board sagging
Joint cracking
None of the above

Use _____ screw to connect ¾ inch single-layer panels to steel studs?

1 inch Type S bugle head
1⅛ inch Type S bugle head
1¼ inch Type S bugle head
2¼ inch Type S bugle head

Stack panels face up with ends resting on 2" x 2" lumber, center of panel resting on floor and allow to remain overnight or until panels show _____?

1" space between adjacent panels
At least a 2" permanent bow
No stains or discoloration on face paper
All of the above

Maintain and control heat in the range of 55 degrees to 70 degrees Fahrenheit 24 hours _____ gypsum board finishing?

Before
During
After
All of the above

Board sags in ceiling are often caused by _____?

Improperly fitted panels
Insufficient support of board
High-humid conditions
All of the above

Long partition runs shall have _____ to compensate for hygrometric and thermal expansion?

Relief joints
Expansion joints
Control joints
All of the above

All but which will cause cracking of compound joints in veneer plaster finishing?

Maximum air circulation
Rapid drying
Possible shrinkage
All of the above

Maximum frame spacing for ⅜ inch single-layer ceiling application is _____ o.c.?

12 inches
16 inches
24 inches
In compliance with local building codes

Where single-nailing is used, drive nails at least _____ from ends or edges of gypsum board?

¼ inch
⅜ inch
½ inch
⅝ inch

Joint defects generally occur in a straight-line pattern and in most cases result from _____?

Incorrect framing
Incorrect joint treatment
Uncontrolled climatic conditions
All of the above

Wood furring strips over wood framing shall be _____ minimum size for nail-on application?

1" x 1"
1" x 2"
1" x3"
2" x 2"

It is desirable to limit deflection to _____ and never exceed L/120 for drywall assemblies?

L/120
L/180
L/240
L/360

The blade end of a drywall hammer is used for all of the following except _____?

Compressing gypsum panel face
To wedge panels
To pry panels
To cut panels

Where screws are used, drive screws at least _____ from ends or edges of gypsum board?

¼ inch
⅜ inch
½ inch
⅝ inch

A board sagging between ceiling support is caused by _____?

Improper ventilation
Extended exposure to strong sunlight
Low humidity
High humidity

Minimum temperature _____ degrees Fahrenheit shall be maintained during gypsum board application?

45
50
55
70

Using a 1½ inch Type W bugle head screw, fasten gypsum panel to _____?

Gypsum panels
Wood framing
Plywood
Steel framing

Tape overlapped at joint intersections _____ in veneer plaster?

Is recommended to strengthen the joints
Is only recommended when the joints are at angles
Is only recommended if the joints are out of alignment
Can cause joint cracking

_____ of panels may be subject to scuffing and may develop paper bond failure or paper delamination from the gypsum core after application?

Board sag
Too much adhesive
Water damage
Strong sunlight

Where gypsum panels are attached to furring channels use, _____ screw?

Type S bugle head
Type S-12 trim head
Type W bugle head
Type G bugle head

Firecode C Core gypsum panels are available in lengths of _____ feet?

8,9,10,12
8,10,14,16
8,9,10,12,14
9,10,12,14

Maintain a minimum temperature of _____ degrees Fahrenheit during gypsum board application?

30
40
50
60

_____ to prevent joint darkening?

Always use white paint in finishing
Always finish joints in humid conditions
Be sure joints are thoroughly dry before painting
None of the above

_____ after joint treatment are signs of edge cracking?

Straight narrow cracks along edges of tape
Cracks along edges of door and/or window opening
Cracks on edges of any curved application
Cracks along sides of pre-finished panels

In large ceiling areas, _____ are recommended to relieve internal stress buildup?

Control joints
Seismic joints
Cladding joints
Stress joints

Structural movement and most cracking problems are caused by _____?

Change in materials due to temperature and humidity changes
Deflection under load
Seismic forces
All of the above

_____ systems consist of reinforcing tape and joint compound?

Reinforcing
Joint treatment
Finishing
Bonding

When installing wood studs and joists, apply gypsum boards first _____?

To the ceiling and then to the walls
To bottom of wall, then top of wall, then ceiling
To walls first in any order, then to ceiling
Parallel, in any order

Joint compounds and textures are seriously affected by lower temperatures; _____?

Suffer loss of strength
Lose its workability
Crack from thermal shock
All of the above

Where screw application is used for attaching gypsum panel to either wood or steel framing, screwhead shall be driven _____ but not deep enough to break the paper?

To just above
Flush with
Slightly below face panel
Deep enough to just slightly break

_____ screw is used to attach ½ inch or ⅝ inches of single-layer gypsum panel and base to steel framing?

1 inch Bugle Head Type S
1 ⅛ inch Bugle Head Type S
1 ¼ inch Bugle Head Type S
1 ⅝ inch Bugle Head Type S

⅜-inch gypsum board applied with long dimension perpendicular to framing has a bending radius of _____ feet?

20
9.5
6
5

Certain interior wall surface should be isolated with surface expansion joints or other means where; _____?

Construction changes within the plane of the wall
Tile and thin brick surfaces exceeds 16 feet
A wall abuts a structural element or dissimilar wall
All of the above

Gypsum products shall be installed at comfortable working temperatures _____ degrees Fahrenheit?

Above 50
Below 72
Both A and B
None of the above

_____, gypsum panels can be prebowed?

When applied to a curved surface
When it is determined that humidity will warm them
Where fasteners at the vertical joints are objectionable
None of the above

To prevent serious problems with gypsum board, such as boards sagging between supports, protect panels from _____?

High humidity
Wind-blown rain
Standing water on floors
Both B and C

What type of screws are used to attach ½ inch gypsum board to metal studs?

Type A
Type S
Type C
Type Z

Fire-code gypsum board is also known as _____.

Type S
Green board
Fire rock
Type X

When installing drywall on a 90-degree outside corner the proper way to finish is to use _____.

Corner bead and joint compound
Joint compound
Tape and joint compound
Z-channel

The maximum spacing for a control joint in a gypsum sheathed wall is _____ feet.

75
50
30
45

Gypsum products may not be stored in temperatures that exceed _____ degrees.

115 F
125 F
130 F
135 F

The maximum spacing for nails in wood framed construction when installing drywall on walls is
_____.

2 inches
4 inches
6 inches
8 inches

Question Set #2

1. Is standard gypsum wallboard acceptable to us in wet areas?

2. ¼" drywall is typically used for _____ .

3. Which type of gypsum panel complies with ASTM requirements for Type X gypsum board?

4. Gypsum board that is green in color is known as _____ .

One of the most effective, lowest cost methods of reducing sound transmission when installing drywall is?

When fastening steel studs to runners, which fastener is required?

When installing resilient channel, what type of fastener is required?

When installing 5/8" gypsum panels to wood studs, what is the minimum length screw required?

When attaching steel framing components to poured concrete and block surfaces, which fastener is required?

When single layer drywall board is applied over metal studs, which fastener is used?

What is the minimum length drywall screw used for installing 5/8" drywall to wood studs?

What is the thickest drywall you can install using a 1 ½" annular drywall nail?

Which type of drywall joint compound hardens quick enough to provide same day finishing?

How many gallons of joint compound will it take to cover 1,000 square feet of drywall?

How should the metal furring channels be attached to bar joists with a furred ceiling?

What is the maximum span for ½" single layer panels in one span using 25 ga. Metal furring channels with 16" o.c. spacing, when framing a ceiling?

How should drywall be stored?

What is the minimum temperature you can apply joint compound?

What is the minimum temperature you can hang sheetrock?

When installing sheetrock, how far must you stay from the edges with the drywall screws?

When placing sheetrock over wood framing, which answer is true?

When installing sheetrock, what is the proper arrangement of drywall joints over wood framing?

With gypsum multi-layer adhesive applications, the joints should be offset a minimum of how many inches?

When installing gypsum in soffit areas, a control joint should be installed how often?

What is used to reinforce the outside corners of sheetrock?

When fastening 200-A & 200-B metal trim to drywall, what is the spacing of the nails?

27. When drywall fasteners are replaced, the heads of the screws should be covered with _____.

1/4" & 3/8" sheetrock are NOT recommended for what purpose?

29. The main reason for drywall problems is _____.

ANSWER KEY

Question Set #1

D
D
D
B
C
C
B
D
D
D
D
B
D
D
D
C
D
B
D
B
A
D
C
A
C
C
C
A
A
D
B
A
D
C
A
C
D
A
C
D
B
D
A
C
B
D

Question Set #2

1. No	Page 3
2. Curved walls	Page 5
3. Fire resistant	Page 5
4. Moisture resistant	Page 7
5. Resilient Channel	Page 31
6. Type S pan head	Page 38
7. 1¼" Type W or Type S bugle head screws	Page 39
8. 1 ¼" Type W Bugle Head	Page 39
9. Tapcon	Page 39
10. 1" Type S	Page 42
11. 1 ¼"	Page 42
12. ¾"	Page 44
13. Powder setting joint compound	Page 49
14. 9.4 gallons	Page 51
15. 24" on center maximum, at right angles to the bar joists	Page 81
16. 5'9"	Page 82
17. Flat and in the center of a dry room	Page 104
18. 55 degree's	Page 105
19. 50 degree's	Page 105
20. 3/8"	Page 110
21. Apply gypsum to the ceiling, then to the wall	Page 116
22. Arrange joints on opposite sides of partition so they occur on different studs	Page 116
23. 10"	Page 118
24. A maximum of 30 feet	Page 128
25. Corner Bead	Page 167
26. 9" on-center	Page 170
27. Joint compound	Page 177
28. Sound control	Page 331
29. Poor workmanship	Page 367

2012 Residential Building Contractor Practice Exam

1. Insulation materials used for wall assemblies, roof assemblies and crawl spaces shall have a MAXIMUM flame spread index of

    1. 25.
    2. 75.
    3. 200.
    4. 300.

2. A detached one- and two-family dwelling in Seismic Design Category D, E or F with a maximum height of 3 stories constructed with stud bearing walls can have plain concrete foundations and basement walls provided the MINIMUM thickness is

    1. 6.5".
    2. 7.0".
    3. 7.5".
    4. 8.0".

3. What is the MINIMUM thickness of a solid masonry wall for a single story dwelling?

    1. 6"
    2. 8"
    3. 10"
    4. 12"

4. What MAXIMUM height off the finished floor can the sill of an emergency egress window be installed?

    1. 44"
    2. 45"
    3. 46"
    4. 47"

5. What is the MINIMUM thickness of foundation walls built with rubble stone?

    1. 12"
    2. 14"
    3. 16"
    4. 18"

6. What is the MINIMUM uniformly distributed live load for a sleeping room in a residential dwelling?

  1. 10 psf
  2. 20 psf
  3. 30 psf
  4. 40 psf

7. What MIMIMUM distance clearance shall be maintained from combustible materials around the outside surfaces of a masonry heater?

  1. 36"
  2. 40"
  3. 44"
  4. 48"

8. A 6 mil vapor retarder shall be installed under which one of the following concrete floors?

  1. Garages
  2. Basement floors
  3. Utility buildings
  4. Accessory structures

9. Exterior insulation finishing systems ("EIFS") when installed on a home shall terminate what MINIMUM distance above the finished ground?

  1. 3"
  2. 4"
  3. 5"
  4. 6"

10. When admixtures are used for water reduction and setting time modification, they shall conform to which one of the following Standards?

  1. ASTM C260
  2. ASTM C494
  3. ASTM C845
  4. ASTM C1017

11. Foam plastic spray insulation applied to a sill plate and header shall have a MAXIMUM thickness of

  1. 2.75".
  2. 3.00".
  3. 3.25".
  4. 3.50".

12. When 29 gage steel siding is installed horizontally, what is the MAXIMUM fastener spacing?

    1. 12"
    2. 14"
    3. 16"
    4. Same as stud spacing

13. What is the MINIMUM width of the material used for lining an open valley on a residential roof?

    1. 18"
    2. 24"
    3. 30"
    4. 36"

14. When handrails are being installed in a residential home, at what height shall the handrails be mounted?

    1. 30" to 34"
    2. 32" to 36"
    3. 33" to 37"
    4. 34" to 38"

15. When a permit application is submitted, what is the MINIMUM number of sets of construction documents required to accompany the application?

    1. 1 set
    2. 2 sets
    3. 3 sets
    4. 4 sets

16. What MINIMUM amount of under-floor space ventilation is required for the area between the floor joists and the earth below with no vapor barrier?

    1. 1 sq. foot for each 100 sq. feet of under-floor area
    2. 1 sq. foot for each 150 sq. feet of under-floor area
    3. 1 sq. foot for each 175 sq. feet of under-floor area
    4. 1 sq. foot for each 200 sq. feet of under-floor area

17. What shall be the MAXIMUM outside diameter of Type I round handrails installed in a dwelling?

    1. 1-1/4"
    2. 1-1/2"
    3. 1-3/4"
    4. 2"

18. What is the net cross-sectional area of a 12" x 16" rectangular flue in a masonry chimney?

    1. 131 sq. inches
    2. 173 sq. inches
    3. 181 sq. inches
    4. 222 sq. inches

19. Weepholes will be provided in the outside wythe of exterior masonry walls with a MAXIMUM spacing of

    1. 27" on center between holes.
    2. 30" on center between holes.
    3. 33" on center between holes.
    4. 36" on center between holes.

20. What MAXIMUM size floor joists can be used for a dwelling before they must be supported laterally with solid blocking or diagonal bridging?

    1. 2" x 6"
    2. 2" x 8"
    3. 2" x 10"
    4. 2" x 12"

21. Water-resistant gypsum board is being used for the ceiling in a shower with 16" on center framing spacing. What is the MINIMUM thickness of gypsum board required?

    1. 3/8"
    2. 1/2"
    3. 5/8"
    4. 3/4"

22. What is the MINIMUM distance that the foundation anchor bolts should be embedded into the concrete or grouted cells of the concrete masonry units?

    1. 6"
    2. 7"
    3. 8"
    4. 9"

23. What MINIMUM thickness roof sheathing should be used when rafters are spaced 24" apart?

    1. 1/2"
    2. 5/8"
    3. 3/4"
    4. 1"

24. What is the MINIMUM thickness of the concrete footings required for a masonry chimney?

    1. 12"
    2. 14"
    3. 16"
    4. 18"

25. Fire escapes shall be designed to what MINIMUM amount uniformly distributed live load?

    1. 10 psf
    2. 20 psf
    3. 30 psf
    4. 40 psf

26. What MINIMUM distance above finished grade shall a concrete or masonry foundation extend at all points?

    1. 3"
    2. 4"
    3. 5"
    4. 6"

27. What is the MINIMUM nominal thickness in the least dimension for wood framing supporting gypsum board?

    1. 1"
    2. 2"
    3. 3"
    4. 4"

28. When glazing is used in walls, enclosures or fences of saunas, whirlpools and hot tubs, if the bottom of the exposed edge of the glazing is located less than what MINIMUM distance (measured vertically) above the standing surface, it shall be considered a hazardous location.

    1. 48"
    2. 54"
    3. 60"
    4. 66"

29. What is the MINIMUM nominal size wood column used for support in a residential house?

    1. 4" x 4"
    2. 4" x 6"
    3. 6" x 6"
    4. 6" x 8"

30. What is the MAXIMUM span of a 2" x 10" Southern pine #1 grade floor joist used for a residential sleeping area with joist spacing of 16" and a dead load of 20 psf?

    1. 14' 4"
    2. 15' 2"
    3. 16' 1"
    4. 17' 11"

31. What is the MAXIMUM smoke-developed index for 6" thick foam plastic insulation?

    1. 350
    2. 400
    3. 450
    4. 500

32. What is the MINIMUM thickness of a masonry chimney wall built with solid masonry units or hollow units filled with grout?

    1. 4"
    2. 6"
    3. 8"
    4. 10"

33. When drilling or notching a top plate more than 50% of its width, a galvanized metal tie shall be fastened across the opening and shall have a MINIMUM width of

    1. 1".
    2. 1-1/4".
    3. 1-1/2".
    4. 2".

34. Mechanical and gravity outdoor air intakes shall be located what MINIMUM distance from any hazardous or noxious contaminants?

    1. 10 feet
    2. 15 feet
    3. 20 feet
    4. 25 feet

35. All of the following information should be included in roof truss design drawings EXCEPT the

    1. location of all joints.
    2. name of designer and license number.
    3. required bearing widths.
    4. lumber size, species and grade for each member.

36. How many coats of exterior portland cement plaster shall be required when applied over metal lath?

    1. Not less than 2 coats
    2. Not less than 3 coats
    3. Not less than 4 coats
    4. Not less than 5 coats

37. A dwelling unit separation wall between townhouses that has no plumbing, mechanical, ducts or vents in the wall shall be a MINIMUM

    1. 1.0 hour fire-resistance rated wall.
    2. 1.5 hour fire-resistance rated wall.
    3. 2.0 hour fire-resistance rated wall.
    4. 2.5 hour fire-resistance rated wall.

38. What is the MINIMUM size access opening through a perimeter wall to the under-floor areas of a residential house?

    1. 16" x 24"
    2. 18" x 26"
    3. 20" x 30"
    4. 22" x 36"

39. What MINIMUM number of fasteners shall be used per wood shake when attached to the roof sheathing?

    1. 1 fastener
    2. 2 fasteners
    3. 3 fasteners
    4. 4 fasteners

40. In a building when making the truss to bearing wall connection, what number and size of screws should be used in each truss?

    1. 1 No. 8 screw
    2. 2 No. 8 screws
    3. 1 No. 10 screw
    4. 2 No. 10 screws

41. What is the MINIMUM thickness of standard unit glass masonry blocks for wall construction?

    1. 3"
    2. 3-1/8"
    3. 3-7/8"
    4. 4"

42. When an emergency situation requires the replacement or repair of equipment, how soon must the permit application be submitted to the building official?

    1. Within the next working day
    2. Within 2 working days
    3. Within 3 working days
    4. Within 4 working days

43. If ambient temperatures on a job are above or below the recommended temperature for placing and curing concrete, a record shall be kept of the protection used for the concrete. What is the temperature range?

    1. 35°F to 90°F
    2. 40°F to 95°F
    3. 45°F to 90°F
    4. 50°F to 95°F

44. What is the MAXIMUM spacing between screws on 1/2" gypsum used for wall board without adhesive and studs that are 24" on center?

    1. 10"
    2. 12"
    3. 14"
    4. 16"

45. Each end of a ceiling joist or rafter that is bearing on a concrete or masonry surface shall have what MINIMUM amount of bearing on that surface?

    1. 1-1/2"
    2. 2"
    3. 2-1/2"
    4. 3"

46. Wood foundation walls below grade shall have a moisture barrier installed. What thickness polyethylene film should be applied?

    1. 3 mil
    2. 4 mil
    3. 6 mil
    4. 8 mil

47. What type of valley lining material has a MINIMUM thickness of 0.027"?

    1. Aluminum
    2. Copper
    3. Lead
    4. Zinc alloy

48. Which one of the following building projects is required to have a permit?

    1. New deck, 300 square feet and 5 feet off the ground
    2. New one story accessory building, 180 square feet
    3. New privacy fence, 6 feet tall
    4. New retaining wall, 2.5 feet tall

49. What is the MINIMUM thickness lumber used for floor sheathing when joist or beam spacing is 16" and sheathing is installed diagonal to the joist?

    1. 1/2"
    2. 5/8"
    3. 3/4"
    4. 11/16"

50. Light-weight concrete shall contain aggregate that meets the density specifications determined by

    1. ASTM C33.
    2. ASTM C330.
    3. ASTM C496.
    4. ASTM C567.

51. What is the MINIMUM ceiling height for a bathroom in a residential home?

    1. 6' 6"
    2. 6' 7"
    3. 6' 8"
    4. 6' 9"

52. Which of the following jobs requires the contractor get a permit for the work?

    1. Fences less than 7 feet tall
    2. Retaining walls not over 4 feet tall
    3. One-story detached accessory buildings less than 200 sq. feet
    4. Installing a new shingle roof

53. What is the MAXIMUM allowed length of a building built with structural insulated panel ("SIP") construction?

    1. 60 feet
    2. 70 feet
    3. 80 feet
    4. 90 feet

54. What is the MINIMUM depth of a masonry or concrete fireplace firebox?

    1. 18"
    2. 19"
    3. 20"
    4. 21"

55. A window well used for emergency escape and rescue shall have a permanently affixed ladder if the vertical depth is greater than

    1. 40".
    2. 44".
    3. 48".
    4. 52".

56. What is the MINIMUM size access opening to the attic of a dwelling with a combustible ceiling?

    1. 22" x 30"
    2. 24" x 30"
    3. 30" x 30"
    4. 30" x 36"

57. What is stamped on construction documents after they have been reviewed by the building department?

    1. "Accepted for Code Compliance"
    2. "Reviewed for Code Compliance"
    3. "Processed for Code Compliance"
    4. "Approved for Code Compliance"

58. What is the MINIMUM size vertical attachment flange required for a weep screed used for an exterior plaster wall?

    1. 2.5"
    2. 3.0"
    3. 3.5"
    4. 4.0"

59. Cement and what two types of mortar are approved for filling the cellular spaces in isolated piers to support beams and girders?

1. Type O or Type S
2. Type N or Type O
3. Type M or Type N
4. Type M or Type S

60. A dwelling that contains two-family dwelling units shall have what type of wall separation between units?

1. 30-minute fire-resistance rating
2. 1-hour fire-resistance rating
3. 90-minute fire-resistance rating
4. 2-hour fire-resistance rating

61. What size corrosion-resistant mesh screen shall be used for protecting exterior air intakes supplying combustion air to a fireplace?

1. 1/16"
2. 1/8"
3. 1/4"
4. 3/8"

62. How long shall the building department maintain construction documents after the project is completed?

1. 90 days
2. 180 days
3. 240 days
4. 360 days

63. What is the MAXIMUM slope that can be used for the construction of residential ramps?

1. 1 unit vertical in 9 units horizontal
2. 1 unit vertical in 10 units horizontal
3. 1 unit vertical in 11 units horizontal
4. 1 unit vertical in 12 units horizontal

64. When a building foundation is built with wood, what MINIMUM size studs are used for the foundation walls?

1. 2" x 4"
2. 2" x 6"
3. 2" x 8"
4. 2" x 10"

65. Wood shingle roofs shall have an ice barrier that extends from the roof edge to what MINIMUM distance inside the exterior wall line?

    1. 18"
    2. 24"
    3. 30"
    4. 36"

66. In areas of the country where snow is a factor on concrete and clay roof tiles, what MINIMUM amount of fasteners are required on each tile?

    1. 1 fastener
    2. 2 fasteners
    3. 3 fasteners
    4. 4 fasteners

67. What is the MAXIMUM flame spread index allowed for fire-retardant-treated wood used for roof framing?

    1. 10
    2. 15
    3. 20
    4. 25

68. Each dwelling unit shall be provided with at least one egress door that has a MINIMUM clear height of

    1. 76" and shall not require a key to open.
    2. 78" and shall not require a key to open.
    3. 80" and shall not require a key to open.
    4. 82" and shall not require a key to open.

69. What is the MINIMUM height of a parapet from the point it intersects with the sloped roof's surface to the top of the parapet?

    1. 24"
    2. 30"
    3. 36"
    4. 42"

70. What is the MAXIMUM square footage of an accessory structure located on the same lot as a residence?

    1. 1,000 sq. feet
    2. 2,000 sq. feet
    3. 3,000 sq. feet
    4. 4,000 sq. feet

71. What MINIMUM distance above the top of the fireplace opening shall the ferrous metal damper be located on a masonry fireplace?

    1. 6"
    2. 8"
    3. 10"
    4. 12"

72. What is the MINIMUM amount of clearance required in front of a water closet in a residential home?

    1. 21"
    2. 22"
    3. 23"
    4. 24"

73. When installing a foundation on Soil Group I, Soil Classification SM, comprised of silty sands and sand-silt mixtures, what is the frost heave characteristic of this type of soil?

    1. Unsatisfactory
    2. Poor
    3. Good
    4. Medium

74. A truss design drawing must be submitted and approved before the trusses are installed. Who receives the truss design drawings?

    1. Building official
    2. Building contractor
    3. Testing agency
    4. Plans examiner

75. Precast wall panels shall have a MINIMUM of two ties per panel with a nominal tensile strength of

    1. 10,000 lbs. per tie.
    2. 15,000 lbs. per tie.
    3. 20,000 lbs. per tie.
    4. 25,000 lbs. per tie.

76. What is the MINIMUM thickness of slab-on-ground concrete floors supported directly on the ground?

    1. 3"
    2. 3.5"
    3. 4"
    4. 4.5"

77. What is the MAXIMUM thickness of stone veneer that is installed over a backing of wood or cold-formed steel?

    1. 4"
    2. 5"
    3. 6"
    4. 7"

78. What is the MINIMUM tread depth that can be used for a residential stairway?

    1. 8 inches
    2. 9 inches
    3. 10 inches
    4. 11 inches

79. All of the following cast-in-place construction activities are covered under the ACI 318 Structural Concrete Building Code EXCEPT

    1. footings.
    2. foundation walls.
    3. tanks.
    4. slabs-on-ground for dwellings.

80. Interior spaces intended for human occupancy shall have a heating system capable of maintaining what level of temperature measured 3 feet off the floor?

    1. 68°F
    2. 69°F
    3. 70°F
    4. 71°F

81. What MINIMUM amount of fasteners shall be used on a roofing strip shingle?

    1. 2 fasteners
    2. 3 fasteners
    3. 4 fasteners
    4. 5 fasteners

82. Openings in exterior masonry veneer shall have additional ties used around the openings when the size of the openings exceed

    1. 14" in either direction.
    2. 16" in either direction.
    3. 18" in either direction.
    4. 20" in either direction.

83. What size floor joist shall be used when joist spacing is 24" with #2 Hem-fir wood and a dead load of 20 psf to achieve a 12 foot span used for a residential living area?

    1. 2" x 6"
    2. 2" x 8"
    3. 2" x 10"
    4. 2" x 12"

84. Where shall the permit for a job be kept until the job is completed?

    1. In the contractor's office
    2. In the contractor's truck
    3. On the job site
    4. At city hall

85. What MINIMUM distance shall a wall tie be embedded in the mortar joints of solid masonry units?

    1. 3/4"
    2. 1-3/8"
    3. 1-1/2"
    4. 1-5/8"

86. Glass unit masonry panels shall be provided with expansion joints along the top, bottom and sides at all structural supports. What is the MINIMUM thickness of the expansion joints?

    1. 1/4"
    2. 3/8"
    3. 1/2"
    4. 5/8"

87. A cold formed 33 KSI steel floor joist with the designation of 1000S162-54 is being used for a building having a live load of 30 psf and a joist spacing of 24". What is the MAXIMUM distance the joist can span?

    1. 16' 8"
    2. 17' 3"
    3. 18' 6"
    4. 19' 9"

88. What type of separation is required between a garage and all habitable rooms located above the garage?

    1. 1/2" gypsum board or equivalent
    2. 1/2" Type X gypsum board or equivalent
    3. 5/8" gypsum board or equivalent
    4. 5/8" Type X gypsum board or equivalent

89. When admixtures are used in producing flowing concrete, they shall conform to which of the following Standards?

    1. ASTM C260
    2. ASTM C494
    3. ASTM C845
    4. ASTM C1017

90. Particle board used for floor underlayment shall conform to Type PBU and shall have a MINIMUM thickness of

    1. 1/4".
    2. 3/8".
    3. 1/2".
    4. 5/8".

91. How long before a permit becomes null and void if work is not started?

    1. 90 days
    2. 120 days
    3. 180 days
    4. 360 days

92. A double top plate shall have end joints offset at what MINIMUM distance?

    1. 18"
    2. 24"
    3. 30"
    4. 36"

93. Concrete used for basement walls that are exposed to moderate weather shall have what MINIMUM strength?

    1. 2,500 lbs.
    2. 2,800 lbs.
    3. 3,000 lbs.
    4. 3,200 lbs.

94. What is the MAXIMUM height for a riser on a residential stairway?

    1. 7"
    2. 7.25"
    3. 7.5"
    4. 7.75"

95. Concrete walls constructed with a thickness of more than 10" shall have reinforcement placed in 2 layers in both directions and also 2 bars. What size bars shall be used?

    1. No. 3 bars
    2. No. 4 bars
    3. No. 5 bars
    4. No. 6 bars

96. What MINIMUM amount of glazing is required to give a room natural light?

    1. 6% of the floor area of the room served
    2. 8% of the floor area of the room served
    3. 10% of the floor area of the room served
    4. 12% of the floor area of the room served

97. What is the MINIMUM lumber framing material recommended for structural insulated panel ("SIP") walls?

    1. No. 2 Southern pine
    2. No. 2 Hem-fir
    3. No. 2 Douglas-fir-larch
    4. No. 2 Spruce-pine-fir

98. The doubled cantilevered joists used for the cantilever of the first floor of a one story building shall extend what MINIMUM distance toward the inside of the building?

    1. 5 feet
    2. 6 feet
    3. 7 feet
    4. 8 feet

99. When installing glass unit masonry, what is the required thickness of the bed and head joints?

    1. 1/4"
    2. 3/8"
    3. 1/2"
    4. 5/8"

100. A kitchen is required in each dwelling unit. What is required to be installed in every kitchen?

    1. Stove
    2. Sink
    3. Range
    4. Refrigerator

101. Hallways in homes are used for egress. What is the MINIMUM allowed width of hallways?

    1. 34"
    2. 35"
    3. 36"
    4. 37"

102. When digging exterior footings, what is the MINIMUM distance a footing shall be placed below undisturbed soil?

    1. 12"
    2. 16"
    3. 20"
    4. 24"

103. When a crawl space is located under a floor that is not insulated, the crawl space walls shall be insulated from the floor down to the finished grade and an additional

    1. 20".
    2. 22".
    3. 24".
    4. 26".

104. When installing a foundation on Soil Group III, Soil Classification CH, comprised of inorganic clays of high plasticity or fat clays, what is the drainage characteristic of this type of soil?

    1. Unsatisfactory
    2. Poor
    3. Medium
    4. Good

105. What is the MAXIMUM amount of roof eave projection for a detached garage located within 2 feet of a lot line?

    1. 4"
    2. 6"
    3. 8"
    4. 10"

106. Exterior concrete that is exposed to the freezing-and-thawing cycle is listed as a Category F concrete. Which class of Category F concrete is exposed to the freezing-and-thawing cycles and in continuous contact with moisture?

    1. F0
    2. F1
    3. F2
    4. F3

107. All of the following steel roof framing members should be attached with No. 10 screws EXCEPT

    1. roof sheathing to rafters.
    2. truss to bearing wall.
    3. gable end truss to endwall top track.
    4. ceiling joist to top track of load-bearing wall.

108. Masonry chimneys shall have a cleanout located what distance from the base of each flue?

    1. 2"
    2. 4"
    3. 6"
    4. 8"

109. What is the MINIMUM clear width of a spiral stairway at and below the railing in a residential home?

    1. 25"
    2. 26"
    3. 27"
    4. 29"

110. All of the following masonry units can be used for load bearing construction EXCEPT

    1. clay.
    2. cement.
    3. solid.
    4. glass.

111. On what MINIMUM design roof slope can a liquid-applied roofing material be installed?

    1. One-eighth unit vertical in 12 units horizontal
    2. One-fourth unit vertical in 12 units horizontal
    3. One-third unit vertical in 12 units horizontal
    4. One-half unit vertical in 12 units horizontal

112. Wood foundations built in soil that is Class II, III and IV shall be equipped with a drainage system including a sump that is installed at least

    1. 24" below the bottom of the basement floor.
    2. 26" below the bottom of the basement floor.
    3. 28" below the bottom of the basement floor.
    4. 30" below the bottom of the basement floor.

113. In ceilings that do not have an attic space, what is the MINIMUM amount of insulation that will be required?

    1. R-26
    2. R-28
    3. R-30
    4. R-32

114. When a cold formed steel framed wall is being attached to a foundation by anchor bolts, the anchor bolts shall extend a MINIMUM of

    1. 12" into a masonry foundation.
    2. 13" into a masonry foundation.
    3. 14" into a masonry foundation.
    4. 15" into a masonry foundation.

115. What MINIMUM distance shall be maintained between adhered masonry veneer and a paved surface area?

    1. 1"
    2. 2"
    3. 3"
    4. 4"

116. Foam plastic insulation used for thermal insulating or acoustic purposes shall have a MINIMUM density of

    1. 10 pounds per cubic foot.
    2. 15 pounds per cubic foot.
    3. 20 pounds per cubic foot.
    4. 25 pounds per cubic foot.

117. What is the MAXIMUM cantilever span for a floor joist supporting an exterior balcony using 2" x 10" members with 16" spacing and a ground snow load of 50 psf?

    1. 39"
    2. 49"
    3. 54"
    4. 67"

118. Masonry fireplaces shall have the firebox lined with fire brick that has a MINIMUM thickness of

    1. 1-1/4".
    2. 1-1/2".
    3. 1-3/4".
    4. 2".

119. Structures built with an unvented under-the-floor crawl space shall have a Class 1 vapor barrier installed over the exposed earth. There is a second requirement for ventilation of the crawl space which can be a continuously operating mechanical exhaust system or a conditioned air supply. What rate of flow shall be needed to meet the ventilation requirement of exhaust or supply?

    1. 1 cubic foot per minute flow per 20 sq. ft. of floor area.
    2. 1 cubic foot per minute flow per 30 sq. ft. of floor area.
    3. 1 cubic foot per minute flow per 40 sq. ft. of floor area.
    4. 1 cubic foot per minute flow per 50 sq. ft. of floor area.

120. What is the MAXIMUM span of a 2" x 8" Hem-fir SS grade ceiling joist used for a residential living area and joist spacing of 16" with a live load of 40 psf and a dead load of 10 psf?

    1. 11' 11"
    2. 12' 0"
    3. 12' 10"
    4. 13' 4"

121. What shall be the MINIMUM fire separation distance for exterior walls with a 0 hour fire-resistance rating?

    1. $\geq$ 3 feet
    2. $\geq$ 4 feet
    3. $\geq$ 5 feet
    4. $\geq$ 6 feet

122. How long shall the records of concrete inspection be kept by the inspecting engineer or architect after the project is completed?

    1. 6 months
    2. 1 year
    3. 1.5 years
    4. 2 years

123. What MINIMUM clearance is required for all combustible materials including wood beams, joists and studs from the front faces and sides of masonry fireplaces?

    1. 2" clearance
    2. 3" clearance
    3. 4" clearance
    4. 5" clearance

124. The base flashings used against a vertical sidewall shall direct water away from the sidewall and be continuous or step design. What is the MINIMUM size of the flashing?

    1. 3" x 3"
    2. 4" x 4"
    3. 5" x 5"
    4. 6" x 6"

125. When a window greater than 16" in either dimension is located in a wall with a masonry veneer, the metal ties around the perimeter of the opening shall be placed within

    1. 12" of the wall opening.
    2. 14" of the wall opening.
    3. 16" of the wall opening.
    4. 18" of the wall opening.

126. In Seismic Design Categories D_0, D_1 and D_2, what size vertical reinforcement bar should be used for masonry stem walls?

    1. No. 3
    2. No. 4
    3. No. 5
    4. No. 6

127. How many and what type of fastener should be used to secure the following roof element: ceiling joists to plate?

    1. 3 - 6d common, toe nailed
    2. 3 - 8d common, toe nailed
    3. 3 - 10d common, toe nailed
    4. 3 - 16d common, toe nailed

128. Grade No. 2 wood shingles that are 24" length and installed on a 3:12 pitch roof shall have how much weather exposure?

    1. 4.5"
    2. 5.0"
    3. 5.5"
    4. 6.0"

129. What is the MINIMUM net clear opening square footage required for an emergency escape and rescue opening?

    1. 5.7 sq. feet
    2. 5.8 sq. feet
    3. 5.9 sq. feet
    4. 5.10 sq. feet

130. What size ceiling joist shall be used when rafter spacing is 16" on center and has a dead load of 10 psf with #1 Southern pine to achieve a span of 20 feet for uninhabitable attics without storage?

    1. 2" x 4"
    2. 2" x 6"
    3. 2" x 8"
    4. 2" x 10"

131. What is the MAXIMUM spacing between lateral ties used for reinforcement in a masonry column?

    1. 6"
    2. 8"
    3. 10"
    4. 12"

132. Every dwelling built shall have at least one habitable room with MINIMUM square footage of

    1. 100 sq. feet.
    2. 110 sq. feet.
    3. 120 sq. feet.
    4. 130 sq. feet.

133. Wood roof shakes that are preservative-treated taper sawn, made of No. 1 Southern Yellow Pine, and are 24" long shall have an exposure on a MINIMUM 4:12 roof of

1. 5-1/2".
2. 7-1/2".
3. 10".
4. 12".

134. All of the following information shall be included on the Certificate of Occupancy EXCEPT the

1. building permit number.
2. name of the building official.
3. address of the dwelling.
4. legal description of the property.

135. What is the MINIMUM thickness of aluminum used for valley lining material?

1. 0.0162"
2. 0.0179"
3. 0.024"
4. 0.027"

136. If a permit extension is granted to the permit holder, how long is each extension good for?

1. 30 days
2. 60 days
3. 90 days
4. 180 days

137. Exterior masonry veneer that is anchored with metal strand wire ties shall have an air space between the veneer and the sheathing. What is the MAXIMUM allowed amount of air space?

1. 3.0"
2. 3-1/2"
3. 4.0"
4. 4-1/2"

138. Fire-retardant-treated lumber used for roof framing shall use chemicals in a closed vessel pressure process with a MINIMUM of

1. 30 psig.
2. 40 psig.
3. 50 psig.
4. 60 psig.

139. Footings that are poured on piles shall be what MINIMUM depth above the bottom reinforcement?

1. 6"
2. 8"
3. 10"
4. 12"

140. A skylight on a roof sloped less than a 3:12 pitch shall be mounted on what MINIMUM height curb above the roof?

1. 2"
2. 4"
3. 6"
4. 8"

141. What is the MINIMUM length of a hearth extension on a fireplace with an opening of 6 square feet or larger?

1. 16" in front of the fireplace
2. 18" in front of the fireplace
3. 20" in front of the fireplace
4. 22" in front of the fireplace

142. What MINIMUM lap is required when installing horizontal fiber cement siding?

1. 1"
2. 1.25"
3. 1.50"
4. 1.75"

143. What is the MAXIMUM length of glass sections used in louvered windows or jalousies?

1. 48"
2. 52"
3. 56"
4. 60"

144. What is the MINIMUM square footage of a manufactured home when completely erected on site?

1. 300 sq. feet
2. 320 sq. feet
3. 340 sq. feet
4. 360 sq. feet

127. How many and what type of fastener should be used to secure the following roof element: ceiling joists to plate?

    1.   3 - 6d common, toe nailed
    2.   3 - 8d common, toe nailed
    3.   3 - 10d common, toe nailed
    4.   3 - 16d common, toe nailed

128. Grade No. 2 wood shingles that are 24" length and installed on a 3:12 pitch roof shall have how much weather exposure?

    1.   4.5"
    2.   5.0"
    3.   5.5"
    4.   6.0"

129. What is the MINIMUM net clear opening square footage required for an emergency escape and rescue opening?

    1.   5.7 sq. feet
    2.   5.8 sq. feet
    3.   5.9 sq. feet
    4.   5.10 sq. feet

130. What size ceiling joist shall be used when rafter spacing is 16" on center and has a dead load of 10 psf with #1 Southern pine to achieve a span of 20 feet for uninhabitable attics without storage?

    1.   2" x 4"
    2.   2" x 6"
    3.   2" x 8"
    4.   2" x 10"

131. What is the MAXIMUM spacing between lateral ties used for reinforcement in a masonry column?

    1.   6"
    2.   8"
    3.   10"
    4.   12"

132. Every dwelling built shall have at least one habitable room with MINIMUM square footage of

    1.   100 sq. feet.
    2.   110 sq. feet.
    3.   120 sq. feet.
    4.   130 sq. feet.

133. Wood roof shakes that are preservative-treated taper sawn, made of No. 1 Southern Yellow Pine, and are 24" long shall have an exposure on a MINIMUM 4:12 roof of

    1. 5-1/2".
    2. 7-1/2".
    3. 10".
    4. 12".

134. All of the following information shall be included on the Certificate of Occupancy EXCEPT the

    1. building permit number.
    2. name of the building official.
    3. address of the dwelling.
    4. legal description of the property.

135. What is the MINIMUM thickness of aluminum used for valley lining material?

    1. 0.0162"
    2. 0.0179"
    3. 0.024"
    4. 0.027"

136. If a permit extension is granted to the permit holder, how long is each extension good for?

    1. 30 days
    2. 60 days
    3. 90 days
    4. 180 days

137. Exterior masonry veneer that is anchored with metal strand wire ties shall have an air space between the veneer and the sheathing. What is the MAXIMUM allowed amount of air space?

    1. 3.0"
    2. 3-1/2"
    3. 4.0"
    4. 4-1/2"

138. Fire-retardant-treated lumber used for roof framing shall use chemicals in a closed vessel pressure process with a MINIMUM of

    1. 30 psig.
    2. 40 psig.
    3. 50 psig.
    4. 60 psig.

139. Footings that are poured on piles shall be what MINIMUM depth above the bottom reinforcement?

    1. 6"
    2. 8"
    3. 10"
    4. 12"

140. A skylight on a roof sloped less than a 3:12 pitch shall be mounted on what MINIMUM height curb above the roof?

    1. 2"
    2. 4"
    3. 6"
    4. 8"

141. What is the MINIMUM length of a hearth extension on a fireplace with an opening of 6 square feet or larger?

    1. 16" in front of the fireplace
    2. 18" in front of the fireplace
    3. 20" in front of the fireplace
    4. 22" in front of the fireplace

142. What MINIMUM lap is required when installing horizontal fiber cement siding?

    1. 1"
    2. 1.25"
    3. 1.50"
    4. 1.75"

143. What is the MAXIMUM length of glass sections used in louvered windows or jalousies?

    1. 48"
    2. 52"
    3. 56"
    4. 60"

144. What is the MINIMUM square footage of a manufactured home when completely erected on site?

    1. 300 sq. feet
    2. 320 sq. feet
    3. 340 sq. feet
    4. 360 sq. feet

145. What is the MINIMUM nominal thickness for concrete wall members that are vertical or horizontal and made with a waffle-grid wall system?

    1.　4"
    2.　6"
    3.　8"
    4.　10"

146. A permanent wood foundation built for a crawl space shall have a base of gravel or crushed stone under the footing with a MINIMUM thickness of

    1.　3".
    2.　4".
    3.　5".
    4.　6".

147. What is the MINIMUM height that nonabsorbent walls shall extend above the floor of a shower?

    1.　5 feet
    2.　5.5 feet
    3.　6 feet
    4.　6.5 feet

148. What is the MAXIMUM length of an eave overhang on a residential home when measured horizontally?

    1.　20"
    2.　24"
    3.　28"
    4.　32"

149. What is the MINIMUM lap amount for horizontal lap siding that is rabbeted?

    1.　0.5"
    2.　0.75"
    3.　1.0"
    4.　1.5"

150. Metal shingle roofs shall have an ice barrier that consists of two layers of underlayment cemented together that extends from the roof edge to what MINIMUM distance inside the exterior wall line?

    1.　18"
    2.　20"
    3.　24"
    4.　30"

CORRECT ANSWER KEYS

1. Key 1	39. Key 2	77. Key 2	115. Key 2
2. Key 3	40. Key 4	78. Key 3	116. Key 3
3. Key 1	41. Key 3	79. Key 3	117. Key 2
4. Key 1	42. Key 1	80. Key 1	118. Key 4
5. Key 3	43. Key 2	81. Key 3	119. Key 4
6. Key 3	44. Key 2	82. Key 2	120. Key 3
7. Key 1	45. Key 4	83. Key 4	121. Key 3
8. Key 2	46. Key 3	84. Key 3	122. Key 4
9. Key 4	47. Key 4	85. Key 3	123. Key 1
10. Key 2	48. Key 1	86. Key 2	124. Key 2
11. Key 3	49. Key 2	87. Key 3	125. Key 1
12. Key 4	50. Key 4	88. Key 4	126. Key 1
13. Key 2	51. Key 3	89. Key 3	127. Key 2
14. Key 4	52. Key 4	90. Key 1	128. Key 3
15. Key 2	53. Key 1	91. Key 3	129. Key 1
16. Key 2	54. Key 3	92. Key 2	130. Key 3
17. Key 4	55. Key 2	93. Key 3	131. Key 2
18. Key 1	56. Key 1	94. Key 4	132. Key 3
19. Key 3	57. Key 2	95. Key 3	133. Key 3
20. Key 4	58. Key 3	96. Key 2	134. Key 4
21. Key 3	59. Key 4	97. Key 4	135. Key 3
22. Key 2	60. Key 2	98. Key 2	136. Key 4
23. Key 2	61. Key 3	99. Key 1	137. Key 4
24. Key 1	62. Key 2	100. Key 2	138. Key 3
25. Key 4	63. Key 4	101. Key 3	139. Key 4
26. Key 2	64. Key 2	102. Key 1	140. Key 2
27. Key 2	65. Key 2	103. Key 3	141. Key 3
28. Key 3	66. Key 2	104. Key 2	142. Key 2
29. Key 1	67. Key 4	105. Key 1	143. Key 1
30. Key 4	68. Key 2	106. Key 3	144. Key 2
31. Key 3	69. Key 2	107. Key 1	145. Key 2
32. Key 1	70. Key 3	108. Key 3	146. Key 4
33. Key 3	71. Key 2	109. Key 2	147. Key 3
34. Key 1	72. Key 1	110. Key 4	148. Key 2
35. Key 2	73. Key 4	111. Key 2	149. Key 1
36. Key 2	74. Key 1	112. Key 1	150. Key 3
37. Key 1	75. Key 1	113. Key 3	
38. Key 1	76. Key 2	114. Key 4	

1 Exam Prep
Modern Masonry
Questions and Answers

In masonry work, what tool is used to make long horizontal joints?

      Sled runner jointer
      Joint raker
      Line jointer
      Line runner

Concrete pours of up to how high can be consolidated by rodding or vibration?

      8 inches
      10 inches
      12 inches
      14 inches

What type of brick is used in dry conditions and exposed to freezing weather?

      SW
      MW
      NW
      FBX

Brick that will come in contact with ground water and freezing conditions should be type_____.

      MW
      NW
      SW
      FBA

With masonry, what unit of measure is used in a modular grid system?

      1"
      3"
      4"
      5"

What is the nominal size of a modular brick?

    2" x 2 1/3" x 8"
    3" x 2 2/3" x 8"
    4" x 2 1/3" x 8"
    4" x 2 2/3" x 8"

What percentage of a brick must be solid for it to be considered solid?

    95%
    85%
    75%
    65%

What is the white powder that forms on a masonry wall after exposure to moisture?

    Efflorescence
    Chalk dust
    Fluoropolymer
    Sodium bicarbonate

Five stretcher courses of brick with one header course describe what type of bond?

    Running
    Flemish
    English
    Common

When laying brick and all the vertical joints align, this is a_____.

    Dutch bond
    Stack bond
    Flemish bond
    American bond

Which brick pattern is considered the weakest bond?

    English cross bond
    Common bond
    Stack bond
    Running bond

What type of mortar joint is recommended in areas exposed to high winds and heavy rains?

Weathered joint
Concave
Troweled joint
Raked joint

What type of facing tile is used when a high degree of mechanical perfection is required?

FTX unglazed
FTS unglazed
SCR acoustile
SCR unglazed

What is the weight of an 8 x 8 x 16 CMU made of sand & gravel?

28 lbs.
35 lbs.
40 lbs.
42 lbs.

What is the highest strength aggregate in an 8 x 8 x 16 CMU?

Shale
Sand and gravel
Expanded slag
Scoria

Which CMU weighs the least per cubic foot of concrete?

Sand
Limestone
Air-cooled slag
Pumice

What is the standard size of a mortar joint when using standard concrete masonry units?

1/8"
¼"
3/8"
½"

What is not an advantage of a two core block CMU versus a three core block design?

        Reduced heat conductor
        Lighter
        More space for placing conduit
        The shell is narrower at the center web

The nominal size of an 8 inch stretcher block is_____.

        6 x 6 x 18
        8 x 8 x 16
        8 x 8 x 12
        10 x 10 x 18

A standard glass block mortar joint is how thick?

        1/8 inch
        ¼ inch
        ½ inch
        1/3 inch

To prevent moisture from entering the top of a masonry wall, you should use_____.

        Ceramic tile copings
        Plaster copings
        Wood copings
        Stone copings

What is the best stone to protect against moisture on sills?

        Limestone
        Granite
        Sandstone
        Slate

What is mortar mainly composed of?

        Blended cement
        Portland cement
        Hydrated lime
        Aggregate

What type of lime is used in mortar?

       Type N hydrated
       Type M hydrated
       Type S hydrated
       Type K hydrated

What is the primary aggregate used in mortar?

       Sand
       Quartz
       Crushed oyster shells
       Gravel

To avoid hardening due to hydration, mortar should be used within what time span after mixing?

       1 hour
       1 ½ hours
       2 hours
       2 ½ hours

What type of mortar is best suited for use below grade?

       Type S
       Type N
       Type M
       Type O

What is the most important property of hardened mortar?

       Compressive strength
       Bond strength
       Durability
       Weather ability

Which of the following is not a masonry mortar?

       Type P
       Type O
       Type K
       Type N

What is added to mortar to increase strength?

      Admixture
      Cement
      Aggregate
      Polymer

What type of mortar is used where wind speeds will exceed 80 miles per hour?

      Type K
      Type O
      Type S
      Type N

What type of mortar is used for interior non-load bearing partitions where high strength is not needed?

      Type S
      Type M
      Type N
      Type K

How many cubic feet of mortar are required for a single wythe brick wall that measures 200 square feet, has 3/8" mortar joints and has 655 non-modular brick units per 100 square feet?

      6.8 cubic feet
      11.6 cubic feet
      12.8 cubic feet
      14.4 cubic feet

Per 100 sq ft, using a 3/8" mortar joint, you will need how many brick and how many cubic feet of mortar?

      655 brick and 5.8 cubic feet of mortar
      616 brick and 7.2 cubic feet of mortar
      470 brick and 5.8 cubic feet of mortar
      432 brick and 4.5 cubic feet of mortar

The maximum height of grout lifts is usually how high?

       3 feet
       5 feet
       7 feet
       9 feet

With masonry, what gauge wire is ordinarily used for continuous horizontal joint reinforcement?

       5, 6, 7 & 8
       6, 7, 8 & 9
       7, 8, 9 & 10
       8, 9, 10 & 11

What is the closest an adjustable truss type brick tie should be from the edge of the brick?

       3/8"
       ¾"
       5/8"
       ½"

When masonry walls intersect, they may be connected with a?

       Strap anchor
       "L" bent bar anchor
       Hex coupling
       Acorn nut

When the cut edge will be hidden by the mortar, which hand tool is used to cut brick?

       Masonry saw
       Brick hammer
       Brick trowel
       Brick set chisel

When laying brick, what area of the building contains the leads?

       The foundation
       The first course
       The corners
       None of the above

Wall ties in a brick masonry cavity wall should be placed what distance from either edge of the masonry unit?

    3/16"
    3/8"
    5/8"
    ½"

Which masonry joint provides the best moisture protection?

    Weathered joint
    Toweled joint
    Raked joint
    Tooled joint

What is the recommended air pressure setting when sandblasting brick with a ¼" nozzle?

    50 – 100 lbs
    80 – 120 lbs
    60 – 120 lbs
    75 – 150 lbs

When sandblasting, what size nozzle should be used?

    1/8"
    1/4"
    3/8"
    2/3"

What is the best cleaning chemical for brick?

    Hydrochloric or muratic acid
    Sulfuric acid
    Diluted bleach
    Diluted ammonia

What is a two-wythe wall allowing each wythe to react independently to stress known as?

    Solid masonry wall
    Cavity wall
    Composite wall
    Reinforced concrete masonry wall

When using 9 gage ties in a composite wall, what is the proper separation of ties?

> One for every 4 1/4 square feet
> One for every 2 1/2 square feet
> One for every 4 1/2 square feet
> One for every 2 2/3 square feet

When constructing a two wythe wall, what is the most common cavity size?

> 1"
> 1.5"
> 2"
> 2.5"

What type of CMU is commonly used with reinforcement?

> Double bull nose block
> 2 core block
> 3 core block
> Sash block

What is used to anchor brick veneer to the structure?

> Corrugated metal ties
> Strap anchors
> Flat head anchor
> Veneer nails

When blocks are laid, they are positioned how?

> Narrow flange on top
> Wide flange on bottom
> Wide flange on top
> Narrow flange on bottom

When laying block, what distance should be maintained between the block and the mason's line?

> 1/16"
> 1/8"
> ¼"
> ½"

When laying an 8" concrete block wall, string out the blocks for the first course without mortar to check layout. Allow for _____ each mortar joint.

¼"
½"
3/8"
5/8"

The lead corner is usually laid up how many courses high?

Two to three courses
Three to four courses
Four or five courses high
Five to six courses

What diameter bar is used to make a 3/8" concave mortar joint?

1/8 inch
3/8 inch
5/8 inch
1/4 inch

What are the minimum cubic yards of cement required for 6 cubic yards of sand?

1 cubic yard
1.5 cubic yards
2 cubic yards
2.5 cubic yards

What type of footings are used for free standing columns or piers?

Stepped
Isolated
Combined
Continuous

Foundation walls that are being damp-proofed should be parged how many inches above the finish grade?

6"
5"
8"
10"

What are masonry exterior non-load bearing walls not supported at each story?

Panel wall
Cavity wall
Curtain walls
Solid masonry wall

How long must the outer wythe of a cavity wall be on each side of an external corner before expansion joints are recommended?

30 feet
50 feet
60 feet
65 feet

A brick veneer wall will not support loads.

True
False

What masonry structural member is placed over an opening in a wall used to support the loads above that opening?

Chases
Recesses
Lintel
Stirrups

Welded wire mesh for masonry should be lapped to what minimum distance?

One full wire grid spacing plus 1 inche
Two full wire grid spacing plus 1 inches
One full wire grid spacing plus 2 inches
Two full wire grid spacing plus 2 inches

How thick are terrazzo toppings typically?

¼"
½"
3/8"
¾"

What is filling voids in masonry with fresh mortar known as?

Tuck pointing
Joint tucking
Re-grouting
Joint pointing

What type of float is used to float large flat slabs?

Hand float
Bull float
Power float
None of the above

67. Open, unsupported stacks of brick should not exceed _____ feet in height.

A.   5"
B.   6"
C.   7"
D.   8"

68. To use a ladder safely be sure it extends at least _____ feet above the point where you plan to step off.

2"
2.5"
3"
3.5"

If a plan is drawn 1/4" = scale, how long on the drawing would a 40' wall be?

10 feet
10 inches
4 feet
4 inches

70. If a plan is drawn to ½" **size**, how long on the drawing would a 40' wall be?

10 feet
10 inches
4 feet
4 inches

71. A hollow masonry unit is one whose cross-sectional area in any plane is less than _____ % solid material.

        85
        80
        75
        70

The term that describes a white powder or salt like deposit on masonry walls is _____.

        Efflorescence
        Chalk dust
        Fluoropolymer
        Sodium bicarbonate

The simplest mortar joint to make is the _____ joint.

        Flush
        Rough cut
        Raked
        Both A and B

Hollow load bearing block, ASTM C90, Grade N will have an average minimum compressive strength of _____ psi (individual unit).

        600
        800
        900
        1000

An 8" x 8" x 16" block has actual dimensions of _____.

        7 5/8" x 7 5/8" x 15 5/8"
        7 5/8" x 7 3/8" x 15 7/8"
        7 3/8" x 7 3/8" x 15 3/8"
        7 15/16" x 7 15/16" x 15 15/16"

Stone is divided into three categories. They are all of the following EXCEPT:

        Metamorphic
        Quartzite
        Igneous
        Sedimentary

Mortar can be retempered by adding water but must be used within _____ hour(s) after original mixing.

    1 hour
    1.5 hours
    2 hours
    2.5 hours

What ASTM type mortar is used for general use in above ground exposed masonry?

    Type N
    Type O
    Type S
    Type M

For cavity walls where wind velocity exceeds 80 MPH use type_____mortar.

    Type N
    Type O
    Type S
    Type M

0.33 cu. ft. of cementious material and 0.99 cu. ft. of sand will make approximately _____cu. ft. of mortar.

    5
    2
    1.5
    1

How many cu. ft. of mortar is needed for 100 sq. ft. of wall laid with 8" x 8" x 16" block?

    1.2 cu. ft.
    1.3 cu. ft.
    1.5 cu. ft.
    1.6 cu. ft.

The minimum recommended compressive strength of grout is_____ psi.

    800
    1000
    2000
    3000

Grout should be placed within _____ hour(s) after water is first added.

    1
    1.5
    2
    2.5

Weepholes in cavity walls should be placed a maximum of _____ on center.

  1'
  2'
  3'
  4'

A tie for brick veneer walls is required for every _____ sq. ft. of wall area.

  2
  2 1/3
  2 2/3
  3 1/3

Control joints at the ends of lintelsare formed by raking the mortar joint out to a depth of _____ inches.

  1/2
  2/3
  3/4
  1/3

"Normal" Portland cement is Type _____.

  I
  II
  III
  IV

The most commonly used accelerating admixture is _____.

  Pozzolan
  Fly Ash
  Calcium hypochlorite
  Calcium Chloride

A(n) _____ is a piece of material that prevents the concrete from moving past a certain point in the form.

  Bulkhead
  Straightedge
  Builder's level
  Form wall

When placing concrete it should not be allowed to drop more than _____.

  2' to 3'
  3' to 4'
  4' to 5'
  5' to 6'

The first finishing operation on a concrete slab is _____.

      Screeding
      Floating
      Troweling
      Brooming

Control joints should be cut in _____ to _____ hours after the slab has been finished.

      8 to 12
      6 to 12
      4 to 10
      4 to 12

Type I air-entrained concrete will achieve a strength of _____ psi after 3 1/2 days of curing.

      1000
      1500
      1750
      2000

To encourage complete hydration concrete should be cured for at least _____ days.

      1
      2
      3
      4

An 8" concrete block wall is to be constructed with one window opening of 8'-0" wide and 6'-0' high. According to the *Modern Masonry*, the minimum recommended length of precast lintel to span the window opening is _____.

      8'-4"
      8'-8"
      9'-0"
      9'-4

How many bricks 4" x 2 2/3" x 8" will be required to veneer a wall 4' high by 24' long? A 3/8" mortar joints is to be used. How many cubic feet of mortar is required?

      655
      648
      616
      581

How much mortar will be needed to lay a wall 40'long and 8" high using 6" x 4" x 12" SCR bricks with ½"will be required to veneer a wall 4' high by 24' long? A 3/8" mortar joints is to be used. How many cubic feet of mortar is required? The wall has three window openings 3' wide by 4' high.

21.02cu ft.
7.4 cu ft.
21.01 cu ft.
0.074 cu ft

—What is the sum of the following numbers?

$8\frac{1}{16} + \frac{3}{4} + \frac{3}{8} + \frac{1}{2}$

$8\frac{9}{16}$
$9\frac{15}{16}$
$9\frac{1}{2}$
$9\frac{11}{16}$

The space between the inner and outer walls in a concrete masonry cavity wall is _____ inches or more wide. "

1" to 2"
2"to 3"
2"to 4"
3"to 4"

Normal-weight concrete weighs more than _____ lb./cu. ft.

75
100
125
150

Mortar should be used _____ hours after mixing to avoid hardening due to hydration.

1
1-1/2
2
2-1/2

Efflorescence on masonry units is caused by _____ in wet brick or block being carried to the surface as water evaporates.

Rust
Soluble salts
Hydrated lime
Algae

Concrete masonry units should be wet down _____.

On very dry days
Before setting up
Never
None of the above

Which type of mortar bond is general the weakest?

Flemish
Block or stack
Common
English

105. What is the actual size and weight of a 8" x 8" x 16" cmu?

7-5/8" x 7-5/8" x 15-5/8" – 40 lbs.
8" x 8" x 16" – 35 lbs.
7-1/2" x 7-1/2" x 15-1/2" – 40 lbs.
7-5/8" x 7-5/8" x 15-5/8" – 27 lbs.

A concrete wearing surface like terrazzo is typically _____ inch think.

1/16
3/8
½
5/8

Which type of the following is not a masonry mortar type?

P

N

M

S

Jack arch construction should be supported by steel if the opening is over _____ feet.

5

4

3

2

The outside of a masonry basement wall should be parged from the footing to _____ inches above the finished grade.

4

6

8

12

ASTM mortar type _____ has high compressive strength and greater durability than other mortar types; its uses include structures below grade, manholes and catch basins.

M

S

K

N

1 Exam Prep
Modern Masonry
Answers

7th Ed. Page Numbers

1.	A	Page 12, top left of page186
2.	C	Page 13
3.	B	Page 72
4.	C	Page 72
5.	C	Page 73
6.	D	Page 74
7.	C	Page 77
8.	A	Page 79
9.	D	Page 83
10.	B	Page 84
11.	C	Page 84
12.	B	Page 85
13.	A	Pages 90-91
14.	C	Page 105
15.	B	Page 105
16.	D	Page 105
17.	C	Page 107
18.	D	Page 107
19.	B	Page 108
20.	B	Page 115
21.	D	Page 126
22.	A	Page 126
23.	B	Page 131
24.	C	Page 132
25.	A	Page 132
26.	D	Page 134
27.	C	Page 134
28.	B	Page 134

29. A	Page 134
30. B	Page 134
31. C	Page 135
32. D	Page 135
33. B	Page 138, (refer to figure 8-8, double the amount).
34. A	Page 138
35. B	Page 139
36. D	Page 144
37. C	Page 146
38. A	Page 149
39. B	Page 156
40. C	Page 158
41. C	Page 169
42. D	Page 169
43. C	Page 176, right side of page
44. B	Page 176, right side of page
45. A	Page 176
46. B	Page 181
47. D	Page 181
48. C	Page 181
49. B	Page 182
50. A	Page 182
51. C	Page 185
52. A	Page 186, right side of page, 3rd paragraph
53. C	Page 187
54. C	Page 188
55. C	Page 189
56. A	Page 210
57. B	Page 217
58. A	Page 218
59. C	Page 224
60. B	Page 230
61. A	Page 231

62. C	Page 237
63. B	Page 273
64. B	Page 307
65. A	Page 377
66. B	Page 16
67. C	Page 24
68. C	Page 26
69. B	Page 35
70. A	Page 35
71. C	Page 77
72. A	Page 79
73. D	Page 86
74. B	Page 106
75. A	Page 107
76. B	Page 120
77. C	Page 133
78. A	Page 134
79. C	Page 135
80. D	Page 137
81. D	Page 137
82. C	Page 139
83. B	Page 139
84. B	Page 230
85. C	Page 231
86. C	Page 237
87. A	Page 264
88. D	Page 266
89. A	Page 287
90. B	Page 298
91. A	Page 299
92. D	Page 301
93. B	Page 302
94. C	Page 303

95. D   Page 237   8 ft. + 8 in. + 8 in = 9'4"

96. B   Page 65

97. A   Page 66

98. D   Page 55

99. B   Page 227

100. C   Page 271

    D

    B

    C

    B

    A

    C

    A

    D

    B

    A

1 Exam Prep
Finish Carpenters Manual
Questions and Answers

The smooth, even surfaces we install have to fit right because they're_____.
always in full view.
two dimensional.
three dimensional.
cut to the exact size

The basic clothing and safety equipment needed by a professional finish carpenter include
_____?

Hard hat.
Gloves.
Air Scrubber
Workpants, workboots, hearing and eye protection.

3. _____ pouch tool bets are traditional.

Synthetic
Canvas
Leather
Linen

4. A _____ air compressor is recommended because a _____ can blow a 20-amp 120-volt circuit.

½ horse power, ¾ horse power
¾ horse power, 1 horse power
1 horse power, 1 ½ horse power
¼ horse power, ½ horse power

5. The advantage of using a _____ is that it doesn't require an air compressor and hoses for operation.

TrackFast
Finish Nailer
Impulse-fired finish gun
Brad tracker

6. The term_____ refers to horizontal finsish elements, such as base, crown and chair-rail moldings.

A. Running molding
B. Standing molding
C. Compression molding
D. Flexible molding

7. A man-made wood composed of compressed wood fibers and glue is_____?

    Plywood
    MDF Board
    Hardee Backer
    Particle Board

    A rough opening for a door should be _____ inches wider and _____ inches higher than the door.
A. 3 1/4
B. 4 C.
2 D. 1 ½

    A door should swing into_____.

A. A hallway.
B. Open space.
C. A corner wall.
D. the light switch side.

10. How many inches from the top should a hinge be spaced_____?

    11
    12
    6
    7

    When backing is missing at an inside corner drive a long finish nail at a _____ degree angle into the corner.

    22
    35
    90
    45

    Installing French doors is basically like hanging two _____ doors at the same time- though in other ways it's like hanging bypass or bifold doors.

    Passage
    Louver
    Impact Glass
    Half Glass

13. If the molding pattern you need is no longer available the best option is to_____.

A. Modify stock molding with a combination of router bits.
B. Modify stock molding using a combination of planes and scrapes.
C. To have molding custom made.
D. Remove all existing molding and replace it all.

14. After the doors are installed the next step is to install the _____?

    Locks
    Peep hole
    Casing
    Door knob

15. One of the main causes for hinges sagging is_____?

A. The door is too heavy.
B. The contractor did not tighten the screws enough.
C. The contractor did not install enough hinges.
D. The contractor did not properly reinforce the frame to support the door.

16. The best way to fix "grannies" is by using _____ on stain grade work.

    Non-shrinking or cracking fill.
    A iron and a damp cotton rag.
    A stainable wood fill.
    Bondo

17. What tool should be used to seat the railing in place over the balusters and newel post?

    Hammer
    Rubber Hammer
    Level
    Beating block

18. Contemporary window opening installations are simply wrapped by _____?

    Marble
    Quartz
    Exotic woods.
    Drywall.

    In a home framed with 2 x 6 instead of 2 x4, with windows designed for 4" studs, you'll have to install_____?
A. A different window made for 2 x 6.
B. Frame the opening with 2 x 4 secured to a 2 x 6.
C. Extension jambs.
D. The window into 2 x 6 opening.

Using a _____ speeds up the work and makes it easier to hold the drill bit at the proper angle without any guesswork.

Jig.
Speed square.
Laser level.
2 ft. level.

21. A _____ is useful for holding the joint tight, of a surround frame, while the glue dries.

C-Clamp.
Joint Master Angle Clamp.
Quick-grip pipe Clamp.
Spring Clamp.

22. If the rail is designed to be installed at 36 inches above the finished floor, the newel height is?

A. 36 inches plus the rail.
B. 36 inches minus the rail.
C. 34 inches.
D. 36 inches.

23. The _____ joint generally keeps a good tight joint throughout the life of the molding.

Mitter
Dowel
Coped
Splined

When a wood floor is ready to be finished the quickest way to get a room flat and ready to finish is by using a _____.

A. Random Orbit Sander.
B. Drum Sander.
C. Disc Sander.
D. Belt Sander.

25. Before starting any stair trim-out, be sure the stair carriage and proposed design will meet _____.

A. The owner's specifications.
B. The contractor's and owner's specifications.
C. An engineer's specifications.
D. Local building code specifications.

1 Exam Prep
Finish Carpenters Manual
Answers

No.	Answer	Page
1	A	5
2	D	7
3	C	8
4	B	20
5	C	17
6	A	28
7	B	27
8	D	34
9	C	39
10	D	43
11	D	177
12	A	50
13	C	175
14	C	54
15	A	172
16	B	57
17	B	170
18	D	60
19	C	61
20	A	167
21	D	67
22	B	165
23	C	85
24	B	145
25	D	151

1 Exam Prep

ASTM Standard Practice for Installation of Rigid Poly (Vinyl Chloride) (PVC) Siding and Soffit Questions

All fasteners such as nails, staples, and screws must be corrosion-resistant.

> True
> False

This flat material is used on the face of the house, applied between the studs and the siding to provide an even surface for the installation of vinyl siding.

> Flashing
> Fascia board
> Backerboard
> Siding

3. _____ is an accessory strip used to receive and hold the crimped edge of horizontal or vertical siding that has had its normal lock removed.

   A. Undersill trim
   B. Furring strip
   C. Snaplock ear
   D. Starter strip

4. A crimp is small protrusions approximately _____ inch long, _____ inch wide, and projecting _____ inch formed by a crimper.

   ¾, ½, ½
   ½, 1/8, 1/8
   ¼, ¼, ¼
   2/3, 1/8, ½

5. A crimper can also be referred to as _____.

   Unlocking tool
   Nail hole slot punch
   Snap lock punch
   Snap lock ears

When storing cartons which of the following should be followed:

   Store cartons in stacks of 12 boxes or less
   Store cartons on a flat surface and support the entire length of the cartons
   Store cartons away from areas where falling objects could impact them and keep cartons dry
   All of the above

7. The trim covering the ends of roof rafters is referred to as _____.

    Fascia
    Fascia board
    Fascia cap
    Buttlock

8. Staples should be a minimum of _____ gage and corrosion-resistant.

    19
    16
    8
    12

Fascia board is attached to the ends of the rafters between the roofing material and the _____overhang.

    Gable
    Soffit
    Fascia
    Undersill trim

This wooden or steel framing material is usually a nominal 1 by 2 in. used to even the surface in preparation for installation of siding.

    Furring strip
    Flashing
    Starter strip
    Utility trim

11. The inclined and usually projecting edge of a sloping roof is called _____.

    A. Gable
    B. Soffit
    C. Eave
    D. Rake

12. _____ is the action of fastening directly on the "face", or exposed surface, of a panel (instead of using the nail slot).

    A. Flashing
    B. Snap lock punch
    C. Crimp
    D. Face nail

13. The horizontal underside surface of roof overhangs is called the _____ .12

    Gable
    Soffit
    Eave
    Rake

14. Materials such as siding and soffit should not be stored in in any location where the temperature could exceed _____ °F.

    150
    130
    125
    105

15. _____ is the board or molding placed along the sloping sides of a gable to cover the ends of the siding.

    A. Rake
    B. Soffit
    C. Eave
    D. Fascia

16. When applied, vinyl siding products must be attached "loosely", leaving approximately a _____ inch. space between the vinyl and the fastener head or crown to permit thermal movement.

    A. 15/16
    B. 1/32
    C. ½
    D. ¾

17. _____ is special membrane pieces used to supplement siding panels in weather protection around joints and openings, designed and intended to move incidental water to the building exterior.

    Weather proofing
    Weather strip
    Flashing
    Weather-resistant furring strip

18. Provide _____ parallel slots to hold and support soffit panels.

    8
    4
    6
    2

This is an accessory applied directly to the surface of the building and used to secure the first course of siding to a home.

> Undersill trim
> Backerboard
> Snaplock ear
> Starter strip

20. The bottom of a siding or soffit panel located opposite the nail hem and locks into the preceding panel is referred to as _____ .

> Buttlock
> Rake
> Snaplock ear
> Starter strip

Which of the following is **not** true?

> Do not apply vinyl siding directly to studs without sheathing.
> Driving of fasteners directly into sheathing or existing siding is permitted in accordance with the siding manufacturer's instructions, where substantiated by windload testing conducted in accordance with Specification D3679.
> Masonry and uneven surfaces require wood furring strips nominal 1 by 2 in. (25.4 by 50.8 mm) applied horizontally and typically spaced 16 in (406 mm) on center for vertical siding.
> Do not use caulk where it could restrict the normal expansion of the vinyl siding."

22. Ends of starter strips should be kept _____ to _____ inch apart.

> A. ¼ to ¾
> B. ½ to ¾
> C. ¼ to ½
> D. ¾ to 1

Proper ventilation is not important for any home or dwelling.

> True
> False

When installing horizontal siding panel, it is necessary to lap the next panel over the first by approximately one-half of the factory cut notch, provided the overlap is at least ¾ in. (25.4 mm) but not greater than _____ inch.

> 2
> 1.5
> 1.25
> 1

25. When installing fascia, cut the fascia cover to the proper width and punch snaplock ears along the top of the fascia every _____ to _____ inches and snap into the undersill trim.

    A. 4 to 8
    B. 6 to 12
    C. 6 to 10
    D. 4 to 10

26. When installing horizontal siding panel, allow _____ inch clearance at the edges for insertion into each side of the J-channel.

    A. 1
    B. 1/4
    C. ½
    D. ¾

27. If a vertical siding panel is cut on the flat surface, place a piece of _____ , backed by furring, into the receiver of the corner post.

    Furring
    Flashing
    Starter strip
    Undersill trim

Nailing into a panel without pre-drilled holes has the potential to crack or kink the vinyl.

    True
    False

29. If necessary, use _____ to maintain the proper plane of siding.

    Furring
    Flashing
    Starter strip
    Utility trim

When applying vertical siding, cut the panels at windows and doors to fit the opening allowing inch for expansion.

    15/16
    1/4
    ½
    ¾

31. When installing shutters, drill expansion holes through the siding (siding only) where attachment screws will be located, a minimum of _____ inch larger than the diameter of the screws

    15/16
    1/4
    ½
    ¾

The following are typical siding profiles except:

    Vertical
    Double Dutch Lap
    Triple
    Single Dutch Lap

Weather-resistant barrier-Vinyl siding must be installed over a weather-resistant barrier system that includes:

    A continuous weather resistant material
    Properly integrated flashing around all penetrations and where vinyl siding interfaces with other building products.
    Referring to the manufacturer's installation instructions and minimum requirements of local building code for specific requirements
    All of the above

34. To determine the width of the final horizontal siding panel under an eave, measure from the _____ of the eave or soffit to the bottom of the preceding panel lock in several places along the full length of the panel and subtract _____ inch.

    A. Bottom, 1/2
    B. Top, 1/4
    C. Bottom, 1/4
    D. Top, ½

35. Each leg of corner posts should be attached with fasteners spaced not over _____ inches apart centered in nailing slots except the top fastener which is located at the upper end of the nailing slot.

    6
    8
    10
    12

ANSWER KEY

1. A 7.5
2. C 3.2.1
3. A 3.2.16
4. B 3.2.3
5. C 3.2.13
   D 5.2, 5.3, 5.4
7. A 3.2.6
8. B 7.5.2
9. B 3.2.6.2
10. A 3.2.8
11. D 3.2.10
12 D 3.2.5
13. B 3.2.14
14. B 5.1
15. A 3.2.11
16. B 9.1.1
17. C 3.2.7
18. D 11.2.1
19. C 3.2.15
20. A 3.2.2
   C 8.2, 8.3, 8.4, 8.7
   C 9.2.1
   B 11.1.1.1
   C 9.3.3
   B 11.4.2
   B 9.3.6
   D 10.10.2
   A 9.3.8.3
   A 9.3.8.3
   B 10.9
   B 12.3.2
32. D Fig. 3
33. D 8.1
34. C 9.3.9
35. D 9.2.2

1 Exam Prep
ANSI ICC A117.1-2017: Accessible and Usable Buildings and Facilities
Questions and Answers

1. All handicapped accessible parking spaces must be at least _____ inches in width.

    96
    110
    120
    92

2. Which of the following is the maximum slope allowed for ramps along accessible routes?

    1:8
    1:12
    1:16
    1:50

In new buildings and facilities, turning spaces shall be a circular space with a _____ inch minimum diameter.

    24
    32
    48
    67

4. The space between a wall and a grab bar shall be _____ inches.

A. 2 ¼
B. 1 ¼
C. 1 ½
D. 1 5/8

In new buildings, the maximum unobstructed height of an elevator call button shall not exceed_____.

A. 60 inches
B. 48 inches
C. 36 inches
D. 3 feet

Objects with leading edges more than 27 inches and not more than 80 inches above the floor shall protrude _____ inches maximum horizontally into a circulation path.

    2
    6
    4
    8

7. Elevator call buttons shall be _____ inch minimum in the smallest dimension.

    ¼
    ½
    ¾
    1

Openings in floor surfaces shall be of a size that does not permit the passage of a _____ inch diameter sphere.

    ¼
    ½
    ¾
    1

9. The front of a kitchen sink shall be _____ inches maximum above the floor.

    24
    34
    48
    60

10. _____ is a walking surface that has a running slope steeper than 1:20.

    Ramp
    Gangway
    Curb ramp
    Use zone

11. Handrails shall be permitted to protrude _____ inches maximum.

A. 2 ¼
B. 2 ½
C. 3 ½
D. 4 ½

12. The clear width of an interior accessible route shall be _____ inches minimum.

    28
    36
    48
    60

13. Thresholds at doorways shall be _____ inch maximum in height.

A. 2 ½
B. 1 ½
    ½
    ¾

    For a private residence elevator, the level of illumination at the car controls shall be _____ foot candles minimum.

    10
    8
    5
    3

    Visual characters for signs shall be _____ inches minimum above the floor of the viewing position, measured to the baseline of the character.

    40
    42
    48
    52

    Grab bars shall be installed in a horizontal position _____ inches minimum above the floor measured from the top of the gripping surface.

    28
    33
    36
    42

    Ramp handrails shall extend horizontally above the landing _____ inches minimum beyond the top and bottom of the ramp runs.

    9
    10
    12
    15

Where accessible parking spaces are required to be identified by signs, such signs shall be _____ inches minimum above the floor of the parking space, measured to the bottom of the sign.

48
52
56
60

19. Access aisles serving car and van parking spaces shall be ____ inches minimum in width.

56
60
72
96

Knee clearance shall be permitted to extend ____inches maximum under an element at 9 inches above the floor.

24
25
32
35

21. Spout outlets of wheelchair accessible drinking fountains shall be _____ inches maximum above the floor.

40
38
36
34

Clearance around a water closet shall be ____ inches minimum in depth, measured perpendicular from the rear wall. .

56
60
72
96

Van parking spaces shall be _____ inches minimum in width where the adjacent access aisle is 96 inches minimum in width.

96
102
122
132

24. Parking spaces and access aisles shall have surface slopes not steeper than _____.

    1:12
    1:16
    1:48
    1:50

    Grab bars 18 inches minimum in length installed in a vertical position in water closets and toilet compartments shall be mounted _____ inches maximum above the floor.

    33
    41
    39
    42

26. Doorways shall have a clear opening width of _____ inches minimum.

    42
    38
    36
    32

27. Toe clearance shall be permitted to extend ____inches maximum under an element.

    24
    25
    32
    35

    Emergency control buttons in an elevator shall have their centerlines _____ inches minimum above the floor.

    35
    34
    32
    30

29. The height of water closet seats shall be _____ inches maximum above the floor.

    17
    18
    19
    20

30. Ramp runs with a rise greater than _____ inches shall have handrails complying with Section 505.

    10
    8
    6
    4

1 Exam Prep
ANSI ICC A117.1-2017: Accessible and Usable Buildings and Facilities
Answers

1. A   502.2
2. B   405.2
3. D   304.3.1.1
4. C   609.3
    B   407.2.1.1 / 308.2.1
    C   307.2
    C   407.2.1.2
    B   302.3
    B   1103.12.4.2
    A   107.5, ramp
    D   307.2, exception
    B   403.5.1
    C   404.2.4
    C   409.4.5
    A   703.2.9
    B   609.4.1
    C   505.10.1
    D   502.7
    B   502.4.2
    B   306.3.2
    C   602.2.3
    A   604.3.2
    D   502.2
    C   502.5
    B   604.5.1.2
    D   404.2.2
    B   306.2.2
    A   407.4.6.4.1
    C   604.4
    C   405.8

1 Exam Prep
Painting: General Mathematics and Calculations
Questions and Answers

How many cubic yards of material will be excavated from a trench 6' deep x 3' wide x 100' long?

_____

○ 66.67

○ 75.70

○ 75.67

75.69

A Painting job can be completed in 12 hours by 3 professional painters. The same job can be completed in 6 hours by 6 professional painters. All professional painters paint at the same rate. What is the total amount of time it would take 9 professional painters to complete the same painting job?

_____

○ 40 hours

○ 14 hours

○ 4 hours

3 hours

Two houses painters can paint 3 houses in 4 hours. How long would it take 5 house painters to paint 2 houses if they work at the same rate as the 2 house painters? _____ hrs.

_____

○ 17/15

○ 16/13

○ 12/15

16/15

The local painters union recieved an unusual and urgent request to paint 2 houses in 4 hours. If each painter can paint one house in 10 hours, how many painters will it take to accommodate this request?

- ○ 5
- ○ 6
- ○ 7
- ○ 10

Ten people can paint 60 houses in 120 days, so five people can paint 30 houses in _____ days.

- ○ 170
- ○ 121
- ○ 120
- ○ 220

How is 0.145 expressed as a common fraction?

- ○ 14.5/1000
- ○ 145/1000
- ○ 14/100
- ○ 1.45/100

A contractor is given $460.00, which is 40% of his contract price of?

- ○ $1,300.00
- ○ $1,200.00
- ○ $1,150.00
- ○ $1,100.00

The circumference is calculated how?

○ 3.14 x diameter

○ 3.16 x diameter

○ 3.12 x diameter

○ None of the above

Baseboards are sold in 16 feet sections. How many baseboards are needed to install in a room with 322 linear feet?

○ 15

○ 30

○ 20

○ 21

10

A cube shaped piece of metal must be coated with a teflon covering. If the cube has a side of 15 cm, what is the total surface area that needs to be coated?

○ 9005 cm

○ 600 cm

○ 900 cm

1350 cm

What is a vertex?

○ Point where 3 straight lines come together

○ Point where the 2 straight lines com together to form the angle

○ Middle of the circle

○ Two straight lines

3 1/2 + 5 1/3 =

_____

○ 8 3/6

○ 8 5/6

○ 2 5/6

○ 4 5/6

5/2 ÷ 3/4 =

10/3

10/8

13/4

1

_____

○ A

○ B

○ C

○ D

Sales for the year are $10,000.00, and overhead is $2,000.00, what percentage is the overhead?

_____

○ 25%

○ 22%

○ 20%

○ 24%

A cube shaped piece of metal must be coated with a teflon covering. If the cube has a side of 15 cm, what is the total surface area that needs to be coated?

○ 9005 cm

○ 600 cm

○ 1350 cm

○ 900 cm

1 Exam Prep
Painting: General Mathematics and Calculations
Answers

Question 1
The right answer is 66.67.

Question 2
The right answer is 4 hours.

Question 3
The right answer is 16/15.

Question 4
The right answer is 5.

Question 5
The right answer is 120.

Question 6
The right answer is 145/1000.

Question 7
The right answer is $1,150.00.

Question 8
The right answer is 3.14 x diameter.

Question 9
The right answer is 21.

Question 10
The right answer is 1350 cm.

Question 11
The right answer is Point where the 2 straight lines come together to form the angle.

Question 12
The right answer is 8 5/6.

Question 13
The right answer is A.

Question 14
The right answer is 20%.

Question 15
The right answer is 1350 cm.

1 Exam Prep
PDCA Craftman's Manual and Textbook
8th Edition
Questions and Answers

1. New plaster should be allowed to dry for _____ before painting.

A. 24 hours
B. 48 hours
C. 14 days
D. 30 days

The portion of the bristles nearest the ferrule is called the butt end and the tip of the brush is called the _____ end.

Flag
Heel
Sash
Plug

3. _____ is the dominant color in nature and, as such, is considered relaxing and restful.

Blue
Green
Red
Yellow

4. _____ is (are) a white powdery deposit on the surface of concrete caused by the evaporation of moisture carrying soluble salts.

A. Form release agents
   Flocculence
   Efflorescence
   Laitance

5. Removing contaminants from a surface using water pressure of 25,500 is known as _____.

A. Water blasting
B. Ultra high pressure water jetting
C. High pressure water jetting
D. High pressure water cleaning

6. The pH is based on a logarithmic scale of 0 to 14, readings below _____ are acidic.

    2
    7
    9
    14

7. _____ means union of three, one of the most useful formulas for color harmony.

A. Split complement
B. Mutual complement
C. Double complement
D. Triad

8. What percentage of light is reflected by the color white?

A. 70 — 90
B. 55 — 71
C. 40 — 50
D. 5 — 10

9. Polyester bristle brushes are typically recommended for the application of _____ .

A. Waterborne coatings
B. Shellac dissolved in ethyl alcohol
C. Keytone based coating
D. None of the above

10. 5R 5/12 is the written notation for _____ .

    Vermilion
    Rose
    Orange
    Rust

11. _____ pigments with sulfate can range in color from light yellow to bright orange or scarlet red.

A. Organic coloring
    Inorganic
    Synthetic organic
    Red chromate

12. Where wall covering is to be hung, the first step is to mark a vertical line using _____ .

A. Carpenter's level
B. Seam roller
C. Broad knife
D. Yardstick

13. _____ is an example of an ester solvent.

    Ethylene
    Isobutyl acetate
    Ethyl alcohol
    Methanol

14. Using the Munsell system, NV/ describes the color _____ .

A. Pure black
B. Pure white
C. Neutral gray
D. None of the above

15._____ is a type of wood that should be filled and is not suitable for paint finish.

    Ash
    Chestnut
    Cypress
    Maple

16. _____ was a commonly used cleaning agent in the past.

A. Trisodium phosphate
B. Sodium hydroxide
    Acetone
    Turpentine

17. A liquid coating designed to provide a protective barrier against the environmental and health risks associated with exposure to leaded paint dust and chips is known as _____ .

A. Cover over
B. Non-protective barrier
    Stripper
    Encapsulant

18. Which method was developed to test for moisture in new concrete?

    ASTM D-4263
    ASTM D-2456
    ASTM D-1257
    ASTM D-6363

19. _____ coatings are suitable for above-grade, atmospheric, weathering applications.

A. Vinyl
B. Asphaltic
C. Chlorinated rubber
D. Vinyl Butyral

20. Which of the following is considered a paint roller?

A. Dip
B. Fountain
C. Pressure-fed
D. All of the above

21. Before synthetic resins were developed in the 1920's, _____ was the only source of material for coatings of high gloss.

A. Barrier pigment
B. Oil resin
C. Natural resin
D. Flow agent

_____ has a wide application in the protection of steel and concrete in freshwater and saltwater immersion.

Amine adduct-cured epoxy
Polyamide-cured epoxy
Polyamine-cured epoxy
Coal tar epoxy

23. The primer for wood should have the following characteristics.

A. Provide good adhesion
B. Dry to a soft finish
Flexibility
A & C only

Household bleach diluted _____ part bleach to _____ parts water is a very effective way of removing mild cases of mildew from surfaces.

A. 1, 2 or 3
B. 1, 3 or 4
C. 1, 5 or 6
D. None of the above

25. <u>pigments dimi</u>nish the shrinkage stresses that occur within the paint film during the curing process.

    Barrier
    Inhibitive
    Sacrificial
    Extender

26. A highly elastomeric material that is used on parking lots, sidewalks, and terrace decks is called_____ caulk.

A. Acrylic latex
B. Butyl rubber
    Silicone
    Polyurethane

_____have excellent weatherability, gloss and color retention, and good chemical and moisture retention.

A. Vinyl urethanes
B. Epoxy urethanes
C. Acrylic urethanes
D. Polyether urethanes

    It is important when working with varnish to start with a clean brush and that the surrounding area be clean and free from _____ .

    Water
    Dust
    Uneven surface
    Imperfections

29. _____ was (were) first used in the Orient and is now is made from nitrocellulose, cellulose acetate, butyrate and other similar materials.

    Undercoats
    Shellac
    Vinyl
    Lacquer

30. _____ primers are suitable for painting galvanized metal.

A. Aluminum oxide
B. Iron oxide
C. Copper sulfate
D. Zinc-rich

31. _____ contributes to the ability of a coating to wet a substrate and to penetrate and seal any voids, irregularities or crevices.

    Pigment
    Solvent
    Putty
    Filler

32. Removing contaminants from a surface using water pressure of 9,000 psi is known as _____ .

A. Low water pressure washing
B. Ultra high pressure water jetting
C. Low water pressure washing
D. High pressure washing

_____ gallons of paint are to be purchased for a room measuring 20 ft x 75 ft with a 10 ft high ceiling. Assume that each gallon of paint covers 300 ft^2.

    5
    6
    7
    8

34. The most common substrate on which electrostatic spraying is used is _____ .

    Wood
    Steel
    Concrete
    Plastic

_____ coatings will resist dry heat to temperatures of approximately 750 ⁰F.

A. Silicone resin
    Alkyd
    Inorganic zinc-rich
    Heat resistant pigment

36. Where water vapor must be able to pass through the film to leave the substrate, acrylic and vinyl paints are suitable because they are able to _____ .

    Vaporize
    Breathe
    Solidify
    None of the above

37. A _____ percent solution of phosphoric acid in water can be used to etch the concrete surface.

A. 1 to 5
B. 5 to 10
C. 10 to 15
D. 20 to 25

38. The CAS listed in section 2 of the MSDS refers to the _____ , which gives information about chemical properties

A. Chemical addictive status
B. Cautionary advisement number
C. Chemical abstract service number
D. None of the above

_____ are perhaps the best caulking materials with regard to weatherability, moisture and chemical resistance.

A. Acrylic latex caulks
B. Polyurethane caulks
C. Butyl rubber caulks
D. Silicone caulks

40. A low pressure of _____ psi or less is delivered to HVLP spray systems that use high volumes of air, normally between 15 and 22 CFM.

50
30
20
10

41. Paint has basic _____ components.

Two
Three
Four
Five

_____ is a thin, weak, brittle layer of cement that results from the mixture being overwet or overworked when it was poured.

Laitance
Undercutting
Efflorescence
Cobwebbing

43. _____ is not considered a primary color.

    Red
    Yellow
    Blue
    White

44. _____work (s) by emulsifying greasy dirt.

    Alkalies
    Abrasive blasting
    Stripping with chemicals
    Stripping with heat

45. Primers for use with concrete shall be _____.

A. Water resistant
B. Chemical resistant
C. Alkali resistant
D, Chloride resistant

46. As a rule of thumb, the air volume for compressors should be about _____CFM for each nozzle?

    90
    125
    300
    500

    How much will you spend on paint to paint a 14 x 20 ft room and the ceiling that is 8 feet tall and has two doors and two windows? Assume the doors are 36" wide by 6 ft high and the windows are 36" x 60". Assume each gallon of paint covers 350 ft^2 per gallon and costs $35 per gallon. Select the closest answer.

A.$35.00
B.$70.00
C.$105.00
D.$140.00

48. Pressure washing over _____ is known as ultra high pressure water jetting.

A. 5,000 psi
B. 10,000 psi
C. 20,000 psi
D. 25,000 psi

Paints that are formulated specifically to provide a transition from a primer or to a finish coat are called _____ .

A. Texture coatings
B. Floor coats
C. Tie coats
D. Fire-retardant coatings

50. Folding wall covering paste side to paste side before hanging is known as _____ .

A. Paste stick
   Tacked
   Stroked
   Booked

51. _____, as defined by Federal Specification CCC-W-408C, is the ability to resist transfer of color from wall covering surface when rubbed.

A. Colorfastness
B. Crocking resistance
C. Washability
D. Scrub

52. It is recommended for painters using an airless sprayer to maintain a standoff distance of _____ inches from the nozzle to the surface.

A. 7
B. 8
C. 12
D. 16

53. Two colors directly across the color wheel from each other are _____ .

A. True complement
B. Split complement
C. Double complement
D. Triad

54. The percentage of light reflected by the color medium green is _____ .

   15-20
   15-30
   5-10
   1-4

A room is 20' x 15' by 10' high and has one window that is 5' x 6' and one door that is 4' x 8'. Calculate the amount of paint that is needed to paint the walls and all the baseboards, casings and crown molding if they are 4" high. Assume that one gallon of paint will cover 350 ft^2.

One
Two
Three
Four

If considerable time has passed between the time that the paint has been bought and used, the first step to take is to _____.

A. Stir the paint to see if is okay
  Remove the heavy separation from the top
  Pour the top liquid into another container
  Strain the paint through a cheese cloth

57. The features of the _____ brush increase its capacity to maintain its shape, to hold paint and to spread it smoothly.

A. Horst bristle
B. Nylon bristle
C. Hog bristle
D. Badger bristle

58. When dipping a new brush, do not dip _____.

A. In linseed oil
B. Into the paint and allow the paint to harden in the heel
C. Into the paint too deeply
D. In water

59. _____ produces less overspray and fewer VOC emissions.

  High volume-low pressure spray
  High pressure spray
  Low pressure spray
  Low volume-high pressure spray

60. A defect that may result from the application of airless spray coatings is _____ .

A. Paint streaks
B. Excessive fog
C. Orange peel
D. All of the above

61. Shellac must be applied _____ .

A. Slowly in straight strokes in one direction
B. Rapidly in straight strokes in one direction
C. Slowly in straight strokes back and forth
D. Rapidly in straight strokes back and forth

62. _____ is (are) the leading cause of injury for painters.

A. Toxic exposure
B. Falls from ladders
C. Hazardous chemicals
D. Working in confined spaces

63. Exposure to inhalation of toxic vapors might be reduced by _____ .

A. Wearing respirators
B. Providing a decontamination area
C. Using fans
D. Opening up a window or door

64. A room that has a _____ exposure, will allow a color to be true.

   Eastern
   Southern
   Western
   Northern

   Generally, _____ color is chosen for its high reflectance value to maximize the amount of light in a room.

A. An effervescent
B. The wall
C. The ceiling
D. The background

66. The color _____ is used for traffic or directional markings.

   Red
   Orange
   Green
   White

To produce the right color match, an instrument that uses _____ to read and measure the color components of the sample.

A. Light and a prism
B. A computer
   Specifications
   Microscope

68. When hanging wallpaper around a fireplace, the first step is to _____.

A. Center the first wallcovering strip
B. Place into each corner from the middle of each wall
C. Mark the center of the fireplace opening
D. Measure a distance to half the width of the wallcovering material

69. Applying too thick of a coat of paint may cause _____.

   Sags
   Cratering
   Blushing
   Checking

The Munsell system uses a combination of letters and numbers to indicate specific colors and each hue is divided into _____ .

A. R's and V's
B. R's and NV's
C. 10 steps
D. 20 steps

71. A _____may provide many of the essential properties of a paint like opacity.

   Resin
   Solvent
   Sealant
   Pigment

1 Exam Prep
PDCA Craftman's Manual and Textbook
8th Edition
Answers

1.   D   page 61
2.   A   page 147
3.   B   page 216
4.   C   page 59

Cpages 73 and 47

Bpage 59

Dpage 224

Apage 227

Apage 148

Apage 232

Dpage 13

Apage 263

Bpage 12

Cpage 232

Bpage 132

Apages 342 and 58

Dpage 46

Apages 60 and 55

Bpage 24

Dpage 152

Cpage 15

Bpage 27

Dpage 33

Bpages 91, 47 and 58

Dpage 14

Dpage 51

Cpage 28

Bpage 133

Dpage 37

Dpage 36

Bpage 10

Dpage 67

A   Walk the perimeter of the room. 25 ft + 75 ft + 25 ft + 75 ft = 200 ft. Each wall is 10 ft high. 200 ft x 10 ft = 2,000 ft^2

Assume 300 ft^2 per gallon so 2,000 ft^2 / 300 ft^2 = 6.667 gallons or round up to 7 gallons.

34.   B   page 161
35.   C   page 45
36.   B   page 22
37.   C   page 50
38.   C   page 195
39.   D   page 51
40.   D   page 157
41.   C   page 9

A   pages 60 and 247

D   page 214

A   page 70

C   page 34

C   page 100

C   Divide the room into four walls and one ceiling. The ceiling area is 14' x 20' = 280 sqft

The four walls are 14'+20'+14'+20' = 68' x 8ft high = 544 sqft

Subtract the two doors and the two windows = 2(3 x 6) + 2(3 x 5) = 66 sqft

Add / subtract areas – 280 + 544 – 66 = 758 sqft

758 sqft / 350 sqft per gallon = 2.165 gallons or round up – 3 gallons x $35 per gal = $105

D   page 73

C   page 42

D   page 275

B   page 322

C   page 125

A   page 223

B   page 227

B   The four walls are 20' + 15' + 20' + 15' = 70' x 10ft high = 700 sqft

Subtract the door and the window = 4' x 8' + 5' x 6' = 62 sqft

The baseboard measurement is 20' + 20' + 15' + 15' – 4'(width of door) = 66'

The door and window casing measurement is (8' + 8' + 4') + (5' + 5' + 6' + 6') = 42'

The crown molding measurement is 20' + 15' + 20' + 15' = 70'

Total baseboard, casing and crown molding is 66' + 42' + 70' = 178' x 4"/12 = 59.33 sqft

Total square footage to be painted – 700 – 62 + 59.33 = 697.33 sqft   / 350 sqft in a gallon

Paint to be purchased 1.999 or 2 gallons

56.   A   page 114
57.   C   page 148
58.   C   page 119
59.   A   page 128
60.   D   page 127
61.   D   page 134

62. B page 185
63. C page 200
64. D page 218
65. C page 228
66. D page 229
67. A page 229
68. C page 269
69. D page 241
70. C page 232
71. D page 9

PAINTING: OSHA - CODE OF FEDERAL REGULATIONS QUESTIONS

1) A scaffold used only by painters should be designed for a working load of _____ pounds per square foot (psi), if considered light duty.

A. 15 psf
B. 20 psf
C. 25 psf
D. 50 psf

2) The dimension in the direction of travel on intermediate landings for temporary stairs shall be no less than _____ inches.

A. 40 inches
B. 30 inches
C. 36 inches
D. 24 inches

3) Employees cannot be subjected to noise levels higher than _____ decibels for more than four hours per day according to OSHA Safety and Health Regulations.

A. 95 dB
    10dB
    102 dB
    105 dB

4) A nylon rope eye and eye sling is to be used with a choker hitch to hoist a 1,300 pound piece of machinery, according to OSHA the minimum nominal rope diameter is _____ . Use a safety factor of 9.

A. 1 inch
B. 1-1/16 inches
C. 1-1/8 inches
D. 1-1/4 inches

5) Employees cannot be subjected to noise levels higher than _____ decibels for more than four hours per day, according to OSHA.

A. 95 dB
B. 102 dB
    10dB
    105 dB

6) The range of working loads from light to heavy-duty independent pole scaffolds is _____ pounds per square foot (psi).

A. 20-75 psf
B. 25-70 psf
C. 25-75 psf
D.25-50 psf

7) Where electrical transmission lines are energized and rated at least 50kW or less, a clearance of _____ feet minimum must be maintained by the crane and load.

A. 5 feet
B. 8 feet
C. 10 feet
D. 12 feet

8) The maximum allowable height of a horse scaffold or two tiers is _____ .

A. 4 feet
B. 8 feet
C. 12 feet
D, 10 feet

9) According to OSHA, the minimum distance between side rails of all portable ladders shall not be less than _____ inches.

A. 11-1/2 inches
B. 12 inches
C. 13 inches
D. 14 inches

10) All portable lighting units in tanks, drums or other hazardous damp locations shall be operated at a maximum voltage of _____ .

A. 12 volts
B. 32 volts
C. 110 volts
D. 220 volts

11) When employees are required to be in trenches _____ feet or more in depth, ladders shall be provided for exit, and such ladders shall require not more than _____ feet of lateral travel.

A. 4 feet — 30 feet
B. 5 feet — 30 feet
   4 feet— 25 feet
   5 feet — 25 feet

12) The toe boards of scaffolds shall be a minimum of _____ inches in height.

A 3-1/2 inches
B. 4 inches
C. 6 inches
D. 8 inches

13) A scaffold designed for 75 pounds per square foot (psi) would be usable for _____.

   Painters
   Stone masons
   Carpenters
   All of the above

14) A bricklayer's square scaffold shall not exceed _____ feet in height and _____ feet in width.

A. 4 and 5
B. 3 and 4
C. 5 and 4
D. 5 and 5

15) Rungs, cleats, and steps of portable ladders (except for special applications such as step-stools) shall be spaced not less than _____ inches, no more than _____ inches.

A. 8 — 11
B. 9 — 14
C. 10— 14
D. 12 — 16

16) According to OSHA, the minimum illumination for indoor corridors during construction is foot candles.

A. 3
B. 5
C.10
D. 30

17) Personnel hoistway doors or gates shall be at least _____ high.

4'6"
6'6"
8'6"
None of the above

18) A standard toe board shall be equivalent in strength to 1 inch by _____ inches high.

A. 3 inches
B. 3-1/2 inches
C. 4 inches
D. 4-1/2 inches

One 40 gallon open drum of water with 2 fire pails may be substituted for fired extinguishers having a 2A rating.

A. True
B. False

20) Rungs, steps, and cleats of portable ladders and fixed ladders shall be spaced not less than <u>inches</u> apart.

A. 8
B. 10
C. 12
D. 14

21) According to OSHA, the minimum illumination of an indoor warehouse is _____ floor candles.

3
5
10
D.12

22) All safety nets shall meet accepted performance standards as follows:

A. 17,500 foot pounds minimum impact resistance
B. 24,000 foot pounds minimum impact resistance
C. Withstand five 50 pound sacks dropped simultaneously from a height of 25 feet D.
10,000 pounds rope tensile strength

23) Temporary stairs shall be installed at angles to the horizontal of between _____ and _____degrees.

A. 20 and 40
B. 20 and 50
C. 20 and 30
D. 30 and 50

24) If the personnel hoist wire rope speed is 300 feet per minute, the minimum rope safety factor must be:

9.20
9.50
9.75
10.00

25) OSHA states that compressed air shall not be used for cleaning purposes except where reduced less than psi and then with only effective chip guarding and personal protective equipment meeting OSHA requirements.

A. 30
B. 50
C.70
D. 90

26) The term "ROPS" means:

A. Regional Operating Standards
B. Required Operating Steps
C. Roll over Protective Structure
D. None of the Above

27) OSHA requires that for skeleton steel construction no more than _____ feet or _____ floors of unfinished bolting or welding exist:

A. 20 and 2
B. 24 and 2
C. 30 and 3
D. 48 and 4

28) The greatest angle above the horizontal plan for Type A soil is _____degrees.

A. 34°
B. 45°
C. 52°
D. 90°

29) Class II hazardous locations are those with a presence of:

A. Combustible dust
B. Ignitable fibers
C. Flammable liquids
D. Explosives

30) Open yard storage of combustible materials limits the height of the piles to _____ feet.

A. 12 feet
B. 14 feet
C. 16 feet
D. 30 feet

31) Employees should not be exposed to an impact noise on a job exceeding peak sound pressure of _____.

A. 110 dB
B. 120 dB
C. 130 dB
D. 140 dB

32) Which of the following problems is not caused by asbestos?

A. Lung cancer
B. Gastrointestinal cancer
C. Asbestosis
D. Angina

33) Light duty tube and coupler scaffold must have posts spaced not more than _____ feet longitudinally along the length of the scaffold.

A. 8
B. 9
C. 10
D. 11

34) According to OSHA, the material shall not be stored within _____ inches from a fire door.

A. 24 inches
B. 30 inches
C. 36 inches
D. 48 inches

35) When safety nets are required, the mesh size of the nets shall not exceed _____ inches by _____ inches.

A. 4 — 4
B. 6 — 6
C. 8 — 8
D. 8 — 6

36) The common drinking cup is _____ .

A. Prohibited in hazardous areas
B. Always prohibited
C. Never prohibited
D. Prohibited in areas where running water is not available

OSHA requires a safety factor based on load and speed be used in hoist cables. The safety factor for a cable with a speed of 200 feet per minute is:

A. 7.00
B. 7.65
C. 8.60
D. 6.65

38) If an employee wears prescription glasses, OSHA requires that he must be provided with _____ for certain jobs.

A. Spectacles with protective lenses
B. Goggles over corrective spectacles
C. Goggles with lenses that incorporate lenses mounted behind the protective lenses
D. Either A, B, or C

39) The vertical height of a guard rail shall be:

A, 30 inches
B. 36 inches
C. 42 inches
D. 48 inches

40) When employees are required to be in trenches of _____ or more an adequate means of exit such as a ladder or steps shall be provided.

A. 3 feet
B. 4 feet
C. 5 feet
D. 6 feet

41) An interior hung scaffold is to be suspended from the beams of a ceiling. The suspension rope wire shall be capable of supporting _____ times the intended load.

    4

    5

    6

    7

42) The maximum allowable slope for Type A soil for a simple slope in an excavation of 20 feet or less in depth is _____horizontal and _____vertical.

A. 1 to 1

B. 2 to 1

C. 1/2 to 1

D. 3/4 to 1

43) Openings are defined as a gap or void:

A. 2 inch or less in its least dimension

B. 30 inches or more high and 18" or more wide

C. Less than 12 inches but more than 1 inch in its least dimension

D. 12 inches or more in its greatest dimension

44) According to OSHA the side rails of portable ladders shall extend a minimum of _____above the landing.

A. 22 inches

B. 24 inches

C. 30 inches

D. 36 inches

45) Lifelines shall be secured above the point of operation to anchorage or structural members capable of supporting a minimum of dead weight of _____pounds.

    4,000

    5,000

    5,400

    6,000

46) OSHA states that shore or leant-to scaffolding:

A. Is restricted to structures having 4 or less stories
B. Is restricted to structures having 3 or less stories
C. Has to be made to hold a dead weight load of 20 psi
D. Is prohibited

47) On construction sites, a fire extinguisher rated not less than 2A shall be provided for each _____ square feet of the protected building or major fraction thereof.

A. 1,000 sf
B. 2,000 sf
C. 3,000 sf
D. 4,000 sf

According to OSHA, the proper maintenance for a multi-purpose ABC dry chemical stored pressure fire extinguisher is to:

A. Check pressure gauge monthly
B. Discharge annually and recharge
   Weigh semi-annually
   Check pressure gauge and condition of dry chemical annually

49) Electrical power operated tools shall be either grounded or type _____.

   Approved double-insulated.
   Approved single-insulated
   Three phase
   #12 Romex

50) According to OSHA, the proper maintenance for a carbon dioxide type fire extinguisher is to:

A. Discharge normally and recharge
   Weigh semi-annually
   Check pressure gauge monthly
   Check pressure gauge annually

51) According to OSHA, no more than _____ gallons of flammable or combustible liquids shall be stored in a room outside of an approved storage cabinet.

A. 10 gallons
B. 15 gallons
C. 20 gallons

D. 25 gallons

52) According to OSHA, exposure to impulsive or impact noise shall not exceed <u>dBA peak</u> sound pressure level.

A. 110 dBA
B. 140 dBA
C. 120 dBA
D. 115 dBA

53) Simple slope-short term excavation with a maximum depth of 12 feet can be sloped to a maximum of _____horizontal to _____vertical for Type A soil.

A. 1 to 1
B. 2 to 1
C. 1/2 to 1
D. 3/4 to 1

54) According to OSHA, no more than _____employee(s) shall occupy any given 8 feet of bracket scaffold.

A. 1 employee
B. 2 employees
C. 3 employees
D. 4 employees

The minimum clearance between an operating crane and energized and unprotected electrical distribution lines (rates at 35kV) shall be:

A. 10 feet
B. 14 feet
C. 16 feet
D. 20 feet

56) According to OSHA, oxygen cylinders, regulators and hoses shall be:

A. Stored only in approved containers
B. Prohibited m area where fuel gases other than acetylene are used
   Unpainted
   Kept free of all oil and grease

57) The use of non-self supporting ladders shall be at such an angel that the horizontal distance from the top support to the foot of the ladder is approximately _____ of the working length of the ladder.

A. One half
B. One quarter
C. Three quarters
D. Seven eighths

Two 1" diameter polyester rope slings are to be used with choker hitches (eye and eye sling) to hoist a steel beam. A safety factor of 9 is to be used and there is equal loading on each sling. According to OSHA, the maximum weight of the beam is:

A. 1,200 pounds
B. 2,100 pounds
C. 2,400 pounds
D. 2,600 pounds

59) When a material hoist tower is not enclosed:

A. The hoist platform shall be caged on all sides
B. Shall have 1/2 inch mesh number 14 U.S., gage wire covering
C. Shall have a six foot enclosure at ground level
D. All of the above

60) According to OSHA, life lines used for employee safeguarding shall have a minimum breaking strength of _____ pounds.

A. 500 pounds
B. 1,000 pounds
C. 3,500 pounds
D. 5,400 pounds

A fire breaks out in a main electrical junction box at a construction site; an electrician is close by and asks you to get a fire extinguisher. Which of the following extinguishers should you bring back?

A. Soda acid
B. Stored pressure (water type)
   CO2
   Foam

62) A class C fire is a _____ type fire:

A. Combustible metal
B. Flammable liquid
   Trash
   Electrical

63) The _____ has the first responsibility for assuring that the required personal protective equipment is worn by workers on a construction site defined by OSHA.

A. Employee
B. Owner
C. Prime Contractor
D. Employer

64) The use of a spiral stair for construction purposes shall be:

A. Not permitted
B. Permitted if permanent part of structure
C. Normally prohibited
D. At least 7 feet in diameter

65) Danger signs shall be:

A. Red on the upper panel, with black borders and white lower panel
B. Black on the upper panel, with red borders and a white lower panel
C. Yellow on the lower panel, yellow letters on black background on upper panel
D. None of the above

66) The maximum air pressure for nailers, staplers and other similar type of equipment is _____ at the tool unless the tool shall have a safety device on the muzzle to prevent the tool from ejecting fasteners.

A. 30 psi
B. 60 psi
C. 100 psi
D. 150 psi

67) All ladder Jack scaffolds shall be limited to light duty and shall not exceed a height of _____ feet above the floor or ground.

A. 10
   20
   30
   40

68) Toe boards, where required on scaffolds, shall be a minimum of _____ inches in, height.

3
4
3-1/2
4-1/2

According to OSHA, the recommended slope for sides of excavations for average soil (Type B) is:

45°
55°
60°
70°

70) The minimum rate fire extinguisher required for 3,000 square foot building is:

2A
2B
2C
2D

71) The word "shall" in OSHA, means:

Might
Sometimes
Mandatory
Recommended

72) The contents of a first aid kit must be checked _____.

Monthly
Weekly
Bi-weekly
Semi-annually

73) All employees using abrasive wheels shall be protected:

A. With accessory body and face guards
B. With flexible hooded, ventilated goggles
C. By eye protection equipment
D. By the use of momentary pressure switches

74) The proper way to hang an extension cord over a hallway ceiling during construction is _____ .

A. With wire
B. Under a bent nail
C. With rope
D. With staples

75) Cylinders containing oxygen or acetylene shall not be:

A. Stored in direct sunlight
B. Refilled at the work site
C. Buried underground
D. Taken into confined spaces

76) Every open sided floor or platform _____ feet above the adjacent floor or ground level shall be guarded by a standard railing, or equivalent, on all open sides except where there is an entrance to a ramp, stairs, or fixed ladder.

   3
B. 4
C.   5
D. 6

   The maximum allowable slope for excavations less than 20 feet deep for compacted sharp sand (Type C soil) is:

   90°
   63°
   45°
   34°

78) The side rails of portable ladders shall extend a minimum of _____ inches above the landing.

   36
   40
   32
   30

79) The factor that determines if a compressed air hose requires a pressure reduction safety device at the air source is _____ .

   Pressure
   Length
   Inside diameter
   The number of fittings

80) According to OSHA, when materials are dropped more than _____ feet outside the exterior walls of a building an enclosed shoot must be utilized.

A. 10 feet
B. 15 feet
C. 20 feet
D. 25 feet

81) The maximum loading of a medium duty scaffold is _____ PSF.

A. 40
B. 50
C. 60
D. 70

82) OSHA defines a hole as a void or gap measuring _____ inch(es) or more in its least dimension.

One
Two
Three
Four

83) The maximum distance a man wearing a safety belt may drop or work is:

A. 3 feet
B. 6 feet
C. 12 feet
D. 15 feet

Two manila rope slings with a safety factor of 5 are used to lift a 2-ton load. Using a basket hitch with an endless sling, sling set at 60° horizontally to the load, the minimum diameter rope required to lift the load is _____ inches).

A. 9/16
B. 10/16
C. 11/16
D. 13/16

85) A scaffold used only by painters should be designed for a working load of _____ pounds per square foot (psf) if considered light duty.

A. 1. 5 psf
B. 20 psi
C. 25 psf
D. 50 psf

OSHA states the required tests shall be performed on all cord sets and receptacles, which are not part of the permanent wiring of the building, which are fixed and not exposed to damages, at intervals not exceeding _____ months.

2

3

4

6

88) In excavations where employees must enter, excavated or other materials may be stored:

A. Two feet from the edge of the excavation
B. One foot from the edge of the excavation if properly retained
C. One foot from the edge of the excavation
D. A or B

A stairway abuts a building on one side, and has the opposite side open. The stairway has a total of: 14 risers per flight and is 86 inches wide. OSHA states the stairway:

A. Must be equipped with a least on stair railing on the open side
B. Must be equipped with one handrail on the enclosed side and one stair railing on the open side
C. Does not require any railings or handrails
D. All of the above

90) OSHA states that every open sided floor or platform (other than scaffolding) _____ feet or more above adjacent floor or ground level shall be guarded by a standard railing on all open sides except where there is entrance to a ramp, stairway, or fixed ladder.

6

8

10

12

91) According to OSHA, a carpenter's bracket scaffold:

A. Brackets shall be spaced a maximum of 8 feet
B. May be used if bolted to the wall
C. May be used if hooked over the top of the wall
D. All of the above

92) According to OSHA, a trench is a narrow excavation in which the bottom width is not greater than _____ feet.

A. 5
B. 10
C.15
D. 20

93) A landing platform must be provided at internals not to exceed _____ feet on scaffolds.

A. 25
B. 30
C. 35
D. 40

94) One toilet shall be provided at the construction job site for a maximum of _____.

A. 5 employees
B. 15 employees
C. 20 employees
D. 10 employees

95) The minimum breaking strength of a ½ inch diameter nylon rope is _____.

A. 2,650 pounds
B. 6,080 pounds
C. 3,990 pounds
D. 4,800 pounds

96) The maximum variance in riser height or tread depth shall not be over _____ inches in any stairway system.

A. 1/8
B. 3/16
C. ¼
D. ½

97) Wire ropes shall not be used for material handling if any length of _____ the total number of visible broken wires exceeds 10% of the total number of wires.

A. 12 inches
B. 18 inches
C. One lag
D. 8 diameters

98) _____ tucks are required when making a short splice in a manila rope.

   3

   6

   8

   10

99) OSHA states that the minimum working and clear hot stick distance for 235,000 volts is _____.

A. 3' – 4"
B. 3' – 6"
C. 3' – 8"
D. 5' – 0"

Which of the following types of cables would have the minimum required rated lifting capacity necessary to lift a 9,640 pound load? Answer based on two-leg bridle slings with a 45-degree angle.

A. ¾" diameter, HT, improved plow steel grade rope with independent wire rope core B. ¾" diameter, MS, improved plow steel grade rope with fiber core

Made in the USA
Middletown, DE
09 July 2025

10339222R00183